THE DRAPED BUST HALF DOLLARS OF 1796-1797

Numismatic Background and Census

by Jon P. Amato, Ph. D.

Edited by James L. Halperin and Mark Van Winkle

A Publication of Heritage® Auctions
3500 Maple Avenue, 17th Floor
Dallas, Texas 75219

HERITAGE HA.com AUCTIONS

23454

Ivy Press, Inc.
3500 Maple Avenue, 17th Floor
Dallas, Texas 75219-3941

ISBN #1-59967-729-6

Printed in the United States of America

This research was funded in part by a grant from the Central States Numismatic Society

TABLE OF CONTENTS

INTRODUCTION 5

ACKNOWLEDGEMENTS 7

DEDICATION 11

ORIGIN OF THE DRAPED BUST DESIGN ON U.S. SILVER COINAGE 13

The DeSaussure-Rittenhouse Theory 15

The Gilbert Stuart Theory 16

The Anne Willing Bingham Theory 17

GENESIS OF THE 1796-1797 HALF DOLLAR 19

The Bank of the United States: "Parent" of the 1796-1797 Half Dollar 19

Draped Bust Small Eagle Half Dollar Deliveries to the Bank 20

1796-1797 Half Dollar Mintage 20

Possible Reasons for Low Mintage 20

DRAPED BUST SMALL EAGLE HALF DOLLAR VARIETIES 23

1796-1797 Half Dollar Die Marriages 23

1796 Overton-101 Variety (15 Stars) 24

1796 Overton-102 Variety (16 Stars) 25

1797 Overton-101 Variety 26

1797 Overton-101a Die State 27

1797 Overton-102 Variety 29

COLLECTIONS FEATURING ALL FOUR 1796-1797 HALF DOLLAR VARIETIES 31

The A.C. Gies Collection (Stack's, October 1940) 31

The Dennis Heller Collection (New England Rare Coin Auctions, January 1982) ... 31

The James Brilliant Collection (Bowers and Merena, January 1992) 32

The Jules Reiver Collection (Heritage® Auctions, January 2006) 32

The Bayside New York Collection (Heritage® Auctions, July 2008) 32

DRAPED BUST SMALL EAGLE HALF DOLLAR ANECDOTES 33

The Man Who Swallowed a 1796 Half Dollar 33

Coin Dealer Trades 1796 Dollar for Elderly Woman's 1796 Half Dollar 34

THE RESEARCH METHODOLOGY 35

Previous Rarity and Condition Estimates of 1796-1997 Half Dollars 35

Sources Used in the Study 36

Catalogs of Numismatic Auction Sales 36

Coin Dealer Fixed Price Lists 36

Institutional Collections 37

Private Collections 37

Other 37

Enhanced 1796-1797 Half Dollar Grading Standards 37

Toward a Census of Draped Bust Small Eagle Half Dollars 39

A CENSUS OF 1796-1797 HALF DOLLARS 41

1796 Overton-101 Variety (15 Stars) Examples 43

1796 Overton-102 Variety (16 Stars) Examples 121

1797 Overton-101 Variety Examples 185

1797 Overton-101a Die State Examples 221

1797 Overton-102 Variety Examples 291

THE RESEARCH FINDINGS 329

The 1796-1797 Half Dollar Census Summarized 329

Interpretation of Findings 330

SUMMARY AND CONCLUSION 333

INVITATION FOR READER RESPONSE 334

REFERENCES 335

ABOUT THE AUTHOR 337

LIBERTY
1797
UNITED
OF AMERICA

INTRODUCTION

The Draped Bust Small Eagle half dollars of 1796-1797, from a paltry mintage of 3,918 pieces, hold a special appeal for collectors of early American coins. This two-year design type is the key to a minor coin type set of U.S. coinage, and both dates are needed by early half dollar date collectors. A case might be made for the 1796-1797 half dollar as the most important of *all* U.S. type coins, irrespective of metal content. Perusal of retail and wholesale price guides indicates that it has a higher type value in most grades than any other coin, including the 1796 No Stars and 1808 quarter eagles. While these one-year gold type coins claim a smaller mintage and fewer surviving examples, their lower grade-for-grade values suggest that they are in less demand for type collections than the Draped Bust Small Eagle half dollar. A much larger number of collectors apparently prefer to assemble an early minor coin type set as opposed to a collection of early gold type coins.

Whatever the collector's goal with respect to metal content, a 1796-1797 half dollar is necessary for the completion of a type collection of U.S. coinage. The number of extant Draped Bust Small Eagle half dollars thus limits the number of type sets that can possibly be assembled.

How many 1796-1797 half dollars have survived to the present day, and what is the grade distribution of extant specimens? These questions have guided the author's research on these classic pieces of Americana since early 2001. This research has involved a survey of catalogs of American numismatic auction sales and coin dealer's fixed price lists to locate images of these coins for the purpose of identifying distinct specimens and assessing their grade and surface condition.

A major goal of the study is to arrive at a census, if only preliminary, of the extant population of 1796-1797 halves. Additionally, the numismatic background of the series has been examined, including the economic and historical contexts within which 1796-1797 half dollars were designed and minted, and circulated in the channels of commerce (or conversely, escaped extensive or complete circulation).

This publication summarizes the findings of the author's research. It is hoped that the information contained within its covers imparts to the reader a heightened sense of appreciation for this classic rarity that Q. David Bowers calls the "Holy Grail" of U.S. silver type coins (Bowers, 2005, p. 178).

DEDICATION

My late daughter, Shari Lynn, was my main inspirational source during the conceptual stage of this study. She had little interest in numismatics and even less understanding of the significance of 1796-1797 half dollars. Nevertheless, she was quick to pick up on my passion for the series, and despite reservations that I had about such an undertaking she strongly encouraged that I go forward with it. It is to her memory that I dedicate this book.

During various stages of the study, **Jim Jones** alerted me to several 1796-1797 half dollar appearances in upcoming auctions, and obtained for me some high-resolution images. Moreover, he and his wife **Kim** were most helpful during the summer of 2006 when I was away from Dallas on a family emergency. I thank them for their support during that trying time.

Richard Brainerd, Heritage Auctions' General Counsel, offered valuable suggestions for organizing and writing up a decade of research.

The **Central States Numismatic Society** provided an author's grant to help fund the study. My sincerest appreciation goes to that organization for its confidence in my research.

My thanks go to the many auction houses and rare coin dealers and that sent me images and/or descriptions of 1796-1797 half dollars. These include **Bowers and Merena, Stack's, American Numismatic Rarities, Stack's-Bowers, David Lawrence Rare Coins, Bonhams, J.J. Teaparty, Long Island Numismatics, John Hamrick and Company, Premium Numismatics, MGS & NSI, Dick Osburn Rare Coins**, and **Benchmark Ventures**.

Finally, but certainly not least, I want to thank **Steve Ivy**, Heritage Auctions' CEO, for making the many company resources available to me. The photographic, layout and other complexities involved in the preparation and publishing of the research for this book may well have precluded its completion without Heritage's assistance. My sincerest thanks therefore go to Steve and the entire Heritage executive team.

The **American Numismatic Society** provided images of the two Draped Bust Small eagle half dollars in its collection. **Robert Hoge**, the Society's Curator of North American Coins and Currency, kindly presented me detailed information on their provenance.

Dr. Richard Doty, Curator, National Numismatic Collection, Smithsonian Institution, sent me images and acquisition information on the three 1796-1797 half dollars in the Smithsonian cabinet.

Carrie Wieners, Curator of Exhibits and Collections, The Durham Museum, provided images of the 1796 15 Stars half dollar from the Byron Reed Collection, owned by the City of Omaha, Nebraska, on loan to The Durham Museum. This coin is somewhat special, as it lacks the usually seen crack in the lower-right obverse, indicating it is one of the first 1796 half dollars struck.

I approached **Jim Halperin**, Heritage® Co-Chairman of the Board, in March 2010 to ask if he would be interested in editing my book about 1796-1797 half dollars. I had appreciated his efforts a few years earlier in editing the write-up of the research that Greg Rohan, Mark Van Winkle and I conducted on the Saint-Gaudens ten and twenty dollar gold coinage that culminated in the Heritage-published book entitled *The Coinage of Augustus Saint-Gaudens as Illustrated by the Philip Morse Collection.*

My thanks go out to Heritage Chief Cataloger **Mark Van Winkle** for his editing of the drafts leading up to the final work. He also ensured that a consistent format ran throughout the manuscript and that the half dollar images consisted of the highest clarity possible. Aside from these technical aspects, Mark has been a good friend and a constant source of encouragement, especially during the times I became discouraged with the progress of the research and writing.

Mark Borckardt, Heritage Senior Cataloger/Senior Numismatist, shared with me his numismatic insight on various aspects of this research. Specifically, his thoughts on the survival rates of various early U.S coins forced me to critically assess published rarity ratings, including those of 1796-1797 half dollars. And in his review of an earlier draft of the study he pointed to areas where internal consistencies of data and text were in need of improvement. In a more general sense, I have learned from Mark a great deal about early U.S. coinage, which has helped me tremendously in cataloging for Heritage and in my research.

David Stone, Heritage cataloger, was instrumental in pulling catalogs from the Heritage library for 1796-1797 half dollar photo shoots or edits after I retired (or semi-retired) from Heritage. He also provided catalogs from his personal collection to the Photography Department for these purposes. Moreover, Dave became a close personal friend with whom I shared many culinary experiences.

John Dale Beety, Heritage cataloger, offered many suggestions on inputting text into and generally working with Microsoft Office Word. Moreover, John came to my assistance on several occasions to retrieve or re-input data that I inadvertently lost from Word while preparing the manuscript, or from Lot Description while cataloging coins (his intervention in the latter was particularly welcome as the lost descriptions were often "full pagers").

ACKNOWLEDGEMENTS

I wish to thank those who aided me in this study. They are mentioned in no particular order, but all have my unending gratitude as they all contributed in their various ways to help me complete this book.

Numismatic literature dealer **Karl Moulton** was among the first with whom I shared my interest in the Draped Bust half dollars of 1796-1797. His enthusiasm was a major force in my decision to undertake this work. Along with literature dealers **Bryce Brown**, **David Sklow**, **George Kolbe**, **David Fanning**, **Charles Davis** and **Fred Lake**, Karl also helped to create my extensive library of auction-sales catalogs that contain images of 1796-1797 half dollar appearances.

Frank Campbell, then Head Librarian at the American Numismatic Society, graciously made thousands of auction catalogs available for my search of 1796-1797 half dollar appearances. Roughly once a month between January 2001 and July 2003 I would send Frank a list of catalogs I would like to survey. He would then make these ready for me on my next ANS visit, which usually lasted about three days.

Yelena Morgan did an excellent job inputting most of the manuscript data, no simple feat considering that she had to decipher my handwriting, or lack thereof. And **Mike Morgan** maintained the computerized file of the manuscript, making it readily available to the Heritage® Auctions Marketing Department for layout. I am indebted to them both because data inputting and file maintenance are not among my favorite things to do. Their efforts in these areas thus saved me a tremendous amount of grief!

Mary Hermann, Catalog Production Manager in the Heritage Marketing Department, oversaw the production of the book, and kept all parties, myself included, on task in its completion. Art Directors **Michael Puttonen** and **Lisa Fox** transformed the raw manuscript into a handsome publication. I worked with Mary and Michael in the past on special 1796-1797 half dollar write-ups for the Jules Reiver Collection sale (January 2006) and the Bayside New York Collection of Early Half Dollars in the Baltimore ANA sale (July 2008). Their expertise in those endeavors was again apparent in the preparation of this book, especially in dealing with the several changes I made to the first proof.

The Heritage Auctions Coin Photography Department – **Colleen McInerney**, **Tony Webb**, **Travis Awalt**, **Jason Young**, and **Joel Gonzalez** -- undertook the monumental task of shooting and photo shopping more than 550 images for the book. What is really amazing is that all but three or four of these were in sync with the text in the initial proof! Without the expertise of these folks, this publication is unlikely to have seen the light of day, no matter how good the written text might be.

Dr. Alan Stahl, Curator of Numismatics, Princeton University, made available to me images and pedigree information on the two 1796-1797 half dollars in the university collection.

ORIGIN OF THE DRAPED BUST DESIGN ON U.S. SILVER COINAGE

The half dollars of 1796-1797 are part of the Draped Bust Small Eagle design type of U. S. silver coinage. The draped bust and small eagle motifs first appeared on the silver dollar (1795-1798), and eventually made their way onto the half dime (1796-1797), dime (1796-1797), quarter (1796), and half dollar (1796-1797). This design type can be considered transitional between the Flowing Hair motif on the half dimes, half dollars, and dollars dated 1794 and 1795, and the Draped Bust Heraldic Eagle design on the half dimes (1800-1805), dimes (1798-1807), quarters (1804-1807), half dollars (1801-1807), and dollars (1798-1803) (Fig. 1).

Flowing Hair half dollar

Draped Bust Small Eagle half dollar

Draped Bust Heraldic Eagle half dollar

***Figure 1* — Transition from Flowing Hair to Draped Bust Heraldic Eagle**

The new Draped Bust Liberty was more buxom than the Flowing Hair version and was clothed in drapery on the lower part of the bust. Also, her hair took on a more curled appearance and was partially contained by a ribbon and large bow at the back of her head. This was in stark contrast to the Flowing Hair Liberty's long flowing tresses. Additionally, unlike the 15 stars contained on all Flowing Hair silver denominations, the star count on the Draped Bust Small Eagle obverse varied, depending on the denomination, between 15, 16, and 13.

The 1794-1795 reverse was replaced by one that displayed a smaller eagle with its feet farther apart and its wings entirely within the encircling branches. Its neck was shorter, and it perched on two clouds instead of a rock. The encircling laurel branches in 1794 and 1795 were replaced with a wreath of laurel on the left and a palm branch on the right. On the half dollar, the new reverse included the denomination ½ beneath the juncture of the two branches of the wreath – a fraction that is unique among U.S. silver coinage (fractional denominations also occurred on the Liberty Cap and Draped Bust half cents, and on the Wreath, Liberty Cap, and Draped Bust large cents).

The Draped Bust Heraldic Eagle design type that followed the Draped Bust Small Eagle type retained essentially the same obverse, except that the star count remains at 13. The reverse eagle is now considerably larger, however, and faces left with open wings. The shield of the Unites States covers its central body, and it holds a scroll with the motto E PLURIBUS UNUM in its beak.

The DeSaussure-Rittenhouse Theory

It is unclear who instigated the design change from the Flowing Hair to the Draped Bust motif. Perhaps it was Henry DeSaussure, who took over the Mint directorship from David Rittenhouse in July 1795, and who Bowers (1993, p. 40) says "soon concerned himself with the designs on the silver coinage." Or as Bowers alternatively states: "It may just as easily have been Thomas Jefferson, who as secretary of state, was the cabinet officer in charge of Mint affairs."

Credit: Independence National Historical Park

David Rittenhouse
Mint Director
April 1792 – June 1795

Henry DeSaussure
Mint Director
July 1795 – October 1795

Indeed, it may be that the impetus for the Draped Bust design occurred in the administration of Rittenhouse, and was then implemented during DeSaussure's term. This latter theory has some credence, as DeSaussure was in office for less than four months. This short tenure is likely to have left little time to develop new design concepts and to have them critically reviewed by top officials. The Mint could not afford a major blunder in redesigning precious metal coinage, especially considering the many problems it was facing during this time period, including moves from congressional leaders who wanted to abolish it.

The Gilbert Stuart Theory

James Ross Snowden, Mint Director from June 1853 to April 1861, while writing biographical notes on former Mint Directors (1861), alluded to the aforementioned design change that began with the dollar. He stated:

> "The head of Liberty on the dollar of 1795 was designed by (Gilbert) Stuart, the celebrated portrait painter, at the request of the Director, as we learn from a relation of the family; Stuart facetiously remarking that Liberty on the other coins had run mad – referring to the disheveled hair on the head of Liberty on the previous coins – we will bind it up, and thus render her a steady Matron" (p. 177).

When Snowden said "at the request of the Director'" was he, and/or the family relation of Stuart, referring to DeSaussure or Rittenhouse? It is unlikely that DeSaussure, who had just recently arrived in Philadelphia from his native South Carolina, knew Stuart. Likewise, with respect to Rittenhouse, there is no known documentary evidence that he had engaged Stuart to undertake the design change.

Gilbert Stuart

Another scenario is possible. Instead of either of the two above-mentioned Mint Directors, it may have been President George Washington (who had several portrait sittings with Stuart) who retained the famed artist. Or, Secretary of State Jefferson, who knew Stuart, may have made the design-change request.

One other possibility exists – Gilbert Stuart had nothing whatsoever to do with redesigning early American coinage. After all, the only connection between the famous portraitist and the Draped Bust design was a brief reference that Snowden made about an unnamed "relation of the family." Moreover, no evidence has yet been uncovered in early Mint records that reveals a payment having been made to Stuart. Of course, he may have provided this service gratis.

The present author examined numerous sources on Stuart's life and works in an effort to uncover information on his purported role in designing the Draped Bust motif. These include biographies by George Mason (1879), who apparently had access to Stuart family information, by Dorinda Evans (1999), an authority on Stuart, and anecdotes written by Stuart's daughter, Jane Stuart (1876, 1877). These and other works on Stuart provide not even the remotest hint of him having designed the Draped Bust Liberty.

If Gilbert Stuart did not design the Draped Bust motif, then who might have? One possibility is Chief Engraver Robert Scot. After all, it was he who designed the Flowing Hair Liberty. Perhaps he not only engraved the Draped Bust dies but also created the design. Other possibilities might be Assistant Engraver John Smith Gardner or John Eckstein, a Philadelphia artist.

The Anne Willing Bingham Theory

Anne Bingham (née Anne Willing) is sometimes cited as the model for Liberty on the Draped Bust design. While no documentary evidence exists to substantiate this assertion, Reid Goldsborough, who has written about the Draped Bust Liberty (2001; 2010), contends indirect circumstantial evidence links her to the Draped Bust motif (2010):

Anne Willing Bingham

- She was close personal friends with key players in U.S. Mint policy, specifically President George Washington and Secretary of State Thomas Jefferson.
- She was a personal friend of Gilbert Stuart, who … may have designed the new Liberty on American silver coinage. Though Stuart's proposed Draped Bust sketch has apparently not survived, sketches, portraits, and unfinished portraits of Anne and the Bingham family are part of his repertoire.
- The resemblance of Liberty on the Draped Bust coins to Anne Bingham in the above works, though not exact, is thought to be close enough not to rule out the connection.
- She lived in Philadelphia, site of the U.S. Mint.
- Her father and husband were co-founders of the Bank of North America, also in Philadelphia.

Goldsborough further writes (2001):

> "... information linking Bingham and the Draped Bust Liberty may have been deliberately suppressed at the time. To show a recognizable person on the nation's coins would have been politically dangerous.
>
> "The Mint was under attack in its early days from opponents of President Washington's administration, who charged that the Mint was too expensive and failed to provide a circulating medium. Washington was a Federalist, and Bingham's husband and father were also powerful figures among Federalist leaders.
>
> "A recognizable portrait of a Federalist could have been misrepresented to mean that only the Federalists stood for real Liberty. This would certainly have added fuel to the fire of anti-Mint sentiments" (p. 56).

As is the case with Gilbert Stuart being the purported designer of the Draped Bust motif, it may never be known for certain whether Anne Bingham was indeed the model for the design.

GENESIS OF THE 1796-1797 HALF DOLLAR

The Bank of the United States: "Parent" of the 1796-1797 Half Dollar

Mint records show that Draped Bust Small Eagle half dollars were coined from silver bullion deposited by the Bank of the United States. The Bank, the brainchild of Alexander Hamilton, was a semi-public institution granted a twenty-year charter (1791-1811) by Congress. Its main office was in Philadelphia, with branches in Boston, New York, Baltimore, Charleston, Norfolk, Washington, Savannah, and New Orleans.

Credit: Independence Hall Association

First Bank of the United States

On October 7, 1791, a committee of the Bank's stockholders met in Philadelphia to propose a 25-member board of directors who determined salaries of all Bank officers and clerks, supervised the printing and supply of the Bank's notes, and approved private loan applications. The main board in Philadelphia "... also passed judgment on loans to the government ... soon to be the Bank's largest loan customer" (Cowen, 2000, p. 45). Thomas Willing was elected unanimously to be Bank President by the board of directors on October 25, 1791. The board then chose the Bank's permanent employees, including cashier (essentially the chief operating officer), first and second tellers, first and second bookkeepers, discount (loan) clerk and assistant clerk, runner, and doorkeepers/porters (Cowen, 2000, p. 47). The significance of the Bank's organizational makeup to the present study will become apparent in the section entitled "The Research Findings."

Among the Bank's clients was the U.S. Treasury, which deposited cash receipts in the Bank's vaults. As the government's fiscal agent, the Treasury department deposited the bulk of its funds in the vaults of the Bank and its branches. Consequently, the vaults contained a large quantity of the country's gold and silver supply (Cowen, 2000, p. 139).

The Bank also maintained a close relationship with the U.S. Mint. Neil Carothers (1930, p. 74) writes:

> "The Bank ... adopted the practice of sending foreign coin receipts to the Mint when the machinery was idle through the lack of private deposits. Occasionally it had French coins or other silver pieces recoined on its own account. In the first forty years of the mint's existence much the largest part of the coinage was for the first and second United States Banks."

Draped Bust Small Eagle Half Dollar Deliveries to the Bank

The delivery warrants and dates and number of 1796-1797 half dollars delivered to the Bank of the United States are displayed in Table 1.

***Table 1* — 1796-1797 Half Dollar Deliveries**

Warrant Number	Date	Half Dollars Delivered
81	February 28, 1797	60
84	March 21, 1797	874
90	May 26, 1797	2,984
Total		3,918

Source: U.S. Mint Records

The significant point here is, had the Bank not made silver bullion deposits during this time and requested that they be coined into half dollars, it is quite likely there would have been *no* coinage of Draped Bust Small Eagles halves.

1796-1797 Half Dollar Mintage

Mint records did not break out the 3,918 pieces by date. Overton/Parsley estimate that about 934 coins (23.8%) were dated 1796 and 2,984 pieces (76.2%) bore the 1797 date. These estimates are often repeated in the numismatic literature. As will be seen in the section entitled "The Research Findings," however, the mintage of each date was likely more balanced.

Possible Reasons for Low Mintage

Collectors who own, or who desire to own, a 1796 or 1797 half dollar cannot help but wonder why its original mintage was so small. This question is especially relevant when one views its production figure in relation to early silver coinage as a whole, and to the large mintage of half dollars in general (Table 2). More half dollars were coined (nearly two million pieces) within the pre-Turban era than any other silver denomination, but the 1796-1797 halves accounted for a minuscule share of this production.

Table 2 — **Pre-Turban Silver Coinage, Approximate Mintage**

Coin Denomination	Flowing Hair	Draped Bust Small Eagle	Draped Bust Heraldic Eagle	Total
Half Dimes	86,416	54,757	124,270	265,443
Dimes	-	47,396	422,396	469,406
Quarter Dollars	-	6,146	554,899	561,045
Half Dollars	323,144	**3,918**	1,600,787	1,927,849
Dollars	281,758★	280,000★	870,000★	1,431,758★
Total	691,318	392,217	3,571,966	4,655,501

Sources: *A Guide Book of United States Coins,* 65th Edition, 2012; David Bowers, *Silver Dollars and Trade Dollars of the United States,* Volume I, 1993 (★Bowers' estimates).

While the exact reasons for this minute 1796-1797 half dollar mintage may never be known, some possible answers might be found in the numismatic literature. First, merchants and bankers were reluctant to bring silver bullion to the Mint because of the disclosure of the illegal silver standard of 0.900 fine that was previously in effect instead of the 0.8924+ standard prescribed in the Mint Act of April 2, 1792. The most immediate effect of this practice was that depositors ended up paying an additional 2 ½ grains of silver bullion (about 1% extra) for every dollar they received (Taxay, 1966, p. 89). When this became widely known, bullion deposits brought to the Mint declined significantly in 1796 and 1797. This "silver famine" likely helped to account for the smaller number of all Draped Bust Small Eagle denominations minted during these two years (Table 2).

Second, most bullion depositors wanted dollars for their silver, not half dollars or smaller denomination coins. The dollars were meant for export abroad, and unlike lower denomination coins, were readily accepted by foreign merchants (Bowers, 1993, p.45; Carothers, 1930, p. 75).

Third, a yellow fever epidemic forced the closing of the Mint from late August to late November 1797. Coinage deliveries did not resume until early January 1798, and these included only dollars and gold coins (U.S. Mint Records).

Finally, the large number of 1794-1795 Flowing Hair half dollars minted (323,144 pieces) may have temporarily oversaturated the demand for this denomination.

DRAPED BUST SMALL EAGLE HALF DOLLAR VARIETIES

The 1796 and 1797 half dollars each consist of two varieties as described in Al Overton's *Early Half Dollar Die Varieties*, edited in 1990 and 2005 by Don Parsley. The 1796 issue with 15 obverse stars is Overton-101, and the one with 16 stars is Overton-102. The two 1797-dated varieties, both containing 15 obverse stars and designated Overton-101 and Overton-102, are differentiated according to the placement of the reverse wreath in relation to the peripheral lettering (see below).

1796-1797 Half Dollar Die Marriages

Three obverse and two reverse dies were used to produce the Draped Bust Small Eagle half dollar series (Fig. 2). Overton's Reverse A was used with all three obverses until it began to shatter by the time it was paired with Obverse 3 (1797 Overton-101). The die state with extensive reverse cracks is designated Overton-101a. A new reverse die (Reverse B) was then paired with Obverse 3 (1797 Overton-102).

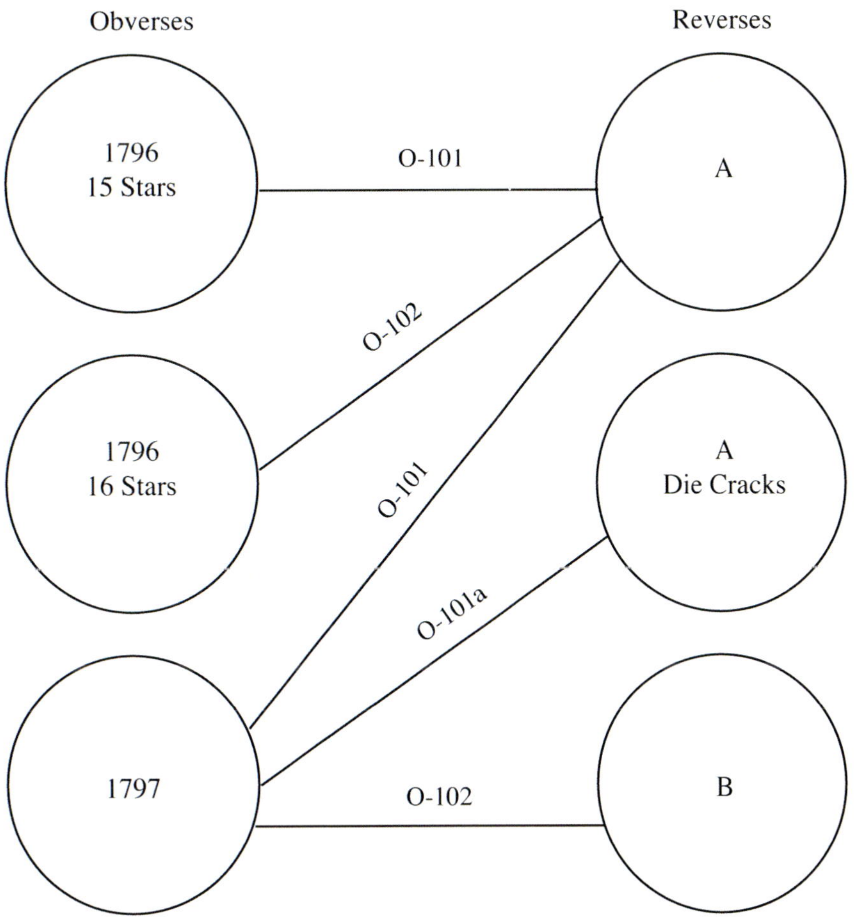

***Figure 2* — 1796-1797 Half Dollar Die Marriage Chart**

1796 Overton-101 Variety (15 Stars)

Most specimens of the 1796 15 Stars variety display a heavy die crack from the rim at 5:00 to Liberty's bust. It then makes a sharp right turn through the drapery and stars 15, 14, and 13, after which it turns right to the rim at about 3:00. This crack shows clearly even on low-grade specimens. Another crack from the 5:00 rim crack travels left through the drapery, where above the 9 in the date it extends upward as a semi-circular crack terminating below the neck curl above the shoulder. This latter crack shows only on high-end VF and finer specimens (Fig. 3).

***Figure 3* — 1796 15 Stars with Obverse Die Cracks**

Previously, only two 1796 15 Stars half dollars were known that lacked the usually seen die crack in the lower-right obverse quadrant. One appeared as lot 1777 in the Stack's John Whitney Walter Sale, May 1999 (Serial # 101 in the present research), and lot 1448 in the Bowers and Merena March 2004 Sale (Serial # 100 in the current study). The present research project has identified four additional specimens that lack this crack (Serial Numbers 119, 145, 162a, and 165a). It can be concluded that these six coins were among the first 1796 15 Stars half dollars struck.

1796 Overton-102 Variety (16 Stars)

Overton/Parsley indicate that: "Most (1796 16 Stars) specimens show a heavy die crack from the milling between the date and star 1, that joins the first four stars then out to the milling" (Fig. 4). However, the majority of examples in the present study lack this crack.

Figure 4 — **1796 16 Stars with Obverse Die Crack**

1797 Overton-101 Variety

The 1797 O-101 variety employed the same reverse die (Reverse A) that was used for both 1796 issues. This reverse is distinguished by the following: a palm leaf extends halfway between the base of F and O in OF; a palm leaf tip ends below the lower serif of the I in AMERICA; and a laurel leaf tip ends below the left serif of the second T in STATES (Fig. 5).

Figure 5 — **Reverse A**

1797 Overton-101a Die State

Reverse A eventually developed myriad die cracks, especially during the time it was paired with the 1797 O-101 obverse. Figure 6 illustrates the location of these cracks at the point Reverse A appears to have reached its "terminal" (or at least near-terminal) die state (1797 O-101a). Additionally, the obverse of 1797 O-101a developed a relatively light crack from the rim through star 2 to the top of Liberty's second curl from the bottom.

Figure 6 — **Reverse A Die Cracks**
Sources: Beistle (1929); Overton (2005); Bowers and Merena (1997); and the author

The present author's research indicates that the first of these cracks to develop on Reverse A occurred when it was paired with the 1796 15 Stars obverse. The enlargement of the upper-right reverse of the high-grade (AU) 1796 15 Stars half from Heritage's July 2008 sale, lot 1668 (Fig. 7), displays this incipient crack through the tops of ES in STATES that extends midway into the field toward the top of O in OF (this is Serial # 112 in the present study). No other reverse cracks are evident on this coin, indicating that it was indeed the first crack to develop on Reverse A.

***Figure* 7 — Initial Crack on Reverse A**

This finding regarding the development and location of the first crack on Reverse A contradicts that originally put forth by Beistle (1929) and Overton (2005). Both of these researchers point to the first crack on Reverse A developing from the rim at about 1:30 to the upper-right side of O in OF.

The second crack identified by the present author to develop on Reverse A, is the one recognized by Beistle and Overton, extending from the rim at 1:30 to the upper-right part of O in OF. It appears to have first developed, however, when Reverse A was paired with the 1796 15 Stars obverse, not with the 1796 16 Stars obverse per Overton or the 1797 obverse per Beistle. Lot 2018 from the Heritage Auctions' September 2008 sale (serial # 113 in the present study) displays this crack, albeit faintly (the Heritage photo archives image, HA.com/1116*2018, shows this second crack even clearer). This crack will eventually travel from the lower-right side of O through the palm wreath to the middle-edge of the right (facing) wing when Reverse A is paired with the 1796 16 Stars obverse. Lot 1865 from Heritage's September 2006 sale (serial # 219 in the present study) displays this extended crack. Later it will travel through the wing into the upper-right part of the right (facing) leg.

What is probably the third crack that forms on Reverse A apparently occurred when it was paired with the latter stages of the 1797 O-101 obverse. It extends from the rim at 10:30 through the first T of STATES and the laurel wreath to the back of the eagle's head. Lot 3837 in the Heritage January 2009 FUN sale (serial #311 in the present study) exhibits this crack.

What is perhaps the fourth crack to develop on Reverse A extends from the rim at 9:30 through the laurel wreath and the top of the left (facing) wing and then to the lower neck. This crack is relatively heavy and is usually visible even on well-worn specimens. For this reason, most catalogers and researchers (the present author included) consider it the major criterion for differentiating the 1797 O-101a die state from its "early die state" 1797 O-101 predecessor.

As evident from Fig. 6, the reverse of the 1797 O-101a die state displays several other cracks, most of which apparently developed after those previously identified. The majority of these were relatively light to begin with and wore down with circulation. Therefore, little else will be said about them in the present study, with one important exception, that being the crack connecting the ones from the rim at 9:30 and 10:30, discussed in the next paragraph.

Examination of high-grade (XF and finer) 1797 O-101a specimens in the study indicates that this connecting crack first developed through the bottoms of ST in STATES, and then extends to intersect the one from the rim at 9:30. When present, this extended crack from the lower-left serif of the first S identifies an O-101a specimen in the study as a "late" (or presumably terminal or near-terminal) die state. If this extended crack is absent, an O-101a coin is designated "intermediate" die state for study purposes.

1797 Overton-102 Variety

Overton's Reverse B that is paired with the 1797 obverse (O-102 variety) differs from Reverse A in the following ways. A palm leaf tip ends just below the left serif of F in OF, and another ends below the upper serif of the I in AMERICA. Finally, a laurel leaf extends across the base of the second T in STATES. Additionally, the obverse crack from the rim through star 2 to Liberty's curl is heavier (Fig. 8).

***Figure 8* — 1797 O-102 with Obverse Die Crack and Reverse B**

COLLECTIONS FEATURING ALL FOUR 1796-1797 HALF DOLLAR VARIETIES

Few numismatists have held all four 1796-1797 half dollar varieties in their collections. In this section, those who have accomplished this difficult feat (as evidenced by the simultaneous sale of all four varieties at public auction) are reviewed. No pretense is made that this list is all-inclusive. Some publicly sold collections containing all four varieties may have inadvertently been omitted from the present study. Likewise, it is possible, even probable, that some collectors owned (and perhaps still own) all four varieties, for which no public record is available.

The A.C. Gies Collection

The Gies Collection appeared in the October 19, 1940 auction sale held by Stack's. The catalog listing is as follows, along with prices realized:

Lot 413	1796 15 Stars H-1★	Very Fine	$125.00
Lot 414	1796 16 Stars H-2★	Very Fine	$155.00
Lot 415	1797 H-1★	Very Fine	$95.00
Lot 416	1797 H-2★	Very Fine	$92.50

★These are Haseltine numbers, an attribution system that pre-dates Overton by more than 80 Years.

The Dennis Heller Collection

The Heller collection appeared in the Florida United Numismatists (FUN) Sale conducted January 7-9, 1982 in Orlando, Florida by New England Rare Coin Auctions (NERCA). The NERCA catalog prefaced the eight 1796-1797 half dollars offered in the sale with the following headline:

"AN UNPRECEDENTED OFFERING OF 1796-1797 HALF DOLLARS FROM THE HELLER COLLECTION."

The catalog goes on to say:

> "All five (die states) are represented in this incredible selection, possibly the finest (and most complete) offering of 1796-1797 halves ever presented at auction. The following eight coins represent years of patient searching by Dennis Heller."

The catalog listing follows, along with prices realized (including 10% buyers fee):

Lot 614	1796 15 Stars	Very Fine 30	$22,550
Lot 615	1796 15 Stars	Very Fine 35	$22,000
Lot 616	1796 16 Stars	Very Good 8	$12,650
Lot 617	1797 O-102	Very Good 10	$11,000
Lot 618	1797 O-101a	Very Fine 25	$18,150
Lot 619	1797 O-101	Very Fine 35	$22,550
Lot 620	1797 O-101	Very Fine 35	$19,250
Lot 621	1797 O-101	Extra Fine 40	$25,300

The James Brilliant Collection

The four 1796-1797 half dollars in the Brilliant Collection were sold by Bowers and Merena in its January 9-10, 1992 sale. The catalog listing, along with the prices realized (including the 10% buyers fee), follows:

Lot 38	1796 15 Stars	Fine 12 to 15	$11,000
Lot 39	1796 16 Stars	Very Fine 30	$19,800
Lot 40	1797 O-101a	Fine 15	$13,750
Lot 41	1797 O-102	Very Good 10	$15,400

The Jules Reiver Collection

The quartet of 1796-1797 half dollar varieties appeared in the January 27, 2006 Signature sale conducted by Heritage Auctions in Dallas, TX. The catalog listing, along with prices realized (including the 15% buyer's fee) follows:

Lot 22512	1796 15 Stars	NCS VF Details	$63,250
Lot 22513	1796 16 Stars	NGC VG8	$46,000
Lot 22514	1797 O-101	NCS XF Details	$69,000
Lot 22515	1797 O-102	NGC VG10	$46,000

The Bayside New York Collection

Heritage Auctions sold all four Draped Bust Small Eagle half dollar varieties in its July 31, 2008 World's Fair of Money sale in Baltimore, MD. The catalog listing and prices realized (including the 15% buyer's fee) follows:

Lot 1668	1796 15 Stars	PCGS AU58	$207,000
Lot 1669	1796 16 Stars	PCGS VF30	$83,375
Lot 1670	1797 O-101a	NGC VF30	$69,000
Lot 1671	1797 O-102	PCGS VF35	$97,750

DRAPED BUST SMALL EAGLE HALF DOLLAR ANECDOTES

Some rare coins (perhaps most notably the 1804 dollar, 1894-S dime, and 1913 Liberty Head nickel) yield their own particular stories. The Draped Bust Small Eagle half dollar, while not having the stature of these rarities, nevertheless possesses interesting anecdotes. The following hopefully add flavor and spice to the background of this important series.

The Man Who Swallowed a 1796 Half Dollar

A presumably satirical article entitled "A Warning to Coin Collectors" in *Mason's Coin Collectors Herald* (1879, p. 13) states:

A WARNING TO COIN COLLECTORS.

WE grieve to announce the following melancholly event, which we find circulating the rounds of the press:

"KILLED BY A COIN.—A young man died in Binghampton last week from the effects of swallowing a silver half dollar, dated 1796, about three weeks ago. He was tossing the coin in the air and catching it in his mouth. to amuse a child, when it lodged in his throat and passed into his stomach."

The sympathies of all true numismatists will be enlisted in behalf of the bereaved family and friends of this unique Coin Collector, and the loss *of the coin* will be sincerely felt! Thus we lose the last hope of completing our series of U. S. Silver Half Dollars. Why will the unsophisticated collector turn his stomach into a Coin Cabinet and destroy at once his own and the coin's circulation?. Perhaps the Coroner is a numismatist: if so, there is yet hope that a *tarnished* 1796 half dollar will, at no distant day, be offered at a public coin sale. Let us wait and hope. No "peace to his remains," until the piece swallowed is exhumed and pronounced genuine! We offer $100 for the recovery of the coin!

Coin Dealer Trades 1796 Dollar for Elderly Woman's 1796 Half Dollar

A short note from 'Echoes from a Coin Dealer's Sanctum' in the August 1892 *The Numismatist* (pp. 20-21) states:

Mr. Henry Ahlborn, one of the oldest coin dealers in Boston, is about as keen a man for a bargain as one can find. He tells how one summer day, trade being unusually dull in store, he started on a pick up trip along the north shore going through the old towns of Salem, Marblehead, Hamilton, and Essex. He stopped in all the country stores, and talked with many an old farmer always with a view of finding some rare coin. He at last heard of a old lady who had in her possession a number of fine old cents and silver coins.

Mr. Ahlborn paid her generous prices for the cents and some silver and was about to go away when the old lady said that she had another piece, that was a gift from her father, and was made in the year she was born, but that she would not part with it for anything. He asked to see it and she brought out the finest 1796 half-dollar he had ever seen.

His eyes snapped, and he immediately considered how he could get possession of of that half-dollar.

A lucky idea struck him, he bethought himself of a fine 1796 dollar he had bagged that morning and taking it out he offered to exchange it with the lady for her half-dollar making prominent the fact that this was a whole dollar, while while hers was only a half-dollar besides it bore the same date and was equally as good. Convinced by this reasoning, she readilly made the exchange and Mr. A went on his way satisfied with his days work.

He afterwards sold it to Mr. Parmelee for $150,00 and I think he holds it to day for $350,00. It bears but very slight traces of circulation.

THE RESEARCH METHODOLOGY

One of the key questions about the Draped Bust Small Eagle half dollar series (or any other rare coin series) centers on the number of examples that have survived to the present day. A related question revolves around the level of preservation of surviving specimens. While population reports prepared by the major grading services provide some insight into these questions, rarity and condition data can often be distorted by the common practice of resubmitting a coin to the same or a different service in the hope of receiving a higher grade. As indicated in the Introduction, the present study seeks to determine the survival rate of 1796-1797 half dollars and the grade distribution of surviving examples, with an eye toward arriving at a census of the extant population.

Previous Rarity and Condition Estimates

Estimates by numismatic researchers of the number of surviving Draped Bust Small Eagle half dollars vary widely. David Lange (1990) suggests "... there are not many more than 100 survivors." Lano Balulescu (2000) gives an estimate of 75 to 200 specimens, and Robert Hilt (1980, p. 44) says about 165 examples have survived. Based on the Rarity Rating Estimates (R values) for each of the four 1796-1797 half dollar varieties provided by the Bust Half Nut Club at the August 2004 Pittsburgh ANA, 184 to 259 total coins are estimated to exist. Donald Parsley's 2005 edition of Al Overton's *Early Half Dollar Die Varieties* estimates between 106 and 270 examples, again based on R values for each of the four varieties.

Most literature referring to the condition of surviving 1796-1797 half dollars points to their survival in lower levels of preservation. Walter Breen (1988) writes they are "Usually in low grades." An August 15, 2000 RARCOA website archives (no longer active) indicated that "Outside of a small number of Mint State coins, most of the survivors are only in well worn condition." Randy Camper (2001) opines that survivors "range from Poor to Uncirculated and are usually seen in lower circulated grades." The March 11-13, 2004 Bowers and Merena catalog, on the other hand contends "There are, in fact, several high quality examples of both 1796 and 1797 half dollars."

Sources Used in the Study

In an effort to determine how many 1796-1797 half dollars have in fact survived to the present day, and to what degree of preservation, the author has tracked the appearances of these coins in catalogs of numismatic public auction sales held in the United States since their advent in the mid 19th century. While auction catalogs served as the major source material in the study, dealer fixed price lists advertised in *Coin World* and *Numismatic News* have also been monitored for such appearances, as have the websites of major numismatic firms. Finally, 1796-1797 halves in institutional and private collections known to the author have been referenced.

Catalogs of Numismatic Auction Sales

Numismatic auction occurrences and dates were obtained from listings in Adams (1982, 1990), Gengerke (1990), Moulton (2001), and other sources. Additionally, since 2001 the author has monitored the sales of all major American numismatic auction firms, and those of several minor ones, for the appearance of 1796-1797 halves. Nearly 4,000 auction catalogs located in the libraries of the American Numismatic Society and Heritage Auctions, and in his personal collection have been surveyed. This survey covered numismatic auction sales from 1855 to the present, and resulted in the identification of more than 1,500 appearances of 1796-1797 half dollars, 702 of which are imaged. Poor photo quality that prevented the determination of a coin appearance's Overton variety, its grade, or its identification markers resulted in 76 of the 702 imaged auction-catalog appearances to be deleted from further analysis, leaving 626 auction appearances in the study (the 76 deleted appearances are listed at the end of the census of each Overton variety/die state in the section entitled "A CENSUS OF 1796-1797 HALF DOLLARS").

Coin Dealer Fixed Price Lists

Most Draped Bust Small Eagle half dollars are sold at auction as opposed to being offered through retail coin sales. Even in his nearly 100 fixed price lists issued between 1885 and 1911, Charles Steigerwalt (the first dealer, according to Adams, to make extensive use of this merchandising form), only showed 50 1796-1797 offerings, the vast majority of which appear to be duplicate specimens, based on several repetitive descriptions. To this author's knowledge, none of these were plated.

In the present day, a number of numismatic retail firms make 1796-1797 half dollar (and other rare coin) offerings. In addition to the 50 fixed price lists cited by Steigerwalt, the author has identified about 75 other such appearances, most occurring after 2001. Of these, 61 are imaged.

Institutional Numismatic Collections

The author canvassed major institutions that might hold 1796-1797 half dollars in their collections. The American Numismatic Society holds a 1796 16 Stars and a 1797 O-101 specimen; the Princeton University numismatic cabinet possesses a 1796 16 Stars and a 1797 O-101 example; the National Numismatic Collection, Smithsonian Institution, holds a 1796 15 Stars, a 1796 16 Stars, and a 1797 O-101a; and the Durham Museum in Omaha, Nebraska has a 1796 15 Stars example from the Byron Reed Collection, on loan from the city of Omaha. All eight of these coins are imaged.

Inquiries to the American Numismatic Association and the British Museum indicated that no 1796-1797 halves are held in their collections. The author knows of no other numismatic institution cabinets that might hold examples of these coins.

Private Collections

Ten collectors who responded to the author's 2001 article in *The Numismatist* sent images of the 1796 or 1797 half in their collection. All but two of these (a Texas collector's 1797 O-102 and an upstate New York collector's 1797 O-102) appeared in previous or subsequent auction or fixed price sales included in the study. The names of collectors who contributed images and other information to the author are kept confidential.

Other

Draped Bust Small Eagle half dollar appearances not falling into any of the above categories are classified under "Other." These include plate coins in Overton's *Early Half Dollar Die Varieties* (1990, 2005) and *Coins* and *Coinage* magazines, PCGS registry set coins, the 1914 American Numismatic Society exhibition of the two H.O. Granberg Collection specimens, and various other appearances. All 16 "Other" appearances are imaged.

The above sources resulted in 713 imaged Draped Bust Small Eagle half dollar appearances to form the core of the study analysis. In sum, 626 appearances are from auction catalogs, 61 from dealers' fixed price lists, eight from institutional cabinets, two from private collections, and 16 from "other" sources.

Enhanced 1796-1797 Half Dollar Grading Standards

The following grading standards used in the study are based in part on ANA, PCGS, and NGC grade criteria. The author felt it was necessary, however, to go beyond these criteria and develop more specific standards for grading 1796-1797 half dollars. The justification for these "enhanced" standards is based on his experience in examining hundreds of images of these coins over the past 10 years and in cataloging about 50 or so different specimens for Heritage Auctions.

The standards used represent "technical" grading based on the amount of wear on a coin, not "market" grading or "net" grading that takes impairments into consideration. A study coin that does exhibit problems is given a technical grade and the impairments indicated separately. Also, the obverse and reverse of each appearance was graded separately, its final grade being the lower of the two.

Mint State (MS 60 to 70)
Mint condition is very difficult to determine from photos. For the present study, reliance is placed on grade assigned by a third party grading service, and/or the author's familiarity with the coin if he cataloged it at Heritage Auctions.

About Uncirculated (AU 50, 53, 55, 58)
Sharp detail except for high-point wear. On reverse, talons completely separated from clouds.

Extremely Fine (XF 40, 45)
Obv.: Liberty's drapery clearly separated from shoulder.
Rev.: All feathers delineated, though there may be some incipient merging in lower part of left (facing) wing. Talons sharp, but those on left (facing) leg may begin to merge with cloud.

Very Fine (VF 20, 25, 30, 35)
Obv.: Liberty's hair worn but shows considerable detail. Drapery line at shoulder worn smooth.
Rev.: Feathers merged in lower part of left (facing) wing. Talons merging with clouds.

Fine (Fine 12, 15)
Obv.: Liberty's hair heavily worn, but some separation still shows. Ear lobe, eye, eye lid, and eye brow worn but visible. Delineation between shoulder and hair. Drapery partially separated (albeit faintly) from left (facing) breast
Rev.: Feathers merged in lower portions of both wings. Talons and clouds merged. Wings and legs separate from torso. Tail feathers separated or nearly so.

Very Good (VG 8, 10)
Obv.: Little or no separation in hair. Only partial detail in ear lobe, eye, and eye lid. Shoulder and hair show little or no separation.
Rev.: Only a few details show in wings. Wings and legs show only partial separation from torso.

Good (Good 4, 6)
Central motifs outlined but show little or no internal detail. Peripheral elements heavily worn but visible.

About Good (AG 3)
Central motifs outlined or nearly so. Date strong but other peripheral elements merging with rim and sometimes partially worn away.

Fair (Fair 2)
Date visible but other peripheral elements and central devices only partially outlined.

Poor (Poor 0, 1)
All design elements smooth or nearly so, but coin identifiable by date and type.

Toward a Census of Draped Bust Small Eagle Half Dollars

The 713 plated appearances of 1796-1797 half dollars were further examined to account for duplicate specimens (Carl Carlson, 1981, pp. 349-364), presents an excellent discussion on the use of photographic plates to track and "isolate" rare coin appearances; images are also important in assessing a particular coin's grade and surface condition.

The 713 imaged 1796-1797 half dollar appearances were first grouped by the four Overton varieties and the 1797 O-101a die state. Second, they were sorted by broad grade categories (e.g., Extremely Fine, Very Fine, Fine, etc.) within their respective Overton variety, and any identification markers noted, such as distinctive toning patterns, streaks, or spots, and the location of adjustment marks, planchet flaws, surface abrasions, rim bruises, plugs, or intentional damage such as digs, punch marks, deep scratches, or graffiti.

Each of the 713 imaged appearances within each grade category within the respective Overton variety was then compared to identify duplicate specimens. This was accomplished by examining and comparing the location of identification markers on the various appearances. This comparative analysis resulted in the identification of 270 1796-1797 half dollars.

Each of these 270 specimens was then assigned a serial number. This number begins with 100 for 1796 15 Stars coins, 200 for 1796 16 Stars pieces, 300 for 1797 O-101 examples, 400 for 1797 O-101a specimens, and 500 for 1797 O-102 examples. The grade, identification markers, provenance, serial number, and any other appropriate information for each of the 270 coins are listed in the next section (auction prices realized include the appropriate buyer's fee, if charged to the hammer price).

A CENSUS OF 1796-1797 HALF DOLLARS

1796 15 Stars Half Dollar Examples
Overton-101

From Bowers and Merena, March 2004

1796 15 Stars, O-101, early die state.

Knoxville Collection Specimen.

Grade: Specimen Strike.

Identification Markers: Minute marks on Liberty's neck and breasts, to the right of stars 2 and 3-4, and to the upper right of the eagle's right (facing) wing. All of these appear to be lint marks. Lacks the usually seen die crack from the border at 5:00 to the bust. One of only six early die state examples in the study without this crack, indicating it is among the first 1796 halves struck.

Provenance: *Knoxville Collection (Jay Parrino's The Mint, June 2003), NGC Specimen 65; Rare Coin Wholesalers (Numismatic News Ad, September 2003), NGC Specimen 65, $1,000,000; Bowers and Merena (March 2004), PCGS Specimen 65, lot 1448, unsold.*

Additional Notes: The Bowers and Merena catalogs states: "Arguably the finest survivor of this design type," and "The obverse die is perfect without any trace of the usually seen die crack from the border to the bust at 5:00." It cannot be determined from the photos whether this or the following Mougey – Granberg – Allenburger – Judd – Walter specimen is the finest known 1796 15 Stars half dollar.

Coin Serial Number: 100.

From Stack's,
May 1999

1796 15 Stars, O-101, early die state.

Mougey – Granberg – Allenburger – Judd – Walter Specimen.

Grade: Specimen Strike.

Identification Markers: Small mark to the upper right of the 6 in the date. Two squiggly lint marks above Liberty's shoulder, and another between star 3 and the curl. A short toning streak bisects the I in UNITED, and a curved lint mark extends from the upper right of the left (facing) wing. Lacks the usually seen die crack from the border at 5:00 to the bust. One of only six early die state examples in the study without this crack, indicating it is among the first 1796 halves struck.

Provenance: *Peter Mougey Collection (Thomas Elder, September 1910), Proof, lot 424, $360; H.O. Granberg Collection (American Numismatic Society Exhibition, January-February 1914); C.A. Allenburger Collection (B. Max Mehl, March 1948), lot 385, $735; Dr. J. Hewitt Judd; Kreisberg and Schulman (January 1963), Brilliant Proof, lot 2963; Kreisberg and Schulman (March 1964), Brilliant Proof, lot 1289; Stack's (October 1990), Brilliant Proof, lot 1646, $121,000; John Whitney Walter Collection (Stack's, May 1999), Specimen 66, lot 1777, $138,000; Coins Magazine Plate Coin, Vol. 52, No. 3, March 2005.*

Additional Notes: This coin apparently served as the host coin for a cast copy counterfeit that appeared in Auction '80 and Auction '86. Jesse Patrick published an article on this counterfeit entitled "An Interesting 1796 Bust Half Dollar" in the December 1996 *John Reich Journal.*

Coin Serial Number: 101.

From American Numismatic Rarities, September 2005

1796 15 Stars, O-101.

Whitney Walter Specimen.

Grade: Mint State.

Identification Markers: Small mark on middle right of Liberty's neck. Mottled toning pattern on central reverse, and a toning streak between TE of UNITED to the wreath. This and most subsequent 1796 15 Stars examples in the study are from later die states and display the crack from the border at 5:00 to the bust. Only the two aforementioned "Specimen Strike" coins and those with serial numbers 119, 145, 162a, and 165a lack this crack. Catalog photo quality precludes determination whether or not specimens under serial numbers 118, 121, 141, 155, 164, 165, and 167 lack this crack.

Provenance: *Superior Galleries (August 1991), NGC MS 64, lot 501, $198,000; John Whitney Walter Collection (Stack's, May 1999), MS 64, lot 1776, $120,750; American Numismatic Rarities (September 2005), NGC MS 64, lot 388, $310,500.*

Additional Notes: None.

Coin Serial Number: 102.

From Heritage Auctions, January 2009

1796 15 Stars, O-101.

Eliasberg Specimen.

Grade: Mint State.

Identification Markers: Upper-left to lower-right adjustment marks in Liberty's upper hair. Darker peripheral toning on obverse. Mark on chest to upper left of cleavage. Mark just beneath eagle's right (facing) wing.

Provenance: *Benjamin H. Collins, January 1896; J.M. Clapp; John H. Clapp; Clapp estate, 1942, to Louis Eliasberg, Sr. (per Bowers and Merena, April 1997); Eliasberg estate (Bowers and Merena, in cooperation with Stack's, April 1997), MS 63 prooflike, lot 1673, $110,000; Heritage Auctions (August 2006), PCGS MS 63, lot 5222, $310,500; Stack's (January 2009), PCGS MS 63, lot 400, unsold; Stack's (July 2009), PCGS MS 63, lot 523.*

Additional Notes: The Bowers and Merena catalog states: "With prooflike fields on obverse and reverse this memorable 1796 half dollar must have been minted on a special occasion."

Coin Serial Number: 103.

From Bowers and Merena, November 2010

1796 15 Stars, O-101.

Clarke – Norweb Specimen.

Grade: Mint State, light obverse Scratch.

Identification Markers: Thin vertical scratch on Liberty's neck from ear lobe to curl. Toning spot in field to lower left of star 9. Semicircular planchet fissure between D and S of UNITED STATES.

Provenance: *T. James Clarke Collection (New Netherlands, April 1956), Proof, lot 1195; Mrs. R. Henry Norweb; Norweb Collection (Bowers and Merena, November 1988), MS 60, prooflike, lot 3024, $99,000; Dennis Irving Long Collection (Bowers and Merena, January 1990), MS 60, prooflike, lot 256, $83,000; Stack's (October 1999), Brilliant Uncirculated, lot 343, unsold; Stack's (October 2000), Brilliant Uncirculated, lot 876, $80,500; American Gold Exchange (May 2001), NGC MS 62, POR; American Numismatic Rarities (November-December 2004), NGC MS 62, lot 1236, $201,250; Bowers and Merena (November 2010), NGC MS 63, lot 1908, $299,000.*

Additional Notes: The ANR catalog states: "A tiny spot around a piece of adhering lint is present under star 9, though since that piece of lint was not present when this coin was sold in 1988 or 1990 we imagine it would be easily removed by a careful hand."

Coin Serial Number: 104.

From Heritage Auctions, February 2008

1796 15 Stars, O-101.

Hagle Specimen.

Grade: Mint State.

Identification Markers: Several flyspeck-like spots in right obverse field, between date and star 1, and between stars 7-8 and Liberty's head. Dark toning area around lower part of last S in STATES. Spot in middle of upper stand of U in UNITED.

Provenance: *Hagle Collection (Bowers and Merena, March 1989), AU 58 to MS 60, prooflike, lot 1990, $74,800; American Numismatic Rarities (August 2004), NGC MS 63, lot 418, $189,750; Heritage Auctions (June 2005), NGC MS 63, lot 6209, unsold; Southwest Collection (Heritage Auctions, February 2008), NGC MS 63, lot 528, $373,750.*

Additional Notes: None.

Coin Serial Number: 105.

From Stack's,
October 2002

1796 15 Stars, O-101.

Parmelee – Hawn – Queller Family Specimen.

Grade: Mint State.

Identification Markers: Small spot right of star 4, two to upper right of star 5, two between lower ribbon and curls, one just above head below right serif of L, two on cheek, and one on lower left serif of Y in LIBERTY.

Provenance: *Lorin Parmelee Collection (New York Stamp and Coin, June 1890), Proof, lot 723, $251; Reed Hawn Collection (Stack's, August 1973), Prooflike, lot 6, $13,000; Queller Family Collection (Stack's, October 2002), Brilliant Uncirculated, lot 22, $86,250.*

Additional Notes: None.

Coin Serial Number: 106.

From Stack's, January 2000

1796 15 Stars, O-101.

1982 ANA Sale Specimen.

Grade: Mint State, Pinscratches.

Identification Markers: Faint pinscratch from bottom of star 10 through portrait to lower hair ribbon, another under right (facing) wing from upper leg into field, and another from rim parallel to diagonal of N in UNITED.

Provenance: *Roy Harte et al. Collections (Bowers and Ruddy, March 1981), Choice Extremely Fine 45, lot 220, $6,000; ANA Sale (Steve Ivy, August 1982), Extremely Fine 45, lot 2304; Americana Sale (Stack's, January 2000), Brilliant Uncirculated, NGC MS 62, lot 1681, $75,900.*

Additional Notes: The Stack's catalog is apparently incorrect in stating: "... a barely detectable hairline scratch ... at the central reverse" instead of at the central obverse.

Coin Serial Number: 107.

From Stack's,
March 1975

1796 15 Stars, O-101.

James A. Stack Specimen.

Grade: Mint State.

Identification Markers: Several spots between neck and stars 13-14. Short linear horizontal mark above eagle's right (facing) wing.

Provenance: *Probably World's Greatest Collection (Numismatic Gallery, April 1945), Uncirculated, lot 60, $575; James A. Stack Collection (Stack's, March 1975), Proof, lot 313, $29,000.*

Additional Notes: The photo quality of the plates in the above catalogs precludes a match with 100% certainty. In the author's opinion, however, there is a high probability that the appearances illustrate the same coin (both appear to display a linear mark above the wing). It is less certain, however, whether or not it duplicates another high-grade 1796 15 Star half dollar in the study.

Coin Serial Number: 108.

From Numismatic Gallery,
June 1950

1796 15 Stars, O-101.

Menjou – Donlon Specimen.

Grade: About Uncirculated.

Identification Markers: Mark in field midway between stars 3 and 4 and the curl (photo quality makes it very difficult to discern this pedigree identifier).

Provenance: *Adolphe Menjou Collection (Numismatic Gallery, June 1950), Uncirculated with prooflike luster, lot 942, $590; William P. Donlon Collection (A. Kosoff, November 1956), Uncirculated with prooflike luster, lot 705.*

Additional Notes: Both catalogs state: "… the lightest trace of a rub on the highest point of the hair." Photos in both catalogs make it difficult to assess the coin's surface condition and pedigree markers. Consequently, it is uncertain whether or not it duplicates another high-grade 1796 15 Star half dollar in the study.

Coin Serial Number: 109.

From Kagin's,
September 1974

1796 15 Stars, O-101.

Sale of the 70's Specimen.

Grade: About Uncirculated.

Identification Markers: Weak dentils upper-left obverse. Mark on upper-left eagle's breast.

Provenance: *Sale of the 70's (Kagin's, November 1973), About Uncirculated, lot 1209, $2,200; Kagin's (September 1974), Near Uncirculated, lot 1660.*

Additional Notes: Photo quality prevents locating any additional identifiers.

Coin Serial Number: 110.

From Superior Galleries,
January 1989

1796 15 Stars, O-101.

Moreira Specimen.

Grade: About Uncirculated, obverse Pinscratches.

Identification Markers: Pinscratches on Liberty's chin, jaw, and neck. Mark on lower-middle neck. Diagonal (upper-left to lower-right) adjustment marks in central reverse. Mark on upper-right eagle's breast.

Provenance: *James Kelly (February, 1964), Choice Extremely Fine, lot 241; Moreira Collection Sale (Superior Galleries, January 1989), Mint State 63, lot 4417, $79,750.*

Additional Notes: The James Kelly catalog states: "Showing only faintest trace of friction on high spots."

Coin Serial Number: 111.

From Heritage Auctions,
March 2011

1796 15 Stars, O-101.

Dupont – Miles – Clarke Specimen.

Grade: About Uncirculated.

Identification Markers: Two planchet defects on the lower reverse, the left one extending through the upper part of the 2 in the fraction and through the middle of the right ribbon.

Provenance: *Anderson Dupont Collection, Part II (Stack's, November 1954), Uncirculated, Proof surface, lot 2031, probably $1,300; R.L. Miles Collection (Stack's, April 1969), Brilliant Uncirculated, Prooflike, lot 1205, $7,000; Dr. E. Yale Clarke Collection (Stack's, October 1975), Brilliant Uncirculated, Prooflike, lot 182, $11,500; Bowers and Ruddy Rare Coin Review (No. 26, Summer 1976), Brilliant Uncirculated, Prooflike, $19,500; Bayside New York Collection (Heritage Auctions, July 2008), PCGS AU 58, lot 1668, $207,000; Heritage Auctions (March 2011), PCGS AU 58, lot 4410, $207,000.*

Additional Notes: The 1969 and 1975 Stack's catalogs state: "Light friction on the high points."

Coin Serial Number: 112.

From Heritage Auctions,
September 2008

1796 15 Stars, O-101.

Noblet – Genaitis Specimen.

Grade: About Uncirculated, light obverse Scratches.

Identification Markers: Two marks between star 2 and curl, mark on mid-shoulder. Light scratches on forehead and adjacent field. Nearly imperceptible horizontal adjustment marks on eagle's lower torso and clouds.

Provenance: *Douglas L. Noblet Collection (Bowers and Merena, January 1999), PCGS AU 55, lot 4, $59,700; Richard Genaitis Collection (Heritage Auctions, August 2001), PCGS AU 55, lot 6090, $50,000; Superior Galleries (February 2006), PCGS AU 58, lot 680; Stack's (November 2007), PCGS AU 58, lot 2009; Heritage Auctions (April 2008), PCGS AU 58, lot 2306, unsold; Heritage Auctions (July 2008), PCGS AU 58, lot 1667; Heritage Auctions (September 2008), PCGS AU 58, lot 2018, unsold; Stack's (January 2009), PCGS AU 58, lot 8345, unsold; Stack's (March 2010), PCGC AU 58, lot 1009, unsold; ANA Sale (Stack's – Bowers, August 2011), PCGS AU 58, lot 7338, apparently unsold.*

Additional Notes: None.

Coin Serial Number: 113.

From Heritage Auctions,
May 2008

1796 15 Stars, O-101.

Bullowa Specimen.

Grade: About Uncirculated.

Identification Markers: Upper-right to lower-left adjustment marks on middle and lower obverse, heaviest in Liberty's middle hair. Two contact marks between star 5 and ribbon, two below chin, and one on upper shoulder. Mark between laurel leaves and lower left (facing) wing.

Provenance: *Coinhunter C.E. Bullowa (January 2007), NGC AU 55, lot 295; Heritage Auctions (May 2008), NGC AU 55, lot 493, $149,500.*

Additional Notes: None.

Coin Serial Number: 114.

From Stack's,
June 2007

1796 15 Stars, O-101.

Prestera Specimen.

Grade: About Uncirculated.

Identification Markers: Spot just right of 1 in the date and another low between 96. Minor rim ding above left serif of Y in LIBERTY, another above final A in AMERICA.

Provenance: *Auction '90 (Stack's session, August 1990), Choice Extremely Fine, lot 195, $46,750; Dr. Tory Prestera et al. Collections (Stack's, June 2007), PCGS AU 53, lot 620, $149,500.*

Additional Notes: None.

Coin Serial Number: 115.

From Harmer, Rooke, November 1969

1796 15 Stars, O-101.

Million Dollar Sale Specimen.

Grade: About Uncirculated.

Identification Markers: Minute rim mark over E of UNITED.

Provenance: *Federal Brand (January 1963), Practically Uncirculated, lot 1083; possibly Million Dollar Sale I (Harmer, Rooke, November 1969), Almost Uncirculated, lot 1083, $10,000.*

Additional Notes: Photo quality in both catalogs makes plate matching extremely difficult. Both appear to show a minuscule rim mark over E in UNITED, possibly indicating the same coin. It is uncertain, however, whether or not it duplicates another high-grade 1796 15 Star half dollar in the study.

Coin Serial Number: 116.

From Stack's,
June 2008

1796 15 Stars, O-101.

Husky Specimen.

Grade: Extremely Fine.

Identification Markers: Mark on upper neck below jaw, another on neck to the upper right of curl, and three more form a triangle on chest. Spot on lower-left serif of L in LIBERTY. Mark on middle inner curve of D in UNITED, another on upper-right eagle's breast, two on right (facing) leg, one on lower-left (facing) leg, and three or four between last-mentioned leg and wing.

Provenance: *New England Rare Coin Auctions (November 1975), Very Fine 35, lot 582, $8,500; Bowers and Merena (March 2005), NGC EF 45, lot 560, $82,800; Husky Collection (Stack's, June 2008), NGC EF 45, lot 2014, $126,500.*

Additional Notes: None.

Coin Serial Number: 117.

From Stack's,
March 1959

1796 15 Stars, O-101, uncertain die state.

Kuitham – H.P. Smith – Nygren – Pelletreau Specimen.

Grade: Extremely Fine, obverse Digs.

Identification Markers: Several digs, including right of star 4, in hair between shoulder and curl, in hair lower left of ear, on upper-middle chest, midway between chin and star 13, between eagle's beak and right (facing) wing, and on cloud below right (facing) leg. Also a dark spot in Liberty's hair near forehead. Photo quality prevents knowing whether or not the usually seen die crack from the border at 5:00 to the bust is present.

Provenance: *E.F. Kuitham Collection (Edward Frossard, March 1884), Fine impression, lot 528, $45; Harlan P. Smith Collection (S.H. and H. Chapman, May 1906), Very Good, lot 576, $80; Arthur C. Nygren Collection (B. Max Mehl, November 1914), Fine, lot 180; Alex J. Rosborough Collection (B. Max Mehl, April 1929), Very Good, lot 84; Robert H. Pelletreau Collection (Stack's, March 1959), Very Fine, lot 724, $1,250.*

Additional Notes: None.

Coin Serial Number: 118.

From Bowers and Ruddy,
February 1977

1796 15 Stars, O-101, early die state.

Blauvelt - Silliphant Specimen.

Grade: Extremely Fine.

Identification Markers: Round mark right of star 4. A complex of lint marks is located between chest and star 14. Minor rim bruise below star 1. Semicircular mark from eagle's left (facing) wing to lower neck. Lacks the usually seen die crack from the border at 5:00 to the bust.

Provenance: *Paramount (August 1967), Choice Extremely Fine, lot 2186, $4,000; Harold A. Blauvelt et al. Collections (Bowers and Rudy, February 1977), Extremely Fine, lot 389; Stirling Silliphant Collection (Heritage Auctions, July 1988), Extremely Fine (45/45), lot 678, $34,000.*

Additional Notes: The Paramount catalog states: "We were tempted to add About Uncirculated as there is little or no wear on any but the highest spots." The Heritage catalog states: "Both sides display traces of the original mint luster." Nevertheless, the author classified the coin as Extremely Fine for the purpose of this study, albeit a very high-end XF.

Coin Serial Number: 119.

From New England Rare Coin Auctions, January 1982

1796 15 Stars, O-101.

Garrett - Heller Specimen.

Grade: Extremely Fine.

Identification Markers: Spot on right part of Liberty's neck, another to the lower right of the 6 in date. Spot between the bases of IT in UNITED.

Provenance: *George Cogan to T. Harrison Garrett, 1883; Garrett Collection, Part I (Bowers and Ruddy, November 1979), Very Fine 20, lot 274, $22,000; Dennis Heller Collection (New England Rare Coin Auctions, January 1982), Very Fine 35, lot 615, $22,000.*

Additional Notes: The NERCA catalog states: "… a trace of adjustment filing at the UNI of UNITED." This filing does not show on the photo.

Coin Serial Number: 120.

From B. Max Mehl,
June 1946

1796 15 Stars, O-101, uncertain die state.

Atwater Specimen.

Grade: Extremely Fine.

Identification Markers: Mark top of T in LIBERTY (photo quality makes it nearly impossible to see; also, it is unclear whether or not the die crack from the bust at 5:00 is present). Spot on eagle's crotch.

Provenance: *William Cutler Atwater Collection (B. Max Mehl, June 1946), Extremely Fine, lot 394, $310.*

Additional Notes: The Mehl catalog states: "A pin-point nick, or rather what appears … to be a very minute planchet defect, at top of T in LIBERTY." Photo quality makes it difficult to say with certainty whether or not this coin duplicates another high-grade 1796 15 Star half dollar in the study.

Coin Serial Number: 121.

From Stack's,
July 1989

1796 15 Stars, O-101.

Auction '89 Specimen.

Grade: Extremely Fine.

Identification Markers: Splotchy toning pattern. Rim ding over star 11. Mark on lower front of Liberty's neck, another just to upper right of nose tip. Semicircular toning streak runs from rim through left base of M in AMERICA and the upper-right palm leaves to the bottom of O in OF.

Provenance: *Auction '89 (Stack's session, July 1989), Very Fine, lot 1711, $21,000.*

Additional Notes: None.

Coin Serial Number: 122.

From Heritage Auctions, July-August 2008

1796 15 Stars, O-101.

2008 ANA Sale Specimen.

Grade: Extremely Fine, Cleaned.

Identification Markers: Mark between star 3 and rim. Linear mark under lower lip. Mark at each end of the two palm leaves below the last S of STATES. Faint crisscross adjustment marks on lower right reverse.

Provenance: *Scotsman Auction (July 2007), NCS XF 45 Detail, Cleaned, lot 560, apparently unsold; ANA Sale (Heritage Auctions, July-August 2008), PCGS Genuine (XF Details), lot 1666, $69,000; Long Beach Sale (Heritage Auctions, September 2011), PCGS Genuine (XF Details), lot 3963; Central States Numismatic Society Sale (Heritage Auctions, April 2012), PCGS Genuine (XF Details), lot 5113, unsold.*

Additional Notes: None.

Coin Serial Number: 123.

From Bowers and Merena, November 2007

1796 15 Stars, O-101.

November 2007 Baltimore Auction Specimen.

Grade: Very Fine, Cleaned.

Identification Markers: What appear to be two pinprick-like marks with upper-right to lower-left alignment are located on Liberty's cheek midway between nose and ear. Another on temple midway between eye and hair, and one centrally located on chest.

Provenance: *Baltimore Auction (Bowers and Merena, November 2007), VF Details, Improperly Cleaned, lot 2147, unsold.*

Additional Notes: Photo quality makes assessment of coin's surface condition difficult, and lessens the certainty that it does not duplicate another mid-grade 1796 15 Star half dollar in the study.

Coin Serial Number: 124.

From Heritage Auctions,
December 2004

1796 15 Stars, O-101.

Oviedo Specimen.

Grade: Very Fine.

Identification Markers: Linear mark between rim and upper left of star 6, round mark between rim and lower left of star 7, large spot between stars 6 and 7. Faint horizontal pinscratch on lower neck. Mark on upper left eagle's breast.

Provenance: *Dr. George F. Oviedo, Jr. Collection (Stack's, September 1983), lot 725; Heritage Auctions (January 2003), PCGS VF 35, lot 7057, $43,700; Heritage Auctions (December 2004), NGC XF 45, lot 6035, $86,250.*

Additional Notes: None.

Coin Serial Number: 125.

From Bowers and Merena, September 1992

1796 15 Stars, O-101.

Ten Eyck – Stack – Moreira Specimen.

Grade: Very Fine obverse, Extremely Fine reverse.

Identification Markers: Planchet defect on rim over B of LIBERTY and another between ER. Mark lower left of curl 3 from bottom. What may be a corresponding rim flaw, or perhaps a rim ding, occurs on the reverse slightly to the right of the fraction. Diagonal pinscratch from eagle's beak to palm leaf tip, mark on upper-right (facing) leg, and another under corresponding wing. Faint pinscratches at UNIT of UNITED.

Provenance: *James Ten Eyck Collection (B. Max Mehl, May 1922), "Strictly very good," lot 432, $92; James A. Stack Collection (Stack's, March 1975), Extremely Fine, lot 314, $7,500; Moreira Collection, Part 3 (Superior Galleries, January 1989), Very Fine 30, lot 4418, $23,100; Bowers and Merena (September 1992), ANA Certificate VF 30/30, lot 1034, $17,600.*

Additional Notes: None.

Coin Serial Number: 126.

From Heritage Auctions,
September 2008

1796 15 Stars, O-101.

Cox – Menlo Park Collection Specimen.

Grade: Very Fine.

Identification Markers: Dark triangular spot just above drapery between 96 of date. Round mark left of star 11. Mark midway between eagle's beak and right (facing) wing. Linear mark from upper-left serif of first T in STATES to its middle stand.

Provenance: *James Kelly Collection (November 1957), Very Fine, lot 1588, $835; R.E. Cox, Jr. Collection (Stack's, April 1962), Very Fine, lot 1576, $3,500; A Gentleman's Study Collection of U.S. Half Dollars (Coronet Coin Shop, Manhasset, NY, no date), close to Very Fine, fixed price list number 97, $3,600; Stack's (June 1993), Very Fine, lot 1093, $13,750; Heritage Auctions (August 2006), PCGS VF 25, lot 5220, $63,263; Menlo Park Collection (Heritage Auctions, September 2008), PCGS VF 25, lot 2017, $86,250.*

Additional Notes: The Coronet booklet refers to a July 1968 numismatic journal, thereby indicating a general time frame of its publication.

Coin Serial Number: 127.

From RARCOA,
July 1988

1796 15 Stars, O-101.

Auction '88 Specimen.

Grade: Very Fine.

Identification Markers: Mark midway between right serif of L in LIBERTY and Liberty's head. Horizontal pinscratch from juncture of chin and neck to curl below ear. Three marks in form of a triangle below juncture of eagle's torso and left (facing) wing.

Provenance: *Auction '88 (RARCOA's session, July 1988), Very Fine, lot 1720, $19,800; Bowers and Merena (March 2009), NGC VF 25, lot 4190, $51,175.*

Additional Notes: None.

Coin Serial Number: 128.

From Heritage Auctions, January 2006

1796 15 Stars, O-101.

Arnold – Reiver Specimen.

Grade: Very Fine, Environmental Damage obverse.

Identification Markers: Streaky toning on obverse. Mark between rim and lower left of star 5. Mark one-third of way between last S of STATES and O in OF. Mark just to the right part of lower left (facing) wing.

Provenance: *C.L. Arnold Collection (Stack's, September 1968), Fine to Very Fine, lot 1117, $3,000; Jules Reiver Collection (Heritage Auctions, January 2006), NCS VF Details, Environmental Damage, lot 22512, $63,250.*

Additional Notes: The Heritage catalog states: "The NCS 'Environmental Damage' designation apparently refers to the areas of lime-green coloration on the obverse that may have been associated with some sort of residue."

Coin Serial Number: 129.

From Bowers and Merena,
January 1991

1796 15 Stars, O-101.

Bartlett – Copeland Specimen.

Grade: Very Fine.

Identification Markers: Linear mark midway between star 4 and curl. Upper-left to lower-right mark right of eagle's beak. Pronounced weakness in dentils between U of UNITED and fraction, including lower part of 2.

Provenance: *C. Ramsey Bartlett Collection (Stack's, February 1966), Fine, lot 588, $3,200; Bernard L. Copeland Collection (Stack's, April 1967), Fine, lot 849, $3,400; Stack's (February 1977), Fine, lot 265; Bowers and Merena (January 1991), Fine 12, lot 1012, $14,850.*

Additional Notes: None.

Coin Serial Number: 130.

From Superior Galleries,
November 1976

1796 15 Stars, O-101.

Gilhousen Specimen.

Grade: Very Fine, reverse Scratched.

Identification Markers: Lightly scratched "X" on right (facing) wing. Part of scratch crosses lower neck then through field to upper left (facing) wing. Minor rim bruise below fraction. Mark high between F in OF and A in AMERICA.

Provenance: *Clarke E. Gilhousen Collection, Part III (Superior Galleries, October 1973), Very Fine, lot 869, $6,750; Superior Galleries (November 1976), Very Fine, lot 457, $7,000.*

Additional Notes: Photo quality in both catalogs makes it difficult to see pedigree markers.

Coin Serial Number: 131.

From Heritage Auctions,
April 2009

1796 15 Stars, O-101.

Thomas Specimen.

Grade: Very Fine.

Identification Markers: A wide diagonal streak (presumably a toning streak) travels from left of Liberty's nose, beneath the ear and through the hair. Small mark above the ribbon in line with the inner point of star 7, and another below the right serif of the L in LIBERTY. Toning spots within the D of UNITED and just left of the adjacent laurel leaf.

Provenance: *Premium Numismatics, Inc. fixed price list (April 2004), NGC VF 30, $67,500; American Numismatic Rarities Numismatic Sun fixed price list (Spring/Summer 2004), NGC VF 30, $72,500; Joseph C. Thomas Collection (Heritage Auctions, April 2009), NGC VF 30, lot 2388, $54,625; Northeast Numismatics fixed price list (May 2009), NGC VF 30, $69,500; Scotsman Auction Co. (July 2010), NGC VF 30, lot 529, $55,775.*

Additional Notes: None.

Coin Serial Number: 132.

From Bowers and Merena,
November 1988

1796 15 Stars, O-101.

Norweb Specimen.

Grade: Very Fine.

Identification Markers: Small scrape just to lower right of star 8. Dark spot on rim over T of LIBERTY. Three or four short diagonal scratches (upper right to lower left) midway between chin and star 13. Spot between 9 of date and drapery. Mark just right of the upper part of the left (facing) wing.

Provenance: *B. Max Mehl, January 1937 to the Norwebs (per Bowers and Merena, November 1988); Norweb Collection, Part III (Bowers and Merena, November 1988), Fine 12, lot 3025, $18,425; Superior Galleries (January 1990), PCGS Fine 12, lot 3420, $19,250.*

Additional Notes: None.

Coin Serial Number: 133.

From Heritage Auctions, June 2008

1796 15 Stars, O-101.

Hoosier Discovery Collection Specimen.

Grade: Very Fine, lightly Whizzed.

Identification Markers: Marks near rim left of star 7. Mark about midway between star 7 and upper ribbon. Mark midway between tip of palm leaf and curvature of upper-right (facing) wing. Splotchy toning on eagle's torso.

Provenance: *Hoosier Discovery Collection (Heritage Auctions, May 2007), ANACS Fine 15 Details, Tooled, Whizzed, lot 2126, $43,125; Anaconda Rare Coins (Heritage Auctions, June 2008), NGC VF 25, lot 961, $69,000.*

Additional Notes: The author cataloged this coin. Any whizzing was very light and tooling was not readily evident.

Coin Serial Number: 134.

From Heritage Auctions,
January 2011

1796 15 Stars, O-101.

January 2011 FUN Sale Specimen.

Grade: Very Fine, Repaired, Whizzed, Re-engraved.

Identification Markers: Vertical milling mark on Liberty's temple. Three milling marks under I of LIBERTY, and a dig between middle and lower ribbon in line with the upper point of star 5. The right obverse field has been smoothed, and both sides have been whizzed. Several marks in field below left (facing) wing. The right (facing) wing has been re-engraved, and ironically appears to resemble the wing of the silver coinage of 1794-1795 more than that of the half dollar coinage of 1796-1797! A repair is evident at 12:00 on obverse and 6:00 on reverse.

Provenance: *Heritage Auctions (May 2004), PCI XF 40 Repaired, lot 7314, unsold; Heritage Auctions (July 2004), PCI XF 40 Repaired, lot 6436, $29,900; Long Island Numismatics fixed price list (March 2008), NCS VF Details, Repaired, Whizzed, $55,000; Stack's (March 2010), NGC VF Details, Repaired, Whizzed, lot 1010, unsold; FUN Sale (Heritage Auctions, January 2011), NGC VF Details, Repaired, Whizzed, lot 5540, $25,300.*

Additional Notes: None.

Coin Serial Number: 135.

From Al Overton,
August 1963

1796 15 Stars.

Blevins Specimen.

Grade: Very Fine.

Identification Markers: Faint mark just to right of nose tip. Faint vertical mark left of second curl below ribbon. Minute mark just below stem end of laurel wreath. A mark below each ribbon end and another to the right of the 2 in fraction. Light rim bruise between IT of UNITED. Except for the rim bruise, all of the remaining marks are difficult to discern in the catalog photos.

Provenance: *1963 ANA Sale (Al Overton, August 1963), Very Fine, lot 1196; H.W. Blevins Collection (Superior Galleries, June 1988), Fine 12, lot 3051, $16,500.*

Additional Notes: Despite the difficulty in plate matching because of photo quality, the author is virtually certain the two appearances represent the same coin. It is less certain, however, whether or not it duplicates another mid-grade 1796 15 Star half in the study.

Coin Serial Number: 136.

From New England
Rare Coin Auctions,
January 1982

1796 15 Stars, O-101.

1982 FUN Sale Specimen.

Grade: Very Fine.

Identification Markers: Faint horizontal mark on shoulder above 7 in date. Mark two-thirds right of forehead between Y in LIBERTY and star 9. Mark on cloud just above left bow ribbon. Faint vertical mark to right of 2 in fraction. Mark low between AT of STATES.

Provenance: *1982 FUN Sale (New England Rare Coin Auctions, January 1982), Very Fine 30, lot 614, $22,550.*

Additional Notes: None.

Coin Serial Number: 137.

From Stack's,
January 2007

1796 15 Stars, O-101.

2006 ANA Sale Specimen.

Grade: Very Fine.

Identification Markers: Faint upper-left to lower-right obverse adjustment marks, most evident from field to rim between 3:00 and 4:00. Mark midway between star 7 and head, another on lower neck right of curl. Minor reverse rim bruise at 6:30. Mark just to right of lower part of left (facing) wing, aligned with juncture of torso and left (facing) leg.

Provenance: *Superior Galleries (February 1991), PCGS VF 20, lot 1631; Harry Labstain Rare Coins fixed price list (Coin World ad, October, 2004), NGC XF 40, inventory number 80187, $89,500; Drew St. John Sale (American Numismatic Rarities, June 2005), NGC XF 40, lot 6, $74,750; Stack's (October 2005), NGC XF 40, lot 1596; Crimson Collection (Stack's, March 2006), NGC XF 40, lot 2575; Ira & Larry Goldberg (May 2006), PCGS XF 40, lot 2907, unsold; ANA Sale (Heritage Auctions, August 2006), PCGS XF 40, lot 5221, unsold; Stack's (January 2007), PCGS XF 40, lot 628, unsold; Ira & Larry Goldberg (May 2007), PCGS XF 40, lot 1131, $89,125; Ira & Larry Goldberg (September 2008), PCGS XF 40, lot 1214, unsold; Ira & Larry Goldberg (February 2009), PCGS XF 40, lot 926, unsold.*

Additional Notes: None.

Coin Serial Number: 138.

From B. Max Mehl,
May 1914

1796 15 Stars, O-101.

Conover – possibly Emmons Specimen.

Grade: Very Fine.

Identification Markers: Shallow reverse rim bruise to upper left of first A in AMERICA extends about one-half way to the F in OF, encompassing roughly three and one-half to four dentils. Additionally, the Conover appearance clearly shows two short upper-right to lower-left cuts at the edge of Liberty's chest, midway between the bottom of the neck and star 15. The photo quality of the Stack's (Emmons) obverse image precludes determination of whether or not these cuts are present.

Provenance: *Charles H. Conover Collection (B. Max Mehl, May 1914), Very Good, fine for coin, lot 322, $84; possibly Dr. Calvert L. Emmons Collection (Stack's, September 1969), Very Fine, lot 611, $3,500.*

Additional Notes: Photo quality of the images in both catalogs prevents a conclusive plate match of the two appearances. Consequently, they may be the same or different coins.

Coin Serial Number: 139.

From Superior Galleries, May 1990

1796 15 Stars, O-101.

Father Flanagan's Boys Town Sale Specimen.

Grade: Very Fine.

Identification Markers: Small mark just to lower right of eagle's beak, another on lower middle neck, and another on upper part of right (facing) leg.

Provenance: *Father Flanagan's Boys Town Sale (Superior Galleries, May 1990), PCGS VF 25, lot 31, $27,500.*

Additional Notes: The above-mentioned marks do not show clearly. Consequently, it cannot be determined with certainty whether or not this coin duplicates another mid-grade 1796 15 Star half dollar in the study.

Coin Serial Number: 140.

From Stack's,
April-May 1986

1796 15 Stars, O-101, uncertain die state.

Lester Bernstein Specimen.

Grade: Very Fine.

Identification Markers: Scalloped mark midway between star 7 and upper ribbon and another between star 9 and Liberty's forehead. Two linear digs between the curve of U in UNITED and the wreath stem. Light scratches in the form of a triangle encompass the eagle's head and extend into the adjacent field. Photo quality prevents determination whether or not the die crack from the border on the obverse at 5:00 to the bust is present.

Provenance: *Lester Bernstein Collection (Stack's, April-May 1986), Very Fine, lot 836.*

Additional Notes: None.

Coin Serial Number: 141.

Punchmarked obverse, as seen in Stack's (May 1961) catalog
From Stack's,
May 1961

Repaired obverse, as seen in Scotsman (February 2007) catalog
From Scotsman Auction Co.,
February 2007

1796 15 Stars, O-101.

Egolf - Rusbar Specimen.

Grade: Very Fine, Repaired obverse.

Identification Markers: The Stack's catalog obverse photo displays seven diamond-shaped punch marks on Liberty's temple, forehead, and adjacent hair. Other pedigree markers include a light rim bruise above star 2, a light mark on jaw below ear, and another just to the lower left of star 14. The reverse exhibits rim dings over the N, I, and stand of D in UNITED, one over the left diagonal of A in STATES, and another at 4:30. A mark occurs at lower left neck of eagle and three more are seen below the right (facing) wing. The Scotsman obverse photo shows all punches removed (except for one on the temple). All other obverse and reverse pedigree marks are still visible. The Bowers obverse photo also shows the punches removed.

Provenance: *Howard D. Egolf Collection (Stack's, May 1961), Very Fine, counterstamped, lot 929, $1,050; Robert W. Rusbar et al. Collections (Bowers and Merena, September 1990), VF 20, lot 273, $18,700; Scotsman Auction Co. (February 2007), VF 20, lot 542, $50,600.*

Additional Notes: The Stack's catalog states: "This curious mark is definitely attributable to a Trinidad counterstamp. Many of our early coins have this mark as they circulated in the Antilles. A description of a similar ... counterstamp can be found in 'Counterstamped Coins of The Americas' by Howland Wood. See page 109, fig. 85."

Coin Serial Number: 142.

From Stack's,
January 2004

1796 15 Stars, O-101.

Gable – Yale University Specimen.

Grade: Very Fine, obverse Graffiti.

Identification Markers: An A or a sideways 4 etched in field between 6 of date and die crack. Mark right of star 7 above ribbon, another midway between L of LIBERTY and Liberty's head. Two ticks just right of ear and one in center of chest. Mark above eagle's beak and another just above right (facing) wing midway between neck and wing curve.

Provenance: *William F. Gable Collection (S.H. Chapman, May 1914), Very Good, lot 854, $105; Yale University Collection (Stack's, December 1971), Fine, lot 254, $3,600; Americana Sale (Stack's, January 2004), Very Fine, lot 3309, $36,800.*

Additional Notes: None.

Coin Serial Number: 143.

From Stack's,
March 1959

1796 15 Stars, O-101.

Pelletreau Specimen.

Grade: Very Fine.

Identification Markers: Horizontal linear mark from juncture of Liberty's jaw and neck extending into hair (unclear whether adjustment mark or scratch). Mark just left of Liberty's eye. Light toning spot midway between 1 of date and star 1, and another to right of upper hair ribbon.

Provenance: *Robert H. Pelletreau Collection (Stack's, March 1959), Fine, lot 725, $800.*

Additional Notes: Photo quality prevents seeing pedigree markers clearly.

Coin Serial Number: 144.

From Bowers and Merena,
November 1991

1796 15 Stars, O-101, early die state.

Frontenac Sale Specimen.

Grade: Very Fine.

Identification Markers: Distinctive toning pattern on Liberty's neck and chest. Small mark between C and A in AMERICA (closer to A). No other marks or spots are readily discernible from the photos. Lacks the usually seen die crack from the border at 5:00 to the bust.

Provenance: *Frontenac Sale (Bowers and Merena, November 1991), PCGS VF 25, lot 3016, $23,100.*

Additional Notes: None.

Coin Serial Number: 145.

From Heritage Auctions,
November 2003

1796 15 Stars, O-101.

Ridings Specimen.

Grade: Very Fine, Plugged, Re-engraved, Smoothed.

Identification Markers: What appears to be a toning streak extends from just left of Liberty's ear diagonally through the hair to the curl end at the top of the head. Moderate contact mark on lower neck just above shoulder. Several marks on both ribbons below bow knot and one on upper right of right bow. Liberty's hair re-engraved, and a plug left of the last A in AMERICA has been smoothed.

Provenance: *Dennis Ridings Collection (Heritage Auctions, February 2003), NCS Genuine, Re-engraved, Damaged, lot 7684, $17,825; Heritage Auctions (November 2003), NCS Genuine, Re-engraved, Damaged, lot 6595, $23,575.*

Additional Notes: The February Heritage catalog states: "Glossy in sheen, both sides appear to be whizzed as well as polished."

Coin Serial Number: 146.

From Heritage Auctions,
October 2006

1796 15 Stars, O-101.

2004 ANA Specimen.

Grade: Very Fine, Smoothed, Whizzed.

Identification Markers: Vertical streak from Liberty's eyebrow to jaw. Vertical cuts on drapery – one above 1 of date, two above 9, and one to the upper right of 6. Two small marks above the cut over the 1, and several more scattered over the central reverse, including three on the upper loop of the left bow ribbon. Both surfaces smoothed and whizzed.

Provenance: *Heritage Auctions (September 2003), NCS Fine 12 Details, Repaired, Improperly Cleaned, lot 6953, $14,950; 2004 ANA Sale (Heritage Auctions, August 2004), NCS Fine 12 Details, Repaired, Improperly Cleaned, lot 6158, $20,700; Heritage Auctions (October 2006), NCS Fine Details, Repaired, Whizzed, lot 1116, $37,260.*

Additional Notes: None.

Coin Serial Number: 147.

From Stack's, March 2005

1796 15 Stars, O-101.

Gardner Specimen.

Grade: Very Fine obverse, Scratches, Fine Reverse.

Identification Markers: Vertical scratch on shoulder, running from above 7 to curl. Short diagonal scratch (upper right to lower left) above upper lip. Two minuscule marks midway between beak and wing.

Provenance: *Laurence H. Gardner Collection from the Buffalo & Erie County Historical Society (Stack's, March 2005), Fine to Very Fine, lot 166, $33,375.*

Additional Notes: The Stack's catalog states: "The right obverse field has been smoothed to obscure old graffiti there."

Coin Serial Number: 148.

From Stack's, November 1956

1796 15 Stars, O-101.

Frank Specimen.

Grade: Very Fine obverse, Damaged, Fine reverse, Damaged.

Identification Markers: Attempted puncture on neck above Liberty's shoulder. Deep horizontal cut across eagle's breast extending halfway through the right (facing) wing. Minor rim bruise above A in STATES.

Provenance: *B. Frank Collection (Stack's, November 1956), Fine, lot 870, $425.*

Additional Notes: Photo quality makes any other marks difficult to discern.

Coin Serial Number: 149.

From Stack's,
December 1985

1796 15 Stars, O-101, early to late die state.

December 1985 Sale Specimen.

Grade: Very Fine obverse, Fine reverse.

Identification Markers: Large spot on Liberty's temple. Two moderate marks on central chest (aligned with 96 in date). Horizontal linear mark extends from upper right of eagle's beak about one-halfway to palm wreath. Faint linear mark (probably a pinscratch) from R of AMERICA to the right (facing) leg, and another curves through the left (facing) wing into the laurel wreath. Appears to lack the usually seen die crack from the border at 5:00 to the bust (but see "Additional Notes" below).

Provenance: *The December Sale (Stack's, December 1985), Very Good, lot 1405, $13,750.*

Additional Notes: The Stack's catalog states: "The crack from the tip of the bust to the rim only lightly in evidence."

Coin Serial Number: 150.

From Heritage Auctions,
January 2009

1796 15 Stars, O-101.

Morrison Family Specimen.

Grade: Very Fine obverse, Fine reverse, Scratches.

Identification Markers: Short horizontal adjustment marks in central hair of Liberty below ear. Minute tick on drapery – bust line above 6 in date. A large but very faint "X" bisects the eagle, a smaller "X" extends from the clouds through the left bow to the 1 of the fraction, and an even smaller "X" is located right of U in UNITED. A moderate mark or spot just to the right of the bow may be on the PCGS holder as it does not appear on the earlier uncertified Stack's offering.

Provenance: *Sotheby's (December 1993), About Very Fine, lot 754; Morrison Family Collection (Stack's, March 2005), Fine, lot 2423, $37,375; FUN Sale (Heritage Auctions, January 2009), PCGS Fine 15, lot 3833, unsold; Bowers and Merena (March 2009), PCGS Fine 15, lot 963, $54,050.*

Additional Notes: None.

Coin Serial Number: 151.

From Bowers and Merena,
January 1992

1796 15 Stars, O-101.

Brilliant Specimen.

Grade: Very Fine obverse, Fine reverse.

Identification Markers: Light rim bruises over stars 5 and 6, and several dentils coalesced over stars 13 and 14. Vertical mark left of star 14. Mark midway between right (facing) wing and leg, aligned with upright of E in AMERICA, and another above tip of each lower, inner palm leaf.

Provenance: *Stack's (March 1987), Fine, lot 687, $14,850; James D. Brilliant Collection (Bowers and Merena, January 1992), Fine 12 to Fine 15, lot 38, $11,000.*

Additional Notes: None.

Coin Serial Number: 152.

From Harry Labstain Rare Coins, November 2009

1796 15 Stars, O-101.

HLRC Inventory Specimen.

Grade: Very Fine obverse, Fine reverse.

Identification Markers: S-shaped mark on upper shoulder between 1 and 7 of date. Mark midway between star 11 and nose. Two marks on upper-middle palm leaf (one beneath last S of STATES, the other between S and O in OF. Round mark on the lower part of the vertical feather on the right (facing) wing.

Provenance: *Harry Labstain Rare Coins fixed price list (November 2009), ANACS, VF Details, Net Fine 12, Repaired, Tooled, inventory number 2403, $27,500.*

Additional Notes: Photo quality makes pedigree markers and any impairments difficult to see.

Coin Serial Number: 153.

From Bowers and Merena,
November 1999

1796 15 Stars, O-101.

Duvall Specimen.

Grade: Very Fine obverse, Fine reverse.

Identification Markers: The obverse displays a distinctive toning pattern on the central part of Liberty's portrait (a triangular area of darker toning with its apex at the temple and its base at the upper shoulder and lower neck). Faint vertical streak from upper part of right (facing) wing to palm leaf.

Provenance: *Gordon Duvall Collection (Bowers and Merena, November 1999), Fine 15, lot 2033, $18,400; possibly Heritage Exclusively Internet Auction (July 2001), NGC VF 20, lot 3310, unsold.*

Additional Notes: Photo quality of the Heritage image restricts plate matching to the obverse toning pattern. Consequently, it is difficult to determine with certainty whether or not these appearances represent the same or different coins, and whether they duplicate another mid-grade 1796 15 Star half dollar in the study.

Coin Serial Number: 154.

From Stack's,
June 1963

1796 15 Stars, O-101, uncertain die state.

Walton Specimen.

Grade: Very Fine obverse, Fine reverse.

Identification Markers: Two side-by-side ticks on Liberty's left (facing) breast (though it is possible they are photographic flaws). Rim bruise between U in UNITED and ribbon end, two above serifs of T, and one above E.

Provenance: *George O. Walton Collection (Stack's, June 1963), strong Fine bordering on Very Fine, lot 1665, $2,700.*

Additional Notes: Photo quality makes it difficult to determine with certainty whether or not this coin duplicates another mid-grade 1796 15 Star half dollar in the study.

Coin Serial Number: 155.

From Superior Galleries, February 1987

1796 15 Stars, O-101.

Hoffecker Specimen.

Grade: Very Fine obverse, Fine reverse.

Identification Markers: Several marks or spots on Liberty's cheek and jaw. Mark midway between star 2 and curl, and two more between star 7 and head. A mark to the upper right of D in UNITED close to the rim. A faint upper-right to lower-left scratch to right of 2 in fraction. Several dentils are nearly coalesced above E of STATES.

Provenance: *L.W. Hoffecker Collection Sale (Superior Galleries, February 1987), Fine 15, lot 3127, $16,500.*

Additional Notes: None.

Coin Serial Number: 156.

From Bowers and Merena,
April 1983

1796 15 Stars, O-101.

Connecticut Historical Society Specimen.

Grade: Very Fine obverse, Fine reverse.

Identification Markers: Two minuscule marks between Liberty's nose and star 9, and another just to the upper left of star 11. Horizontal streak from upper serif of first S in STATES to laurel wreath, and another through the middle of the left upright of the U in UNITED. A mark just to the right of the right upright of U. Two or three coalesced dentils left of the last A in AMERICA.

Provenance: *Connecticut Historical Society Collection (Bowers and Merena, April 1983), Fine 12, lot 627, $17,600.*

Additional Notes: Pedigree markers are difficult to see as they are very minor.

Coin Serial Number: 157.

From Heritage Auctions,
February 2008

1796 15 Stars, O-101.

Stimson Specimen.

Grade: Very Fine obverse, Smoothed, Fine reverse, Plugged, Re-engraved.

Identification Markers: Crudely plugged and tooled at upper-right obverse and lower right reverse borders. Obverse fields extensively smoothed, apparently to remove pockmarks, several of which are visible throughout the reverse fields. TY of LIBERTY re-engraved, as was the lower-right ribbon on the reverse wreath.

Provenance: *John Stimson Sr. Collection, Part Two (Heritage Auctions, February 2008), NCS Fine Details, Plugged, Repaired, lot 527, $18,500.*

Additional Notes: The crack from the rim at 5:00 to the bust has been removed by the smoothing; it is visible from the bust through stars 15-14.

Coin Serial Number: 158.

From Heritage Auctions,
February 2002

1796 15 Stars, O-101.

Patten - Robison Specimen.

Grade: Very Fine obverse, Fine reverse.

Identification Markers: Mark on Liberty's rear jaw to lower right of ear. Mark midway between Y of LIBERTY and lower forehead curl, and another just to lower right of nose, and another to the upper left of star 14. Light vertical streak just to right of stars 4 and 5 (an adjustment mark, according to Dick Osburn). Other vertical and diagonal streaks show on the obverse Heritage image, but they may be on the PCGS holder as they are not apparent on the images in the previous catalogs where the coin is uncertified.

Provenance: *Charles H. Patten Collection (Stack's, May 1973), Fine, lot 252, $6,400; Ellis and Doris Robison Collection (Stack's, February 1982), Fine, lot 1524, $16,000; Stack's (December 1992), Very Fine, lot 1778; Stack's (May 1993), Fine, lot 737; Ohio Collection (Heritage Auctions, February 2002), PCGS Fine 12, lot 5727, $20,700; Dick Osburn Rare Coins fixed price list (April 2002), PCGS Fine 12, $26,900.*

Additional Notes: None.

Coin Serial Number: 159.

From New England Rare Coin Auction,
November 1980

1796 15 Stars, O-101.

Carnegie Specimen.

Grade: Very Fine obverse, Fine reverse.

Identification Markers: Moderate planchet depression above Liberty's upper ribbon. Mark midway between star 5 and middle ribbon, another between star 7 and planchet flaw. Mark to right of chin. Mark just after D in UNITED.

Provenance: *David K. Carnegie Sale (New England Rare Coin Auctions, November 1980), Very Good 10, lot 727, $25,300.*

Additional Notes: None.

Coin Serial Number: 160.

From Heritage Auctions,
March 1011

1796 15 Stars, O-101.

2010 ANA Sale Specimen.

Grade: Very Fine obverse, Fine reverse.

Identification Markers: Round mark halfway between star 2 and curl. Linear mark extending horizontally from upper-right point of star 3. Hairline from upper-left point of star 4 to rim. Mark on eagle's upper torso halfway between wings. Horizontal hairline from lower-right (facing) wing to upper tail.

Provenance: *Macy's Inaugural Auction Catalog (June 1954), About Very Fine, lot 1387, $475; Heritage Auctions (July 2008), PCGS Fine 15 CAC, lot 1665, $69,000; 2010 ANA Sale (Heritage Auctions, August 2010), PCGS Fine 15 CAC, lot 3136, unsold; Heritage Auctions (March 2011), PCGS Fine 15 CAC, lot 4409, $74,750.*

Additional Notes: None.

Coin Serial Number: 161.

From Heritage Auctions,
October 2011

1796 15 Stars, O-101.

Tremblay Specimen.

Grade: Very Fine obverse, Fine reverse.

Identification Markers: A small rim flaw between ER of LIBERTY is also seen on the reverse rim below the twist in the right ribbon.

Provenance: *Heritage Auctions (September – October 1988), Fine 15/15, lot 653, $15,500; Heritage Auctions (February 1989), Fine 12/12, lot 657, $11,500; Pete Tremblay Collection (American Numismatic Rarities, June 2006), ICG Fine 12, lot 1428, $34,500; ANA Sale (Heritage Auctions, October 2011), NGC Fine 12, lot 3673, $46,000.*

Additional Notes: None.

Coin Serial Number: 162.

From the Byron Reed Collection;
owned by the City of Omaha, Nebraska;
on loan to the Durham Museum

1796 15 Stars, O-101, early die state

Byron Reed Specimen.

Grade: Very Fine obverse, Fine reverse.

Identification Markers: Fine scratch extends diagonally from lower right of knob in 6 of date to just below drapery under left (facing) breast. Horizontal scratch in field between drapery and rim, in line with left (facing) breast. Horizontal pinscratch runs from lower hair curl to above 17 in date. Upper-left to lower-right pinscratch extends from beneath chin to lower-left point of star 14. Mark adjacent to upper-left part of third curl from top. Reverse dentilation does not show except along the left border. Tops of AMER weak. Short horizontal mark beneath third vertical feather of right (facing) wing, another midway between eagle's tail and palm wreath, in line with I of AMERICA. Mark between lower-inner laurel leaf and left ribbon bow, closer to former. Photo quality makes all pedigree markers very difficult to see. One of only six 1796 15 Star examples in the study lacking the die crack from border at 5:00 to the bust.

Provenance: *Byron Reed Collection; owned by the City of Omaha, Nebraska; on loan to the Durham Museum.*

Additional Notes: None.

Coin Serial Number: 162a.

From Bowers and Merena, November 2009

1796 15 Stars, O-101.

November 2009 Baltimore Auction Specimen.

Grade: Fine, Cleaned.

Identification Markers: Arrow-like field mark in front of Liberty's mouth. Small spot just to upper left of star 13. A minuscule mark to the right of D in UNITED and two more between right (facing) leg and wing. Dark spot on bottom of third laurel leaf below first S in STATES.

Provenance: *Baltimore Auction (Bowers and Merena, November 2009), NGC Fine Details, Improperly Cleaned, lot 857, unsold.*

Additional Notes: The Bowers and Merena catalog states: "Glossy surfaces and scattered hairlines point to a cleaning."

Coin Serial Number: 163.

Reverse unplated

From Gregory Brunk, 2003

1796 15 Stars, O-101, uncertain die state.

Brunk Plate Specimen.

Grade: Fine obverse, Counterstamped, Scratched.

Identification Markers: LOCK SMITHS NO 3 MOTT. ST. stamped on obverse. Four to five long curved scratches in right field. Photo quality prevents determining whether or not the usually seen die crack from the border at 5:00 to the bust is present.

Provenance: *Thomas Warner, Esq. Sale (S.H. and H. Chapman, June 1884), obverse very good, reverse poor, lot 2710 (unplated), $21; Charles Steigerwalt (October 1884), obverse very good, reverse nearly good (unplated); Gregory Brunk, Merchant and Privately Countermarked Coins, 2003.*

Additional Notes: None.

Coin Serial Number: 164.

From Stack's,
January 1953

1796 15 Stars, O-101, uncertain die state.

Guggenheimer Specimen.

Grade: Fine obverse, Scratched, Very Good reverse.

Identification Markers: Scratch extends from star 4 through Liberty's lower portrait to star 15. Short parallel streaks just left of stars 9 and 10. Short upper-right to lower-left mark between eagle's beak and neck and curve of upper-right (facing) wing. Mark on upper-left torso. Except for the obverse scratch and torso mark, photo quality makes it difficult to see the other pedigree markers. Photo quality prevents determining whether or not the usually seen die crack from the border at 5:00 to the bust is present.

Provenance: *F.S. Guggenheimer Collection (Stack's, January 1953), Fine obverse, Very Good reverse, lot 784, $350.*

Additional Notes: None.

Coin Serial Number: 165.

From Stack's – Bowers, November 2012

1796 15 Stars, O-101, early die state.

November 2012 Baltimore Auction Specimen.

Grade: Very Fine obverse, Re-engraved, Very Good reverse.

Identification Markers: Liberty's hair re-engraved, especially noticeable at the back of the head above the ribbon. Mark to the right of star 1. Parts of eagle and clouds worn smooth. Lacks the usually seen crack from the border at 5:00 to the bust. One of only six early die state examples in the study without this mark, indicating it is among the first 1796 halves struck.

Provenance: *Baltimore Auction (Stack's-Bowers, November 2012), NGC Fine Details, Repaired, Re-engraved, lot 3137, $20,700.*

Additional Notes: The Stack's-Bowers catalog states: "The surfaces show evidence of heating (to accomplish the re-engraving) in the form of finely granular texture."

Coin Serial Number: 165a.

From Heritage Auctions, July 2006

1796 15 Stars, O-101.

1972 NASCA Sale Specimen.

Grade: Very Good obverse, Scratched, Fine reverse, Scratched.

Identification Markers: What appears to be the letter "P" is scratched on Liberty's portrait from the temple to the drapery above the 9 in the date. Three or four marks are visible between the middle curls and stars 3 and 4. Light rim mark left of star 4 and another left of star 8. Three scratches nearly encircle the eagle.

Provenance: *Numismatic Association of Southern California Sale (RARCOA, February 1972), Fine, lot 345, $2,275; Heritage Auctions (July 2006), ANACS VG 8 Details, Repaired, lot 2394, $23,000.*

Additional Notes: The Heritage catalog states: "… Liberty's portrait has been subjected to some sort of abrasive … that has left several mostly-vertical hairline-like scratches that are visible under high magnification."

Coin Serial Number: 166.

Reverse unplated

From H. Chapman,
December 1921

1796 15 Stars, O-101, uncertain die state.

Jenks Specimen.

Grade: Very Good obverse, Scratched, Plugged.

Identification Markers: Horizontal scratch extends from star 14 along Liberty's jaw to the hair ribbon. Several scratches in lower hair and adjacent field (right of star 2, 3, and 4). Photo quality prevents determining whether or not the usually seen die crack from the border at 5:00 to the bust is present.

Provenance: *John Story Jenks Collection (H. Chapman, December 1921), obverse fair, reverse poor, lot 5912, $21.*

Additional Notes: None.

Coin Serial Number: 167.

From Bowers and Merena,
May 1993

1796 15 Stars, O-101.

Stetson University Specimen.

Grade: Very Good obverse, Good reverse.

Identification Markers: Photo quality makes it difficult to conclusively identify pedigree markers. That said, there appears to be a faint mark just to the lower right of star 4, and a round mark left of the curl across from stars 2-3. A diagonal band of streaked toning runs from stars 9 and 10 to Liberty's nose and mouth, and vertical bands extend from the ear and rear jaw to the drapery above 96 in the date. Lower-right reverse border appears to be heavily worn.

Provenance: *Stetson University Collection (Bowers and Merena, May 1993), PCGS Good 4, lot 278, $8,525.*

Additional Notes: Photo quality makes it uncertain whether or not this coin duplicates another low-grade 1796 15 Star half dollar in the study.

Coin Serial Number: 168.

From the National Numismatic Collection, Smithsonian Institution

1796 15 Stars, O-101.

National Numismatic Collection Specimen.

Grade: Very Good obverse, Cleaned, About Good reverse, Cleaned.

Identification Markers: Rim planchet defect above star 10 and on corresponding reverse at 4:30. What appear to be numerous upper-right to lower-left hairlines are visible on both sides. A mark below Liberty's chin. Three prominent marks on the top part of Liberty's head. Minor rim ding above space between AT of STATES.

Provenance: *From "the cabinet started by Eckfeldt and Dubois back in the 1830s at the Philadelphia Mint, transferred to us ... after 1923" (per Dr. Richard Doty, Curator, National Numismatic Collection, January 26, 2012 email).*

Additional Notes: None.

Coin Serial Number: 168a.

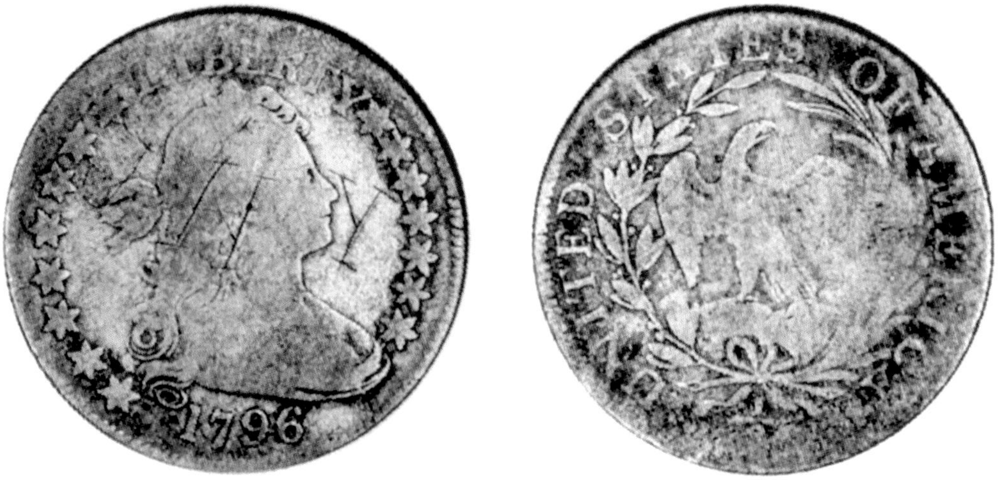

From Superior Galleries,
January 2003

1796 15 Stars, O-101.

2003 Pre-FUN Sale Specimen.

Grade: Good obverse, initials removed, About Good reverse.

Identification Markers: A "J" inscribed in field between stars 6 - 8 and Liberty's head, an "H" on the head centered left of the ear, and a "Y" in the field between the nose and chin and stars 11 - 14. The eagle's right (facing) wing and adjacent palm wreath are worn smooth, as is the bottom of 2 in the fraction. The rim is worn into the tops of letters in AMERICA.

Provenance: *Pre-FUN Sale (Superior Galleries, January 2003), About Good 3, lot 690, $8,625; Dick Osburn Rare Coins fixed price list (May 2003), Good/About Good, Repaired (unplated), $32,500.*

Additional Notes: The author viewed this coin at the summer 2003 ANA sale after the initials were removed. The repair was virtually undetectable. Except for the areas of reverse wear mentioned above, no other identification markers were readily evident.

Coin Serial Number: 169.

From Numismatic Services, Inc., December 2004

1796 15 Stars, O-101.

December 2004 NSI Specimen.

Grade: Good obverse, Fair reverse.

Identification Markers: Photo quality makes it difficult to conclusively identify pedigree markers. Moreover, the coin exhibits heavy wear with no discernible post-strike impairments. The eagle's right (facing) wing, except for its curved upper part, is worn smooth, as is the fraction and the wreath and lettering along the right border.

Provenance: *Numismatic Services, Inc. fixed price list (December 2004), PCGS AG 3, $28,500.*

Additional Notes: None.

Coin Serial Number: 170.

Additional 1796 15 Stars Half Dollar Appearances

Images from the following catalogs are not included in the study because poor photo quality makes it virtually impossible to determine a coin's grade or identification markers. Specimens in some of these catalogs may duplicate coins that have been incorporated into the study, while others might represent new appearances. Grades are those listed in the respective catalogs or represent an approximation by the author.

Proof. John M. Morris Collection (Numismatic Gallery, August 1953), lot 868.
Proof. Farish Baldenhofer Collection (Stack's, November 1955), lot 675.
MS. John G. Mills Collection (S.H. and H. Chapman, April 1904), lot 811.
MS. George W. Rice Collection (St. Louis Stamp and Coin, April 1906), lot 196.
AU. Kriesberg and Schulman (January 1957), lot 2127.
AU. NASCA (November 1977), lot 689.
XF or **AU.** George H. Earle, Jr. Collection (H. Chapman, June 1912), lot 2823.
XF. Federal Coin Exchange, August 1957, lot 1454.
VF. Robert Colton Davis Collection (New York Stamp and Coin, January 1890), lot 584.
VF. Will W. Neil Collection (Max Mehl, June 1947), lot 352.
VF. Mathew A. Stickney Collection (H. Chapman, June 1907), lot 929.
VF. Al Overton (August 1965), lot 1652 (the same as the plate coin in Overton's *Early Half Dollar Die Varieties).*
VF. Michael Higgy Collection (A. Kosoff, September 1943), lot 665.
VF. H.O. Granberg Collection (Max Mehl, July 1913), lot 192.
VF. Griffith Collection (Max Mehl, March 1912), lot 105.
VF. Davis-Graves et al. Collections (Stack's, April 1954), lot 458.
VF. Stack's (April 1957), lot 971.
VF. RARCOA (August 1970), lot 869.
VF. George H. Hall Collection (Stack's, May 1945), lot 1001.
VF. George W. Parsons Collection (H. Chapman, June 1914), lot 1413.
VF. Alex Shufford Collection (A. Kosoff, May 1918), lot 1094.
Fine. James Kelly (August 1951), lot 102.
Fine. Stack's (August 1976), lot 1086.
Fine. W. F. Dunham Collection (Max Mehl, June 1941), lot 674.
Fine. Numismatic Enterprises (August 1968), lot 1786.
Fine. Bowers and Merena (November 1996), lot 1923.
Fine. A. Kosoff (August 1968), lot 42.
Fine. Kriesberg and Schulman (February 1961), lot 2706.
Fine. Kriesberg and Schulman (February 1961), lot 2707.

1796 16 Stars Half Dollar Examples
Overton-102

From Stack's,
May 1999

1796 16 Stars, O-102, early die state.

Mougey (possibly) – Rogers – Whitney Walter Specimen.

Grade: Mint State.

Identification Markers: Minute triangular toning spot in field stemming from the drapery of Liberty's left (facing) breast. Distinctive but minuscule arrowhead-like toning mark to lower left of lower-right ribbon (arrowhead points to fraction bar). The sometimes-seen die crack from the rim through the first four stars is absent on this coin, indicating its early die state.

Provenance: *Possibly Peter Mougey Collection (Thomas Elder, September 1910), Uncirculated, lot 423, $340; Lelan Rogers Collection (Stack's/Akers/RARCOA, November 1995), Gem Brilliant Uncirculated, lot 1250, $330,000; John Whitney Walter Collection (Stack's, May 1999), Specimen 66, lot 1778, $460,000.*

Additional Notes: Despite photo quality of the image in the Mougey appearance, the above-mentioned toning patterns appear to match those in the Rogers and Whitney Walter images, resulting in a fairly high degree of certainty that the three appearances represent the same coin.

Coin Serial Number: 200.

From American Numismatic Rarities,
January 2006

1796 16 Stars, O-102, early die state.

Hawn – Koshkarian – Specimen.

Grade: Mint State.

Identification Markers: Moderate mark on middle jaw, another on cheek bone. Toning spots right of nose, mouth, and between chest and star 15. Fine streak from rim through star 4 and the right sides of stars 3 and 2. Two light streaks from lower curl diagonally through bottom of 1 in date to rim. Heavy crisscross adjustment marks on central and right reverse.

Provenance: *Reed Hawn Collection (Stack's, August 1973), Gem, lot 7, $32,000; Jay Parrino's The Mint (March 1998 Numismatic News ad), NGC MS 64, $195,000; Bowers and Merena (August 1998), NGC MS 64, lot 181, $115,200; Superior Galleries (August 2002), NGC MS 64, lot 943; Haig Koshkarian et al. Collections Sale (American Numismatic Rarities, March 2004), NGC MS 64, lot 575, $276,000; Robert Michael Prescott Collection (American Numismatic Rarities, January 2006), NGC MS 64, lot 527; Ira and Larry Goldberg (May 2006), PCGS MS 64, lot 2908, $414,000; Ira and Larry Goldberg (February 2009), PCGS MS 64, lot 927, unsold; Ira and Larry Goldberg (January 2011), PCGS MS 64, lot 1413, $345,000.*

Additional Notes: None.

Coin Serial Number: 201.

From Bowers and Merena, April 1997

1796 16 Stars, O-102, early die state.

Clapp – Eliasberg Specimen.

Grade: Mint State.

Identification Markers: A prominent horizontal toning streak (rubber band mark?) runs from star 4 through Liberty's hair before terminating on the lower-middle neck. Another conspicuous toning streak runs from the rim above star 8, then along the tops of star 9 and the LI of LIBERTY before returning to the rim above B. A very short upper-left to lower-right mark is visible just to the lower left of the bottom hair ribbon.

Provenance: *John H. Clapp; Clapp estate, 1942 to Louis E. Eliasberg, Sr. (per Bowers and Merena, April 1997); Louis E. Eliasberg, Sr. Collection (Bowers and Merena, April 1997), MS 63, prooflike, lot 1674, $143,000; Coinage magazine plate coin (December 2003).*

Additional Notes: It is interesting to speculate on the pedigree of this piece prior to Eliasberg. In this regard, David Bowers (1996) writes: "John H. Clapp was a buyer in the June 25-29, 1912 sale of the George H. Earle Collection conducted by Henry Chapman." The obverse photo of the 1796 16 Stars Earle specimen (lot 2824) displays a similarly located and aligned diagonal mark to the lower left of the bottom hair ribbon as seen on the Eliasberg coin. The two prominent toning streaks are not present, however (perhaps they occurred subsequent to Earle's custodianship?). Chapman described the coin as a "superb example." Earle purchased the coin from the S.H. and H. Chapman April 1897 sale of the M.A. Brown Collection (lot 376) where it was described as "very fine, slight trace of proof surface around device. Possibly only one or two in equal condition exist."

Coin Serial Number: 202.

From the National Numismatic Collection, Smithsonian Institution

1796 16 Stars, O-102, early die state.

National Numismatic Collection Specimen.

Grade: About Uncirculated, Pinscratches, Hairlines.

Identification Markers: Upper-right to lower-left pinscratches on Liberty's cheek and neck, and hairlines in the left field. Two moderate toning spots near rim left of star 3. Criss-cross hairlines in central reverse. A vertical pinscratch at the end of each palm leaf below the last S in STATES, and another to right of eagle's beak. Toning splotches at ES and between S and O in OF, and along lower-left border from 2 in fraction through U in UNITED. Horizontal hairlines on eagle's neck.

Provenance: *"Simply found in collection" (per Dr. Richard Doty, Curator, National Numismatic Collection, January 26, 2012 email).*

Additional Notes: None.

Coin Serial Number: 202a.

From Heritage Auctions, January 2013

1796 16 Stars, O-102, late die state.

Delp – Bisanz Specimen.

Grade: About Uncirculated.

Identification Markers: Vertical toning streak extends from the drapery above the right of the 6 in the date to the middle of the chest. Small round mark just above the forehead curl aligned with the stand of Y in LIBERTY. Scalloped mark below eagle's beak. Light upper-right to lower-left adjustment marks extend from the right (facing) wing through the lower leg, right cloud, and lower palm wreath to the rim at the lower right of the fraction. The sometimes-seen die crack from the rim through the first four stars is present on this coin, indicating its late die state.

Provenance: *Stack's (June 1968), Extremely Fine, lot 79, $6,750; Winner F. Delp Collection (Stack's, November 1972), Extremely Fine, lot 70; Heritage Auctions (February 1995), PCGS XF 45, lot 5655, $41,800; Bob Bisanz U.S. Type Set (Heritage Auctions, January 2001), PCGS AU 55, lot 7729, unsold; Bowers and Merena (July 2003), PCGS AU 55, lot 1382; Bowers and Merena (January 2005), PCGS AU 55, lot 524, $172,500; 2013 FUN Sale (Heritage Auctions, January, 2013), PCGS AU55.*

Additional Notes: None.

Coin Serial Number: 203.

From Bowers and Merena,
August 1987

1796 16 Stars, O-102, early die state.

Earle – Bebee – Friend Specimen.

Grade: Extremely Fine.

Identification Markers: Faint upper-right to lower-left linear mark on Liberty's jaw. Rim bruise between stars 15 and 16. Upper-left to lower-right adjustment marks on eagle, right cloud, and lower palm wreath.

Provenance: *George H. Earle Collection (H. Chapman, June 1912), Very fine, lot 2825, $205; Austin Collection (Bowers and Ruddy, May 1974), Extremely Fine, lot 678, $8,750; Aubrey and Adeline Bebee et al. Collections (Bowers and Merena, August 1987), EF 45, lot 2148, $28,600; Dale Friend PCGS Set Registry (December 2009), PCGS AU 50.*

Additional Notes: None.

Coin Serial Number: 204.

From Superior Galleries, September 2004

1796 16 Stars, O-102, early die state.

Mills – Menjou – Polis Specimen.

Grade: Extremely Fine, Smoothed Fields.

Identification Markers: Short diagonal adjustment mark runs from drapery atop Liberty's shoulder into hair beneath curl. Mark to right of 6 in date. Faint remnant of an "X" shows under magnification between Liberty's neck and stars 14 and 15, and also between eagle's beak and palm wreath. Mark between tip of left (facing) wing and cloud. Small rim bruise at 5:30 on the reverse, and another between RI.

Provenance: *John G. Mills Collection (S.H. and H. Chapman, April 1904), Very fine, cross in fields, lot 812, $125; Adolphe Menjou Collection (Numismatic Gallery, June 1950), extremely fine, cross in fields, lot 943, $600; Superior Galleries (December 1972), Extra Fine, etched cross obverse and reverse, lot 1703, $9,500; Mount Vernon Sale (Superior Galleries, November 1976), Extra Fine, etched cross obverse and reverse, lot 456, $9,000; California Collection (Superior Galleries, October 1978), Extremely Fine 40 to 45, etched cross obverse and reverse, lot 1260, $10,250; George N. Polis Collection (Bowers and Merena, June 1991), EF 40, lot 1365, $27,610; Superior Galleries (September 2004) MS 60 Detail, Net AU 50, Cleaned, Smoothed Surfaces, lot 2113, $63,250.*

Additional Notes: Most of each "X" on obverse and reverse (each of which was very light) was smoothed off by the time of the September 2004 Superior sale.

Coin Serial Number: 205.

From Heritage Auctions,
September 1998

1796 16 Stars, O-102, early die state.

Parmelee – Reed Specimen.

Grade: Extremely Fine.

Identification Markers: Two upper-left to lower-right adjustment marks in Liberty's hair, one aligned with drapery at upper shoulder, the other left of ear. "S"- shaped mark low between last S of STATES and O in OF.

Provenance: *Lorin Parmelee Collection (New York Stamp and Coin, June 1890), very fine impression, lot 724, $130; Byron Reed Collection (Spink America, October 1996), nearly extremely fine, lot 24, $41,800; Heritage Auctions (September 1998), NGC XF 45, lot 6745, unsold; Bowers and Merena Rare Coin Review # 141 (May - June 2001), PCGS EF 45, $54,950.*

Additional Notes: None.

Coin Serial Number: 206.

From Heritage Auctions, February 1989

1796 16 Stars, O-102, early die state.

Davis Specimen.

Grade: Extremely Fine.

Identification Markers: Short upper-left to lower-right adjustment mark midway between Liberty's ear and neck curl. Small mark at juncture of jaw and neck. Mark on lower-right eagle's torso. Mark to upper right of 2 in fraction.

Provenance: *R.T. Davis Collections (Stack's, February 1968), Very Fine, lot 85, $3,750; Heritage Auctions (September – October 1988), Very Fine 30/30, lot 654, $21,000; Heritage Auctions (February 1989), Extremely Fine 40/40, lot 658, $25,000.*

Additional Notes: None.

Coin Serial Number: 207.

From Mid-American, January 1989

1796 16 Stars, O-102, early die state.

1989 FUN Specimen.

Grade: Very Fine obverse, Extremely Fine reverse.

Identification Markers: Two minute spots just to the lower right of star 1. Three minuscule spots just to middle left of 6 in date and one to right of its serif. Spot to lower left of star 15. Several flyspecks scattered over reverse. Photo quality makes all pedigree markers difficult to discern.

Provenance: *FUN Sale (Mid-American Rare Coin Auctions, January 1989), Extremely Fine (45), lot 2710, $38,500.*

Additional Notes: None.

Coin Serial Number: 208.

From the
American Numismatic Society,
February 2012

1796 16 Stars, O-102, late die state.

American Numismatic Society Specimen.

Grade: Very Fine.

Identification Markers: Distinctive obverse toning pattern, including splotches to right of and above date, and diagonal streaks between stars 2-6 and Liberty's hair. Short, light upper-right to lower-left scratches to right of last S in STATES, and another between ES.

Provenance: *"Gift of Matilda Bruce, acquisition source unknown. Miss Bruce was apparently the daughter of type-foundryman George Bruce, a prominent New York industrialist of the mid-19th century. She was a serious collector, and became a significant partron not only of the ANS but of the Metropolitan Museum of Art as well" (per Robert Hoge, Curator of North American Coins and Currency, ANS, January 26, 2012 email).*

Additional Notes: None.

Coin Serial Number: 208a.

From Bowers and Merena,
January 1992

1796 16 Stars, O-102, early die state.

Brilliant Specimen.

Grade: Very Fine.

Identification Markers: Minuscule vertical mark just above drapery line in center of Liberty's chest. Moderate vertical mark to right of eagle's beak nearly halfway to tip of palm leaf. Mark centrally located on torso. Fine upper-left to lower-right linear mark midway between right (facing) wing and leg.

Provenance: *Stack's (March 1987), Very Fine, lot 688, $20,900; Brilliant Collection (Bowers and Merena, January 1992), VF 30, lot 39, $19,800; Coin Rarities fixed price list Online Ad Archive (February 2009), NGC VF 35, $87,500.*

Additional Notes: None.

Coin Serial Number: 209.

From Heritage Auctions, July 2008

1796 16 Stars, O-102, early die state.

Bayside Specimen.

Grade: Very Fine.

Identification Markers: Three or four spots immediately right of bridge of Liberty's nose, another on front jaw, and a few others scattered about the obverse. Linear abrasion between U of UNITED and ribbon. Milling mark right of tail between right (facing) wing and tip of palm leaf. Large spot in center of left (facing) cloud halfway between ribbon bow and laurel leaf. Spot high between F of OF and first A in AMERICA.

Provenance: *Bayside New York Collection (Heritage Auctions, July 2008), PCGS VF 30, lot 1669, $83,375; Harry Labstain Rare Coins fixed price list (October 2008), PCGS VF 35, $105,000.*

Additional Notes: None.

Coin Serial Number: 210.

From Heritage Auctions,
October 2011

1796 16 Stars, O-102, late die state.

Zug – Yoder Family Specimen.

Grade: Very Fine, Pitted obverse, Scratched reverse.

Identification Markers: Shallow obverse corrosion pits above hair ribbon and in right field. Roughness throughout Liberty's portrait. Moderate scratches in fields around eagle. Rim mark over R of AMERICA, and coalesced dentils between AM.

Provenance: *Charles Gordon Zug Collection (S.H. Chapman, October 1909), obverse corrosion pits, lot 428; Century Sale (Paramount, April - May 1965), Very Fine, obverse surface roughness, lot 1080, $3,050; RARCOA (May 1971), Very Fine, obverse surface roughness, lot 410, $2,700; Nate Smith Collection (Stack's, March 1973), Fine, lot 807, $3,300; Stack's (June 1989), Very Fine, obverse corrosion, lot 1750, $10,450; Yoder Family Collection (Heritage Auctions, May 2008), NCS Fine Details, Corroded, Improperly Cleaned, lot 494, $28,750; Bowers and Merena (November 2009), PCGS Genuine, Damage, VG Details, lot 858; ANA Sale (Heritage Auctions, October 2011), NGC Fine Details, Corrosion, Cleaned, lot 3674, $28,750.*

Additional Notes: None.

Coin Serial Number: 211.

From B. Max Mehl,
November 1914

1796 16 Stars, O-102, late die state.

R.C. Davis – Nygren Specimen.

Grade: Very Fine.

Identification Markers: Upper-right to lower-left adjustment marks on Liberty's neck and adjacent hair. Nick on lower right E in LIBERTY. Two marks on the eagle's lower-right torso. Vertical mark right of beak and neck.

Provenance: *Wm. F. Johnson Sale, formerly owned by late Robert Coulton Davis (New York Stamp and Coin, January 1890), Very good even impression, lot 583, $66; Arthur Nygren Collection (B. Max Mehl, November 1914), Very fine, lot 181, $87.*

Additional Notes: None.

Coin Serial Number: 212.

From Heritage Auctions,
February 2005

1796 16 Stars, O-102, early die state.

February 2005 Long Beach Sale Specimen.

Grade: Very Fine.

Identification Markers: Upper-right to lower-left adjustment marks from back of Liberty's neck into adjacent hair. Mark just to lower left of star 15. Mark just to lower left of eagle's left (facing) leg.

Provenance: *Long Beach Sale (Heritage Auctions, February 2005), PCGS VF 30, lot 6912, $69,000.*

Additional Notes: None.

Coin Serial Number: 213.

From Bowers and Merena,
August 1999

1796 16 Stars, O-102, early die state.

Winsor (probably) – Clarke – Oviedo – Childs Specimen.

Grade: Very Fine.

Identification Markers: S-shaped mark on Liberty's forehead just below hairline. Two marks just above right (facing) wing, and three vertical-diagonal scratches between wing and tail.

Provenance: *Probably Richard B. Winsor Collection (S.H. and H. Chapman, December 1895), Very good, lot 456, $140; George O. Walton Collection (Stack's, October 1963), Very Fine, lot 856;, $3,250 Dr. E. Yale Clarke Collection (Stack's, October 1975), Very Fine, lot 183, $9,000; Dr. George F. Oviedo Collection (Stack's, September 1983), Fine, nearly Very Fine, lot 726; Walter H. Childs Collection (Bowers and Merena, August 1999), VF 20, lot 332, $20,700.*

Additional Notes: None.

Coin Serial Number: 214.

From Bowers and Merena,
November 1995

1796 16 Stars, O-102, late die state.

H.P. Smith – Norweb Specimen.

Grade: Very Fine.

Identification Markers: Upper-left to lower-right adjustment marks extending from Liberty's hair through the temple and neck. Linear mark from star 8 to upper left of hair ribbon. Short vertical mark to right of eagle's beak. Minute rim ding between ER of AMERICA, and another between IC.

Provenance: *Harlan P. Smith Collection (S.H. and H. Chapman, May 1906), Very good, lot 577, $80; David S. Wilson Collection (S.H. Chapman, March 1907), Very good or fine for date, lot 469, $120; Wayte Raymond advertisement, Standard Catalogue of U.S. Coins and Tokens, 1942 edition (plate coin); Norweb Collection, Part III (Bowers and Merena, November 1988), Fine 12, lot 3026, $16,500; Bowers and Merena (November 1993), Fine 12, lot 1133, $15,590; Bowers and Merena (November 1995), PCGS VF 25, lot 2440, unsold; Premium Numismatics (2003 fixed price list), PCGS VF 25.*

Additional Notes: None.

Coin Serial Number: 215.

From Bowers and Merena, November 1991

1796 16 Stars, O-102, early die state.

Kensington – Frontenac Specimen.

Grade: Very Fine.

Identification Markers: Faint vertical hairline scratch from star 9, terminating at upper left of top hair ribbon. Minute mark left of head and midway between stand of L in LIBERTY and upper hair ribbon. Two faint spots just right of 6 in date, and a diagonal mark to their right. Diagonal hairline scratch from middle stand of E in UNITED to laurel wreath. Mark just above left (facing) cloud, another above eagle's tail. Vertical scratch in middle of right (facing) wing. Diagonal scratch from rim at 5:30 to tip of inner palm leaf below wing.

Provenance: *Paramount (August 1974), VF 20, lot 98; Kensington Collection (Bowers and Ruddy, December 1975), Very Fine, lot 323, $7,500; Bowers and Merena (November 1986), Very Fine 30, lot 480; Frontenac Sale (Bowers and Merena, November 1991), PCGS VF 25, lot 3017, $22,550.*

Additional Notes: None.

Coin Serial Number: 216.

From Heritage Auctions,
September 2010

1796 16 Stars, O-102, early die state.

Lahrman – Seller Specimen.

Grade: Very Fine.

Identification Markers: Upper-left to lower-right strike-through in middle of Liberty's jaw. Horizontal linear mark on lower part of eagle's right (facing) wing, two heavy marks near wing tip, and several small to moderate marks in adjacent field. Linear mark on lower middle-inner palm leaf aligned with lower-right of I in AMERICA.

Provenance: *Lee G. Lahrman et al. Collections (A. Kosoff, February 1963), a very fine example, lot 617, $3,500; Seller Collection (Bowers and Ruddy, March 1980), VF 20, lot 3165, $30,000; Heritage Auctions (September 2010), PCGS VF 25, lot 4071, $69,000; Heritage Auctions (August 2012), PCGS VF 25, lot 5141, $105,750.*

Additional Notes: None.

Coin Serial Number: 217.

From Heritage Auctions, June 2006

1796 16 Stars, O-102, early die state.

June 2006 Long Beach Sale Specimen.

Grade: Very Fine, reverse Cuts.

Identification Markers: Upper-right to lower-left scratch midway between star 13 and Liberty's nose tip, mouth, and chin. A deep cut on rim to upper right of O in OF, another above stand of F, and another between F and first A in AMERICA. A longer cut runs from upper-left serif of F through its lower-right serif into the palm wreath.

Provenance: *Long Beach Sale (Heritage Auctions, June 2006), ANACS VF 20 Details, Damaged, lot 1588, $43,125.*

Additional Notes: None.

Coin Serial Number: 218.

From Heritage Auctions,
September 2006

1796 16 Stars, O-102, late die state.

Dupont – Emmons – Queller Family Specimen.

Grade: Very Fine.

Identification Markers: Short horizontal adjustment marks beneath the two curls that drop from Liberty's ear. Faint adjustment marks at the upper-right obverse border. A distinctive cluster of toning spots between the forehead and stars 10 and 11. Two moderate marks just to the upper left of the upper curve of the right (facing) wing, and a toning spot on the lower right of the same wing. Faint, short vertical adjustment marks on either side of the fraction.

Provenance: *Anderson Dupont Collection, Part II (Stack's, November 1954), Very Fine, lot 2032, $925; Dr. Calvert L. Emmons Collection (Stack's, September 1969), Very Fine, lot 612; Queller Family Collection (Stack's, October 2002), Very Fine, lot 23, $32,200; Heritage Auctions (September 2004), NGC VF 25, lot 6575, $57,500; Premium Numismatics fixed price list (November 2004), PCGS VF 25, $68,000; American Numismatic Rarities (January 2005), PCGS VF 25, lot 497, $59,800; Heritage Auctions (September 2006), PCGS VF 30, lot 1865, $69,000; Harry Labstain Rare Coins fixed price list (January 2007), PCGS VF 30, $85,000.*

Additional Notes: None.

Coin Serial Number: 219.

From Bowers and Merena,
September 1992

1796 16 Stars, O-102, late die state.

Whitham and Sansoucy Sale Specimen.

Grade: Very Fine.

Identification Markers: Moderate spot on the upper-right part of Liberty's left (facing) breast. Spot right of star 15 near rim. Photo quality prevents identification of other pedigree markers.

Provenance: *Stewart Whitham and Raymond Sansoucy Collections Sale (Bowers and Merena, September 1992), VF 20/20 (1989 ANA certificate), lot 1035, $17,050; Harry Labstain Rare Coins fixed price list (May 2007), PCGS VF 20, $75,000.*

Additional Notes: None.

Coin Serial Number: 220.

From RARCOA,
August 2000

1796 16 Stars, O-102, late die state.

2000 RARCOA Archives Specimen.

Grade: Very Fine.

Identification Markers: Mark immediately right of star 5, another right of star 6. Mark between star 15 and chin, another just below drapery on left (facing) breast. Apparent mark on the upper-left part of the eagle's right (facing) leg at juncture with torso, and another on left middle torso close to left (facing) wing.

Provenance: *RARCOA Archives (August 2000), PCGS VF 30.*

Additional Notes: None.

Coin Serial Number: 221.

From Stack's,
May 1955

1796 16 Stars, O-102, uncertain die state.

Atwater Specimen.

Grade: Very Fine.

Identification Markers: Photo quality makes pedigree markers virtually impossible to identify.

Provenance: *William Cutler Atwater Collection (B. Max Mehl, June 1946), Very Fine, lot 395, $470; Dr. Charles W. Green Collection (B. Max Mehl, April 1949), Very Fine, lot 2734 (Atwater pedigree per Mehl, $400); Dr. Clifford E. Smith and Son Collection (Stack's, May 1955), Choice Very Fine, lot 1016 (Green pedigree per Stack's, $1,100).*

Additional Notes: While these three appearances apparently represent the same coin, the photo quality of each prevents determining with certainty whether or not it duplicates another mid-grade 1796 16 Stars late die state half dollar in the study.

Coin Serial Number: 222.

Coin under serial number 223 deleted from study because of photo defects.

From Superior Galleries,
May 1987

1796 16 Stars, O-102, early die state.

Ebsen Specimen.

Grade: Very Fine.

Identification Markers: Splotchy toning pattern on obverse, especially in field between left-border stars and Liberty's portrait, and between nose and stars 11 and 12. Light spot on upper chest above 9 in date, and a darker spot to lower right of chin. Rim bruise below left bow ribbon, another to upper-left of first T in STATES, and one above M in AMERICA.

Provenance: *Buddy Ebsen et al. Collections (Superior Galleries, May 1987), Fine 15, lot 1322, $19,800.*

Additional Notes: None.

Coin Serial Number: 224.

From Stack's,
April 1967

1796 16 Stars, O-102, early die state.

King-Copeland Specimen.

Grade: Very Fine.

Identification Markers: Moderate mark between bottom of star 1 and rim. Small mark just to right of forehead curl. What might be a small "X" is located just to the upper left of the curve of the right (facing) wing.

Provenance: *Colin E. King Collection(S.H. and H. Chapman, April 1892), "Fine for coin," lot 780 (obverse only), $69; Bernard L. Copeland Collection (Stack's, April 1967), strong Fine, lot 850, $3,000.*

Additional Notes: None.

Coin Serial Number: 225.

From Stack's,
November 1957

1796 16 Stars, O-102, early die state.

Empire Collection Specimen.

Grade: Very Fine.

Identification Markers: Pedigree markers are indiscernible, owing in part to photo quality and in part because the coin appears to have been well preserved.

Provenance: *Empire Collection (Stack's, November 1957), Very Fine, lot 1267, $875.*

Additional Notes: It is uncertain whether or not this coin duplicates another mid-grade 1796 16 Stars early die state half dollar in the study.

Coin Serial Number: 226.

From Stack's,
July 1985

1796 16 Stars, O-102, early die state.

Miles - Robison Specimen.

Grade: Very Fine.

Identification Markers: Short upper-right to lower-left linear mark midway between star 9 and Liberty's head. Mark between forehead curl and lower-right serif ofY in LIBERTY. Spot between neck curl and shoulder, and another on upper-left (facing) breast, in line with serif of 6 in date. Toning spot between upper-right part of right (facing) wing and upper-middle inner palm leaf.

Provenance: *R.L. Miles Collection (Stack's, April 1969), Very Fine, lot 1206, $3,700; Ellis and Doris Robison Collection (Stack's, February 1982), Very Fine, lot 1525, $17,500; Auction '85 (Stack's session, July 1985), Very Fine, lot 1700.*

Additional Notes: None.

Coin Serial Number: 227.

From Stack's – Bowers,
November 2012

1797 16 Stars, O-102, late die state.

November 2012 Baltimore Auction Specimen.

Grade: Very Fine obverse, Fine reverse.

Identification Markers: Mark just above neck curl. Short vertical mark to right of chin. Moderate spot just to lower right of bottom-right serif of second T in STATES.

Provenance: *Baltimore Auction (Stack's-Bowers, November 2012), PCGS Fine 12, lot 3138, $69,000.*

Additional Notes: None.

Coin Serial Number: 227a.

From Stack's,
May 1976

1796 16 Stars, O-102, late die state.

Mills Specimen.

Grade: Very Fine obverse, Fine reverse.

Identification Markers: Small rim ding above upper right of star 12. Short toning streak extends to lower left of star 13. Coalesced dentils between D of UNITED and first S of STATES. Upper-left to lower-right streak through first S, and wreath to upper wing.

Provenance: *Mills Collection (Stack's, May 1976), Fine, lot 333, $7,000.*

Additional Notes: None.

Coin Serial Number: 228.

From Heritage Auctions, July 2009

1796 16 Stars, O-102, early die state.

Summer 2009 FUN Sale Specimen.

Grade: Very Fine obverse, Re-engraved Stars, Fine reverse.

Identification Markers: All 16 stars have been re-engraved with centrils delineated. Moderate mark on the upper-middle part of Liberty's right (facing) breast. Eagle's torso, upper legs, and lower-right part of left (facing) wing worn smooth. Upper-right to lower-left pinscratch runs from middle breast to tip of left (facing) wing.

Provenance: *Heritage Auctions (April 2008), NCS VF Details, Etched Stars, lot 2307, $37,375; Summer FUN (Heritage Auctions, July 2009), PCGS Fine 15, lot 566 (Re-Engraved Stars), $51,750.*

Additional Notes: None.

Coin Serial Number: 229.

From Superior Galleries,
October 1990

1796 16 Stars, O-102, early die state.

Gregory Specimen.

Grade: Very Fine obverse, Fine reverse, Plugged and Smoothed.

Identification Markers: Plugged and smoothed at 5:00 obverse and between last S of STATES and O in OF. Numerous small spots scattered over reverse and a few on obverse.

Provenance: *Charles Gregory Collections (S.H. Chapman, June 1916), Good, Plugged, lot 2524, $24; S.H. Chapman (June 1917), Very Good, Plugged, lot 413, $42; Superior Galleries (October 1990), Fine 15, Plugged, lot 848, $4,840.*

Additional Notes: None.

Coin Serial Number: 230.

From Heritage Auctions,
May 2005

1796 16 Stars, O-102, late die state.

Blevins Specimen.

Grade: Very Fine obverse, Cleaned, Fine reverse, Cleaned.

Identification Markers: Lower-left to upper-right toning streak (rubber band mark?) from Liberty's hair above shoulder to beneath chin. Short upper-left to lower-right adjustment marks in hair below ear. Light marks just below the horizontal parts of each wing.

Provenance: *ANA Sale (Steve Ivy, August 1982), Very Fine 20 (obverse image only), lot 2903; H.W. "Woody" Blevins Collection (Superior Galleries, June 1988), Fine 12, lot 3052, $17,600; Bowers and Merena (January 2000), Fine 15, lot 165, $17,250; 2005 FUN Sale (Heritage Auctions, January 2005), NCS Fine Details, Improperly Cleaned, lot 30213, $36,800; Heritage Auctions (May 2005), PCGS Fine 12, lot 7100, $46,000.*

Additional Notes: None.

Coin Serial Number: 231.

From Heritage Auctions, August 2001

1796 16 Stars, O-102, late die state.

Seventko Specimen.

Grade: Very Fine obverse, Fine reverse.

Identification Markers: Mark on Liberty's cheekbone. Minute rim ding above star 15. Mark midway between star 1 and rim, just left of die crack. A short horizontal mark just under tip of palm leaf below last S. Short diagonal mark to right of upper right (facing) leg.

Provenance: *Greenwich Collection (Bowers and Merena, January 1991), Fine 12 to Fine 15, lot 1013, $13,750; Dr. Joseph M. Seventko Collection (Heritage Auctions, August 2001), NGC VG 10, lot 6091, $13,000.*

Additional Notes: None.

Coin Serial Number: 232.

From Stack's,
May 1990

1796 16 Stars, O-102, early die state.

GNYNC Sale Specimen.

Grade: Very Fine obverse, Fine reverse, Defective Planchet.

Identification Markers: Planchet chip out of rim above star 5 and over T of UNITED. Mark one-third of way between curl and star 3, and another to right of lower neck below jaw.

Provenance: *Greater New York Numismatic Convention Sale (Stack's, May 1990), Fine or better, lot 1069.*

Additional Notes: None.

Coin Serial Number: 233.

From Heritage Auctions,
December 2010

1796 16 Stars, O-102, early die state.

Gardner Specimen.

Grade: Very Fine obverse, Fine reverse.

Identification Markers: Two milling marks on Liberty's left (facing) breast. Minute mark on upper-middle neck, another on shoulder above serif of 7 in date. Spot on tip of palm leaf just to right of right (facing) wing. Fine vertical pinscratch on torso. Large toning area on left torso may be a smudge on PCGS holder; it is not apparent in the photos when coin is uncertified or in an NGC holder.

Provenance: *Lawrence H. Gardner Collection from the Buffalo and Erie County Historical Society (Stack's, March 2005), Choice Fine, lot 167, $43,125; William H. LaBelle Collection (American Numismatic Rarities, July 2005), NGC Fine 12, lot 1147, unsold; Ira and Larry Goldberg (September 2005), NGC Fine 12, lot 1706, unsold; Bowers and Merena (January 2010), PCGS VG 10, CAC, lot 353, unsold; Heritage Auctions (December 2010), PCGS VG 10, CAC, lot 3613, $41,688.*

Additional Notes: None.

Coin Serial Number: 234.

From Bowers and Ruddy,
November 1979

1796 16 Stars, O-102, early die state.

Garrett Specimen.

Grade: Very Fine obverse, Fine reverse.

Identification Markers: Two minute marks in alignment left of inner point of star 16. Mark just below space between upper laurel and palm leaves. Small field marks around eagle's head and beak. Fine linear mark extending from right (facing) claw to right across tip of palm leaf and into field.

Provenance: *Garrett Collection, Part I (Bowers and Ruddy, November 1979), Fine 12, lot 275, $17,000.*

Additional Notes: None

Coin Serial Number: 235.

From Heritage Auctions, October 2010

1796 16 Stars, O-102, late die state.

2010 Coinfest Specimen.

Grade: Very Fine obverse, Digs, Fine reverse.

Identification Markers: Large dig between LI of LIBERTY. Three moderate, round marks on upper left (facing) breast, one on drapery below said breast, and two above shoulder. Two moderate spots on eagle's middle torso, and a mark to the immediate left of the lower right (facing) wing.

Provenance: *Coinfest Sale (Heritage Auctions, October 2010), PCGS Fine 12 Secure, lot 3640, $52,900.*

Additional Notes: None.

Coin Serial Number: 236.

From Stack's,
February 1976

1796 16 Stars, O-102, late die state.

Tennessee Specimen.

Grade: Very Fine obverse, Fine reverse, Pocket Piece (irregular rim wear).

Identification Markers: Flattened rims from over star 4 to above star 14, between star 16 to 6 of date, above STATE, and above AMERICA. Linear mark from star 9 to top hair ribbon. Short diagonal mark to lower right of beak.

Provenance: *Tennessee Collection (Stack's, February 1976), Fine, lot 977, $4,500.*

Additional Notes: The Stack's catalog states: "No doubt carried as a 'pocket piece' as the outer rims are flatter; a usual result of pocket wear."

Coin Serial Number: 237.

From Krause Publications Calendar

1796 16 Stars, O-102, early die state.

Jenks Specimen.

Grade: Very Fine obverse, Fine reverse.

Identification Markers: Light rim ding between stars 3 and 4. Light scrape near rim between stars 6 and 7. Mark to left of first S in STATES, another to lower right of laurel leaf below E. Moderate spot to lower right of right (facing) leg, just above cloud.

Provenance: *John Story Jenks Collection (H. Chapman, December 1921), Very good, lot 5913, obverse only, $80; 2000 Krause Publications Calendar plate coin.*

Additional Notes: None.

Coin Serial Number: 238.

From Heritage Auctions,
March 2009

1796 16 Stars, O-102, late die state.

Ely – Western Reserve Historical Society Specimen.

Grade: Fine, Plugged, Smoothed.

Identification Markers: Crudely plugged and smoothed in the field under Liberty's left (facing) breast. Horizontal mark on drapery midway between plug and star 16. Upper-left to lower-right pinscratch from juncture of neck and chin in line with star 16. Reverse plug shows between last S in STATES and O in OF.

Provenance: *Hon. Herman Ely Collection (W.E. Woodward, January 1884), fine, perforation at point of bust filled, lot 157, $25; Western Reserve Historical Society Collection (Stack's, September 2002), About Fine but holed and crudely plugged at 5:00, lot 604, $13,800; Heritage Auctions (March 2009), ANACS VG 10 Details, Plugged, lot 1913, $17,250.*

Additional Notes: None.

Coin Serial Number: 239.

From Superior Galleries, January 1989

1796 16 Stars, O-102, early die state.

Jewett-Moreira Specimen.

Grade: Fine.

Identification Markers: Two small marks midway between star 9 and upper ribbon, and two left of base in 1 in date. Small vertical mark just to lower left of star 12 and upper left of star 13. Two small marks on cloud to upper right of ribbon bow.

Provenance: *Henry L. Jewett Collection (S.H. Chapman, June 1909), Good, lot 1422, $68; Moreira Collection Sale, Part 3 (Superior Galleries, January 1989), Fine 12, lot 4419, $16,500.*

Additional Notes: None.

Coin Serial Number: 240.

From Princeton University,
May 2006

1796 16 Stars, O-102, late die state.

Princeton University Specimen.

Grade: Fine.

Identification Markers: Upper-right to lower-left scratch left of Liberty's neck. Numerous toning spots on central portrait of Liberty, and a large spot just above hair ribbon. Mark to upper-left of the curve of the right (facing) wing. Two small spots on the upper-right part of the right (facing) cloud.

Provenance: *Princeton University Collection.*

Additional Notes: Alan Stahl, Curator of Numismatics, Princeton University, stated to the author in a May 25, 2006 email: "1796 was in our collection in 1930 when we began keeping records."

Coin Serial Number: 241.

From New England
Rare Coin Auctions,
January 1982

1796 16 Stars, O-102, early die state.

Heller Specimen.

Grade: Fine obverse, Very Good reverse.

Identification Markers: Moderate mark to right of 6 in date. Mark on upper-middle neck. Short upper-right to lower-left mark about two-thirds of the way left of star 15. Light rim bruise between stars 13 and 14. F in OF, AMERI, and bottom of 2 in fraction very weak.

Provenance: *Dennis Heller Collection (New England Rare Coin Auctions, January 1982), Very Good 8, lot 616, $12,650.*

Additional Notes: None.

Coin Serial Number: 242.

From Heritage Auctions, May 2009

1796 16 Stars, O-102, late die state.

Reiver Specimen.

Grade: Fine obverse, Very Good reverse.

Identification Markers: J-shaped mark on Liberty's temple. Right (facing) wing and adjacent palm leaves worn smooth. Moderate toning spot to lower right of tail, a smaller spot to upper right of beak, and another to lower right of D in UNITED. Reverse rim very weak from 1:00 to 7:30.

Provenance: *Julian Leidman (September 1983); Jules Reiver Collection (Heritage Auctions, January 2006), NGC VG 8, lot 22513, $46,000; Joseph C. Thomas Collection (Heritage Auctions, May 2009), NGC VG 8, lot 718, $54,625.*

Additional Notes: None.

Coin Serial Number: 243.

From Heritage Auctions,
August 2004

1796 16 Stars, O-102, early die state.

2004 ANA Specimen.

Grade: Very Good obverse, Re-engraved, Fine reverse, Re-engraved.

Identification Markers: Horizontal linear mark right of star 4. Moderate mark on shoulder above serif of 7 in date. ER of LIBERTY re-engraved. Fraction re-engraved, as is end of right ribbon. Last A in AMERICA re-engraved. Four round marks of unknown origin right of fraction.

Provenance: *Auction '81, RARCOA session (July 1981), Very Good, formerly mounted, lot 131, $9,750; FUN Sale (Heritage Auctions, January 2002), ANACS VG Details, Net Good 4, Repaired, Whizzed, lot 6900, $10,063; ANA Sale (Heritage Auctions, August 2004), NCS Fine Details, Plugged, lot 6159, $18,400.*

Additional Notes: It cannot be determined from the photos whether or not the coin was "mounted" or "plugged." The repair (re-engraving) at the upper obverse and lower reverse is quite evident, however.

Coin Serial Number: 244.

From Mid-American Auctions,
May 1988

1796 16 Stars, O-102, late die state.

1988 GNA Sale Specimen.

Grade: Very Good, Scratched, Whizzed.

Identification Markers: Heavy scratch between IB of LIBERTY. Heavy "X"-like scratch on upper head. Numerous heavy scratches throughout lower reverse. Both sides whizzed.

Provenance: *Georgia Numismatic Association Sale (Mid-American Auctions, May 1988), Fine 12, lot 837, possibly $7,750.*

Additional Notes: The Mid-American catalog states: "Holed and plugged at ER of LIBERTY."

Coin Serial Number: 245.

From Ira and Larry Goldberg, May 2006

1796 16 Stars, O-102, early die state.

Kramer Specimen.

Grade: Very Good, obverse Scratches.

Identification Markers: Deep scratches in center of Liberty's portrait and in right field. Small mark midway between serif of 9 in date and rim. Small mark just to upper left of upper hair ribbon. Minor bruise on dentil at 4:30. Small round mark on rim above serif of first S in STATES. Right part of right (facing) wing and adjacent palm leaves worn smooth.

Provenance: *Victor Kramer Collection (Ira and Larry Goldberg, May 2006), VG 7, Obverse Scratches, lot 2909, $14,500.*

Additional Notes: None.

Coin Serial Number: 246.

From Superior Galleries,
May 1990

1796 16 Stars, O-102, early die state.

Boys Town Specimen.

Grade: Very Good.

Identification Markers: Short diagonal mark left of Liberty's mouth, and a horizontal mark above eye brow. Two moderate marks to right of star 5, and another to upper left of star 14. Vertical mark from eagle's torso midway between left (facing) wing and leg. Rim bruise above U of UNITED and another to upper left of first A in AMERICA. Planchet chip at tip of palm leaf located immediately right of right (facing) cloud.

Provenance: *Fred J. Casterline and Brooks Hall Collections (Superior Galleries, May 1989), Good 5, lot 2670; Boys Town Sale (Superior Galleries, May 1990), Good 5, lot 32.*

Additional Notes: The 1990 Superior catalog states: "Possibly worked on about the periphery to remove some rim nicks."

Coin Serial Number: 247.

From Gary Adkins,
April 2004

1796 16 Stars, O-102, early die state.

Allison Park Specimen.

Grade: Very Good.

Identification Markers: Obverse dentils weak from above star 9 to star 11. Light horizontal scratch between star 12 and nose. Shallow scrape from upright of D in UNITED to wreath. Linear diagonal mark about midway between last S of STATES and O in OF. Rim weakness extends from above CA of AMERICA to U in UNITED. Moderate mark located between stem-end of palm wreath and rim just to lower left of ribbon end. Photo quality makes all marks difficult to see.

Provenance: *Gary Adkins fixed price list (April 2004), ANACS VG 10, $39,500; J.J. Teaparty fixed price list (April 2004), ANACS VG 10, No. 215, $44,000; Allison Park Collection (American Numismatic Rarities, August 2004), PCGS VG 10, lot 419, $46,000; Bowers and Merena (November 2007), PCGS VG 10, lot 2148, $57,000.*

Additional Notes: None.

Coin Serial Number: 248.

From Numismatic Gallery,
September 1943

1796 16 Stars, O-102, early die state.

Higgy Specimen.

Grade: Very Good.

Identification Markers: A moderate rim mark above the left serif of I in LIBERTY, which then extends above the I toward the upper serif of B (planchet defect or post-strike impairment?). Two small marks midway between chin and stars 14 – 15. Upper-right to lower-left mark about midway between last S of STATES and O in OF. Rim weakness between F and first A of AMERICA, and between last A and fraction.

Provenance: *Michael F. Higgy Collection (Numismatic Gallery, September 1943), Fine, lot 666, $170.*

Additional Notes: Photo quality makes pedigree markers difficult to discern.

Coin Serial Number: 249.

Reverse unplated

From B. Max Mehl,
September 1912

1796 16 Stars, O-102, early die state.

French Specimen.

Grade: Very Good obverse, reverse unplated.

Identification Markers: Rim dent between 79 of date, another to upper left of star 11. Small spot on jaw left of chin. Short horizontal mark midway between chin and star 16.

Provenance: *Robert E. French Collection (B. Max Mehl, September 1912), "classed as very good," lot 96.*

Additional Notes: The Mehl catalog states: "The surface, especially on obverse is roughed." This is not discernible on the image. Despite photo quality and only an obverse image, the author is fairly confident this coin does not duplicate another low-grade 1796 16 Star early die state half dollar in the study.

Coin Serial Number: 250.

From Bowers and Merena,
November 2007

1796 16 Stars, O-102, early die state.

November 2007 Baltimore Auction Specimen.

Grade: Very Good, Cleaned.

Identification Markers: Upper-left to lower-right obverse hairlines. Mark on left (facing) breast just above drapery line. Mark in middle part of right (facing) wing where it joins with torso. Cluster of toning spots between eagle's head and the upper palm and laurel leaves. Photo quality makes all pedigree markers very difficult to see.

Provenance: *Baltimore Auction (Bowers and Merena, November 2007), NCS VG Details, Improperly Cleaned, lot 2149, $40,250.*

Additional Notes: None.

Coin Serial Number: 251.

From Heritage Auctions,
June 2005

1796 16 Stars, O-102, early die state.

2005 ANA Money Show Sale Specimen.

Grade: Very Good.

Identification Markers: Flyspecks on Liberty's head and in the upper-right obverse field. Moderate spot at lower leaf tip below stand of N in UNITED.

Provenance: *ANA Money Show (Bowers and Merena, April 2005), NGC VG 8, lot 545; Heritage Auctions (June 2005), NGC VG 8, lot 6210, $41,400.*

Additional Notes: None.

Coin Serial Number: 252.

From Heritage Auctions, April 2010

1796 16 Stars, O-102, late die state.

Copeland Specimen.

Grade: Very Good, Harshly Cleaned.

Identification Markers: Mark to right of star 4, another between Liberty's forehead and star 11, and a cut at rim over left serif of Y in LIBERTY (partially covered by the tab of the new-generation NGC holder). Mark midway between chin and star 16. Shallow linear abrasion above ES of STATES that extends to the O in OF.

Provenance: *Bernard L. Copeland Collection (Stack's, April 1967), Very Good, lot 851, $2,300; Heritage Auctions (April 2010), NGC VG Details, Harshly Cleaned, lot 2108, $25,300; Stack's (November 2010), PCGS VG 8, lot 4345, $46,000.*

Additional Notes: None.

Coin Serial Number: 253.

Reverse unplated

From Steve Ivy,
August 1982

1796 16 Stars, O-102, late die state.

1982 ANA Specimen.

Grade: Good obverse, reverse unplated.

Identification Markers: Minute rim nick over stand of L in LIBERTY. Two marks just to right of star 4, one other to lower right of Y in LIBERTY. Five to six small to moderate spots on Liberty's lower and middle portrait.

Provenance: *ANA Auction (Steve Ivy, August 1982), VG 8 obverse, Almost Good reverse, lot 599, $4,400; Paul Sims fixed price list (September 1995 Coin World ad), Good/VG obverse, About Good/Good reverse, $8,400.*

Additional Notes: Despite photo quality and only an obverse image, the author is confident this coin does not duplicate another low-grade 1796 16 Stars late die state half dollar in the study.

Coin Serial Number: 254.

From Superior Galleries,
November 2003

1796 16 Stars, O-102, early die state.

November 2003 Santa Clara Sale Specimen.

Grade: Very Good obverse, Counterstamped, About Good reverse.

Identification Markers: The name J.B. Adam is stamped vertically across Liberty's portrait. A horizontal scratch extends from star 5 to just below the top curl, and another runs left from the space between B and Adams. Numerous minuscule pockmarks are located in the right obverse field. The central reverse is worn nearly smooth (see explanation of this in "Additional Notes" section).

Provenance: *Superior Galleries (November 2003), Fine 12, Counterstamped, lot 515.*

Additional Notes: The Superior catalog states: "The counterstamp seems to have been added relatively early in the coin's life: the central reverse became raised above the other features on that side when the counterstamp was affixed, thus wearing smooth as the coin continued to circulate."

Coin Serial Number: 255.

From Superior Galleries,
October 1973

1796 16 Stars, O-102, late die state.

Gilhousen Specimen.

Grade: Very Good obverse, About Good reverse.

Identification Markers: Mark midway between lower curl and rim, just above die crack. Mark in Liberty's hair near neck, aligned with stars 5 and 15. Right part of eagle's right (facing) wing and adjacent palm leaves worn smooth. Rim worn into letters AMERIC and the bottom of 2 in fraction. Short horizontal mark near rim at 5:30 (below end of right ribbon).

Provenance: *Clarke E. Gilhousen Sale – Part 3 (Superior Galleries, October 1973), Very Good obverse, Good reverse, lot 870, $3,000.*

Additional Notes: None.

Coin Serial Number: 256.

From Heritage Auctions,
July-August 1997

1796 16 Stars, O-102, early die state.

1976 and 1997 ANA Specimen.

Grade: Very Good obverse, Re-engraved, Fair reverse, Re-engraved, Plugged.

Identification Markers: Moderate mark or spot just to right of space between stars 4 and 5. Letters in UNITED worn away, as are these in AMERI, and the 2 in fraction. Outer-lower laurel leaves and middle palm leaves worn away, as are middle parts of the right (facing) wing.

Provenance: *Possibly George W. Massamore (September 1882), lot 290, which reads: "Filled between ber of Liberty ... all stars and date bold (unplated), $30; possibly Thomas Ramsden Collection (S.H. and H. Chapman, June 1892), lot 373, which reads: "Very good. Plugged at ER in LIBERTY and the letters replaced by engraving (unplated); possibly Louis A. Risse Collection (S.H. and H. Chapman, June 1903), lot 928, which reads: "Good. Has been plugged at E in LIBERTY and the letter re-engraved (unplated), $25; ANA Sale (Stack's, August 1976), Very Good obverse, Fair reverse, Plugged, Re-engraved, lot 1087, $2,600; ANA Sale (Heritage Auctions, July – August 1997), AG 3, Plugged, Re-engraved, lot 8295, $5,290.*

Additional Notes: While both the Stack's and Heritage catalogs indicate that the coin was plugged and that Liberty's hair was strengthened, these impairments are not readily evident from the photos. Nevertheless, the author defers to the catalogers of both companies in incorporating these impairments into the coin's surface condition.

Coin Serial Number: 257.

From Heritage Auctions, April-May 2011

1796 16 Stars, O-102, early die state.

2011 Central States Sale Specimen.

Grade: About Good obverse, Poor reverse.

Identification Markers: Moderate toning spot left of star 4, another above Liberty's head, and another to right of star 16. Short vertical mark on chest above right side of 9 in date. Reverse virtually smooth.

Provenance: *Bowers and Merena (November 1993), AG 3/0, lot 335, $4,290; Stack's (January 1995), About Good, lot 504; Central States Numismatic Society Sale (Heritage Auctions, April - May 2011), PCGS Fair 2, lot 5138, $27,600.*

Additional Notes: None.

Coin Serial Number: 258.

Additional 1796 16 Stars Half Dollar Appearances

Images from the following catalogs are not included in the study because poor photo quality makes it virtually impossible to determine a coin's grade or identification markers. Specimens in some of these catalogs may duplicate coins that have been incorporated into the study, while others might represent new appearances. Grades are those listed in the respective catalogs or represent an approximation by this author.

XF or AU (plated obverse). Ferguson Haines Collection (W.E. Woodward, October 1880), lot 562 (possibly the same as the plate coin in Overton's *Early Half Dollar Die Varieties*).
XF or AU (plated obverse). George H. Earle Collection (H. Chapman, June 1912), lot 2824.
VF or XF (plated obverse). William J. Jenks Collection (W.E. Woodward, June 1883), lot 170.
VF. NTL Auctions/Scotsman (October 1999), lot 525.
VF. R.E. Cox, Jr. Collection Stack's, April 1962), lot 1757.
VF. George H. Hall Collection (Stack's, May 1945), lot 1000.
VF. RARCOA (August 1970), lot 870.
VF (plated obverse). Lyman Low (October 1904), lot 372.
VF. Dayton, Ohio Sale (James Kelly, November 1957), lot 1589 (photo imperfections, serial number 223).
VF. RARCOA (April 1963), lot 1043.
VF. Kreisberg and Schulman (August 1963), lot 1138.
Fine-VF. James Kelly (February 1964), lot 242.
Fine-VF. Coronet Coin Shop (no date), lot 98.
Fine-VF. Malcolm N. Jackson Collection (United States Coin Co., May 1963), lot 635.
Fine. Al Overton (August 1963), lot 1197.
Fine. Herdegen Collection (Schulman Coin and Mint, December 1973), lot 681.
Fine. Federal Coin Exchange (August 1957), lot 1455.
Fine. John Cobb (April 1964), lot 715.
VG-Fine. Kagin's (August 1977), lot 1393.
VG-Fine. Hathaway and Bowers Galleries Catalog #9 (January-February, 1971).
VG. Steve Ivy (August 1980), lot 2231.
Good (plated obverse). A. Kosoff (February 1970), lot 632.
Good (plated obverse). Allison W. Jackman Collection (H. Chapman, June 1918), lot 498.

1797 Half Dollar Examples
Overton-101

From Stack's,
October 1996

1797, O-101.

World's Greatest Collection – Aspen Specimen.

Grade: Mint State.

Identification Markers: Weak dentils over Y of LIBERTY. Mark on neck right of curl. Horizontal adjustment marks along right reverse border that mix with diagonal ones around the fraction. Two marks just above right (facing) wing near juncture with neck and torso.

Provenance: *World's Greatest Collection (Numismatic Gallery, April 1945), A gem coin ... barely circulated, lot 61; Dr. Nelson Page Aspen Collection (Bowers and Merena), MS 60 or finer, prooflike, lot 273, $99,000; Bowers and Merena (August 1995), NGC MS 62, lot 130; Stack's (October 1996), Choice Brilliant Uncirculated, lot 277, $160,000.*

Additional Notes: None.

Coin Serial Number: 300.

From S.H. and H. Chapman, December 1890

1797, O-101.

Cleneay Specimen.

Grade: Mint State.

Identification Markers: Photo quality makes it difficult to discern pedigree markers. That said, an apparent rectangular swath of darker toning extends from RTY of LIBERTY and star 9 through Liberty's face, neck, and adjacent field to the chest. Spot or mark on drapery-field interface beneath left (facing) breast. Upper-right to lower-left streak on left-middle part of left (facing) wing that extends into adjacent field. Some of these marks may be photo imperfections.

Provenance: *Thomas Cleneay Collection (S.H. and H. Chapman, December 1890), Uncirculated, lot 1104, $250.*

Additional Notes: Photo quality makes it uncertain whether or not this specimen duplicates another high-grade 1797 O-101 coin in the study.

Coin Serial Number: 301.

From Thomas Elder, October 1908

1797, O-101.

Wilson Specimen.

Grade: About Uncirculated.

Identification Markers: Backward L-shaped mark on lower-left part of inner laurel leaf above eagle's head pointing to its upper-left neck (photo imperfection?).

Provenance: *James B. Wilson Collection (Thomas Elder, October 1908), Nearly uncirculated, lot 232, $75.*

Additional Notes: Photo quality in Elder's catalog only fair. Additionally, the images appear "matted," further reducing surface clarity.

Coin Serial Number: 302.

From Thomas Elder,
October 1908

1797, O-101.

Wilson Specimen.

Grade: Extremely Fine.

Identification Markers: Spot on Liberty's rear jaw at the hair line below the ear (photo imperfection?). Short upper-left to lower-right mark adjacent to eagle's beak. Possible rim bruise above ES of STATES.

Provenance: *James B. Wilson Collection (Thomas Elder, October 1908), Fine to V. Fine, lot 233, $45.*

Additional Notes: Photo quality in Elder's catalog only fair. Additionally, the images appear "matted," further reducing surface clarity. The catalog states: "Several very small scratches. Slight edge nick." Only the mark at the beak is visible on the photo; the location of the edge mark is uncertain (possibly above ES?).

Coin Serial Number: 303.

From Bowers and Ruddy,
November 1979

1797, O-101.

Possibly Randall-Garrett Specimen.

Grade: Extremely Fine.

Identification Markers: Mark to upper right of star 3, one to lower left of star 11, another on lower-right neck, and one on left (facing) breast. Adjustment marks at rim right of stars 10 and 11. Weak dentils between F in OF and first A of AMERICA. Short vertical streak from the lower-middle part of the right (facing) wing.

Provenance: *J. Calvin Randall Collection (W.E. Woodward, June 1885), not uncirculated, lot 214; to T. Harrison Garrett (per Bowers and Ruddy, November 1979); Garrett Collection Sale I (Bowers and Ruddy, November 1979), Extremely Fine 40, lot 276, $30,000; New England Rare Coin Auctions (January 1982), Extremely Fine 40, lot 621, $25,300.*

Additional Notes: None.

Coin Serial Number: 304.

From New England
Rare Coin Auctions,
January 1982

1797, O-101.

Winsor – Mills – Heller Specimen.

Grade: Extremely Fine.

Identification Markers: Rim ding above B of LIBERTY and another between stars 9 and 10. Short vertical adjustment marks at rim above BERTY and star 9. Mark just to upper right of star 2, one on rear cheek to right of ear lobe, and another in field immediately above right (facing) breast. Rim bruise above first S in STATES and weak dentils between AM of AMERICA.

Provenance: *Richard B. Winsor Collection (S.H. and H. Chapman, December 1895), Very fine, lot 457, $60; John G. Mills Collection (S.H. and H. Chapman, April 1904), Very fine, lot 813, $45; Henry L. Jewett Collection (S. H. Chapman, June 1909), Fine, lot 1423, $50; Dennis Heller Collection (New England Rare Coin Auctions, January 1982), Very Fine 35, lot 620, $19,250.*

Additional Notes: None.

Coin Serial Number: 305.

Coin under serial number 306 reassigned to number 502

From Bowers and Merena,
November 1999

1797, O-101.

Duvall Specimen.

Grade: Extremely Fine.

Identification Markers: Vertical mark just to right of Liberty's nose. Minute mark midway between eagle's beak and tip of terminal laurel leaf, and a horizontal mark between upper-right part of beak and tip of palm leaf. Fine diagonal marks on each side of neck.

Provenance: *Gordon Duvall Collection (Bowers and Merena, November 1999), VF 30, lot 2034, $26,450.*

Additional Notes: None.

Coin Serial Number: 307.

From Ira and Larry Goldberg, February 2002

1797, O-101.

Benson Specimen.

Grade: Extremely Fine obverse, Very Fine reverse.

Identification Markers: Minute rim ding left of star 4, another on reverse below end of right ribbon. Upper-left to lower-right mark on Liberty's temple, and an upper-right to lower-left mark on the lower-middle neck. Small spot midway between 9 and 7 of date. Mark on left-middle part of eagle's torso. Large spot overlapping the right part of the left (facing) leg and adjacent field, and a smaller spot on the upper part of the second vertical feather from the left of the right (facing) wing.

Provenance: *Julius L. Brown Collection (S.H. Chapman, May 1911), Fine, lot 794, $50; Purchased from James G. Macallister on November 3, 1944 (per Ira and Larry Goldberg, Febrary 2002); Benson Collection, Part II (Ira and Larry Goldberg, February 2002), PCGS VF 20, lot 881, $31,050.*

Additional Notes: The author was informed on August 13, 2004 by the collector owning the coin at that time that it was reholdered NGC VF 30.

Coin Serial Number: 308.

From Bowers and Merena,
May 2001

1797, O-101.

Warner Specimen.

Grade: Extremely Fine obverse, Very Fine reverse.

Identification Markers: Mark midway between curl and upper part of star 2. Diagonal mark left of 1 in date midway between rim and first curl. Spot near rim below star 1.

Provenance: *George O. Warner Collection (Bowers and Merena, March 1997), ANACS EF 40, lot 2363, $28,600; Bowers and Merena (May 2001), ANACS EF 40, lot 1492, $43,700.*

Additional Notes: None.

Coin Serial Number: 309.

From Stack's,
November 1954

1797, O-101.

Dupont – Stack Specimen.

Grade: Extremely Fine obverse, Very Fine reverse.

Identification Markers: Mark on middle of Liberty's jaw, two more in field to lower right of neck. Two milling marks to right of eagle's tail. Because of photo quality, these marks are only visible on images of the Stack's 1954 catalog, and then just barely so.

Provenance: *Anderson Dupont Sale, Part II (Stack's, November 1954), very choice Very Fine, lot 2033, $1,500; James A. Stack Collection (Stack's, March 1975), Very Fine, lot 315; Superior Galleries (February 2000), NGC EF 45, lot 271, $37,950.*

Additional Notes: None.

Coin Serial Number: 310.

From Heritage Auctions, January 2009

1797, O-101.

2009 FUN Sale Specimen.

Grade: Extremely Fine obverse, Cleaned, Very Fine reverse, Cleaned.

Identification Markers: Upper-right to lower-left adjustment marks extend through Liberty's head from the chin on up (mostly in the hair around and below the ear and left of the temple). A mark just to the lower right of star 15, and another on the reverse midway between the rim and the left ribbon. A short diagonal mark on the cloud beneath the talons of the right (facing) leg about halfway to the adjacent palm leaf. Toning spots at top of right (facing) leg.

Provenance: *Al Overton (August 1963), Extremely Fine, lot 1198; Overton plate coin, Early Half Dollar Die Varieties; FUN Sale (Heritage Auctions, January 2009), NCS XF Details, Improperly Cleaned, lot 3837, $57,500; Dick Osburn Rare Coins fixed price list (November 2009), NCS XF Details, Improperly Cleaned, $69,000; Stack's (November 2010), NGC EF Details, Cleaned, Artificially Toned, lot 4346, unsold.*

Additional Notes: None.

Coin Serial Number: 311.

From Stack's,
March 1973

1797, O-101.

Nate Smith Specimen.

Grade: Extremely Fine obverse, Very Fine reverse.

Identification Markers: Mark centrally located between star 1 and 1 in date. Mark above top ribbon, midway between inner point of star 7 and Liberty's head. Mark midway between nose and stars 10-11. Mark midway between middle of laurel leaf and back of eagle's head, another about halfway between neck and curve of right (facing) wing.

Provenance: *Nate Smith Collection (Stack's, March 1973), Extremely Fine obverse, Very Fine reverse, lot 808, $5,000.*

Additional Notes: None.

Coin Serial Number: 312.

From RARCOA, January 1969

1797, O-101.

Saslow Specimen.

Grade: Extremely Fine obverse, Very Fine reverse.

Identification Markers: Horizontal streak from upper serif of first S in STATES to wreath below left diagonal of A (photo imperfection?). Photo quality precludes discerning any other marks.

Provenance: *Richard Saslow Collection (RARCOA, January 1969), Extremely Fine, lot 227, $4,200.*

Additional Notes: Photo quality makes it uncertain whether or not this specimen duplicates another mid- to high-grade 1797 O-101 coin in the study.

Coin Serial Number: 313.

From Heritage Auctions,
January 2008

1797, O-101.

2008 FUN Specimen.

Grade: Very Fine, Smoothed fields, probably Plugged, Re-engraved, Cleaned.

Identification Markers: Upper-right to lower-left streak from jaw to shoulder. Mark on upper neck in line with ear lobe and neck curl, another in upper part of cleavage. Horizontal and diagonal adjustment marks extending from right (facing) cloud into palm leaves below RI of AMERICA. Cluster of small marks left of 2 in fraction. Weak dentils over CA in AMERICA extending to 5:30. BE in LIBERTY and fraction re-engraved, probably over a plug. Fields smoothed on both sides.

Provenance: *Scotsman Auction Co. (October 2005), SEGS XF 40, Repaired Light Surface Tooling, lot 1574, $33,350; Northeast Numismatics fixed price list (February - March 2006), NCS XF Details, Plugged, Tooled, $48,500; FUN Sale (Heritage Auctions, January 2008), NCS VF Details, Repaired, Improperly Cleaned, lot 2847, unsold.*

Additional Notes: None.

Coin Serial Number: 314.

From Heritage Auctions,
April 2009

1797, O-101.

Reiver Specimen.

Grade: Very Fine, obverse Graffiti.

Identification Markers: Graffiti in field right of stars 3 to 6. Faint vertical adjustment marks in field between last 7 in date and star 15. Vertical mark from rim to between 7 and 9 in date, and another extending down from inner point of star 9 to left of star 10. Spot on upper-left eagle's torso. Linear mark midway between beak and tip of palm leaf.

Provenance: *Paramount (April 1965), Very Fine, lot 1081, $3,100; Jules Reiver Collection (Heritage Auctions, January 2006), NCS XF Details, Obverse Graffiti, lot 22514, $69,000; Joseph C. Thomas Collection (Heritage Auctions, April 2009), NCS XF Details, Obverse Graffiti, lot 2390, $43,125.*

Additional Notes: None.

Coin Serial Number: 315.

*From Stack's,
April-May, 1986*

1797, O-101.

Bernstein Specimen.

Grade: Very Fine.

Identification Markers: Horizontal streak from top of star 15 to breast, another from rim between stars 13 and 14 through top of star 14 into field. Minor rim bruise right of star 14. Mark low between star 1 and 1 in date. Spot near rim to lower right of second 7. Minor rim ding above N in UNITED, another above space between TE. Linear horizontal mark between IT. Short horizontal mark right of eagle's mouth. Cluster of minute marks beneath right (facing) wing.

Provenance: *Lester Bernstein Collection (Stack's, April – May 1986), Very Fine, lot 837; Auction '88 (Superior session, July 1988), Fine 12 ("obverse probably a full 'Very Fine'"), lot 156, $23,100.*

Additional Notes: None.

Coin Serial Number: 316.

From Heritage Auctions, July 2008

1797, O-101.

Tollett Specimen.

Grade: Very Fine, obverse Scratch.

Identification Markers: Light horizontal scratch extending from top of star 3 through Liberty's hair and along the neckline. Minute rim ding above C in AMERICA.

Provenance: *Raymond L. Tollett Estate (Stack's, April 1971), Very Fine, lot 53, $4,000; Stack's (October 1978), Very Fine, lot 136, $10,000; Dennis Heller Collection (New England Rare Coin Auctions, January 1982), Very Fine 35, lot 619, $22,550; Bayside New York Collection (Heritage Auctions, July 2008), lot 1670, $69,000.*

Additional Notes: None.

Coin Serial Number: 317.

From Bowers and
Ruddy, October 1976

1797, O-101.

Johansen Specimen.

Grade: Very Fine.

Identification Markers: Planchet chip at rim above right diagonal ofY in LIBERTY and upper-left part of star 9, and above CA in AMERICA. Two minuscule marks to upper right of star 2. Mark just below eagle's mouth, and a fine scratch connecting beak to curve of right (facing) wing.

Provenance: *Paul H. Johansen Collection (Bowers and Ruddy, October 1976), Fine plus, lot 233, $5,600; Auction '82 (RARCOA session, August 1982), Very Fine, lot 747.*

Additional Notes: None.

Coin Serial Number: 318.

From Numismatic Enterprises,
May 1970

1797, O-101.

May 1970 Mail Bid Sale Specimen.

Grade: Very Fine.

Identification Markers: There appears to be a short upper-left to lower-right adjustment mark in Liberty's hair where it joins the upper-left shoulder. Minute rim ding above the inner serif of U in UNITED, and another above the last A in AMERICA. Photo quality makes all of these marks difficult to see.

Provenance: *Numismatic Enterprises Mail Bid Sale (May 1970), "just about VF," lot 804.*

Additional Notes: None.

Coin Serial Number: 319.

From Bowers and Merena,
July 1997

1797, O-101.

July 1997 Rarities Specimen.

Grade: Very Fine, Plugged, obverse re-engraved, reverse Damaged.

Identification Markers: The letters BE of LIBERTY have been re-engraved, as have the hair curls below them. There is evidence of a plug in this area, as well as on the corresponding location on the reverse where the fraction is missing. There are also two deep linear cuts at 6:00 on the reverse, another on the upper part of the right (facing) wing, one on the lower-left part of this wing, and another on the tail right of the right (facing) leg. A scratch extends from the bottom of U in UNITED through the top of N.

Provenance: *Rarities Sale (Bowers and Merena, July 1997), sharpness of VF 25, net AG 3, Holed and Plugged, Tooled, lot 168, $7,700.*

Additional Notes: None.

Coin Serial Number: 320.

From Superior Galleries,
October 1992

1797, O-101.

Clark E. Adams Specimen.

Grade: Very Fine.

Identification Markers: Upper-left to lower-right mark on Liberty's chin, and three more in field between neck and star 14. Moderate mark between bottom-left serif of Y in LIBERTY and lowest curl on forehead. Mark to right of chin about one-third of way to star 13. Scratch on rim above Y and star 9. Short upper-right to lower-left mark to upper left of curve on right (facing) wing. Moderate spot on rim above C in AMERICA.

Provenance: *Clark E. Adams Collection (Superior Galleries, October 1992), Fine 12, lot 490, $9,900.*

Additional Notes: None.

Coin Serial Number: 321.

From the American
Numismatic Society,
February 2012

1797, O-101.

American Numismatic Society Specimen.

Grade: Very Fine.

Identification Markers: Speckled obverse peripheral toning Mintue rim ding over right stand of M in AMERICA.

Provenance: *"Bequest of Arthur J. Fecht, acquisition source unknown. Mr. Fecht was a successful petroleum industry geophysicist and numismatist. The Fecht collection was actually acquired by the ANS following his death in 1945, but ownership was retained in trust by his surviving sister, Neoma Fecht, who was also an ANS benefactress, until her death in 1980" (per Robert Hoge, Curator of North American Coins and Currency, ANS, January 26, 2012 email).*

Additional Notes: None.

Coin Serial Number: 322.

From Stack's – Bowers,
November 2012

1797, O-101.

November 2012 Baltimore Auction Specimen.

Grade: Very Fine, obverse Smoothing.

Identification Markers: Squiggly pinscratch from chin to lower-left point of star 11. Scalloped mark above chest in line with inner point of star 14. Horizontal adjustment marks from rim through C of AMERICA and right (facing) cloud. Shallow dig touching left ribbon near 1 of fraction.

Provenance: *Baltimore Auction (Stack's-Bowers, November 2012), ANACS Very Fine 30 Details, Tooled, Cleaned, lot 3139, unsold.*

Additional Notes: The Stack's-Bowers catalog indicates smoothing in the obverse fields and on the jaw and shoulder.

Coin Serial Number: 322a.

From Heritage Auctions,
January 2005

1797, O-101.

2005 FUN Sale Specimen.

Grade: Very Fine obverse, Scratched, Cleaned, Fine reverse, Scratched, Cleaned.

Identification Markers: Scratch from back of Liberty's jaw to the cleavage, a shorter scratch perpendicular to the latter just above the cleavage, and an upper-left to lower-right mark right of the neck. Rim ding above star 13. Spot about one-third of way between chin and star 12. Heavy scratch nearly in line with back of eagle's neck and head. Lighter scratch just to right of neck, and another just to left of curve of right (facing) wing. Mark to left of last A in AMERICA to lower right stem of laurel wreath. Another smaller mark directly below the latter mark.

Provenance: *Bowers and Ruddy Rare Coin Review (Summer 1976, #26), Fine, $6,250; Superior Galleries (January 1990), Very Fine 30, lot 3420 A, $15,400; FUN Sale (Heritage Auctions, January 2005), ANACS Fine Details, Net VG 8, Scratched, Cleaned, lot 30214, $25,302.*

Additional Notes: None.

Coin Serial Number: 323.

From Bowers and Merena, February 2006

1797, O-101.

Egolf Specimen.

Grade: Very Fine obverse, Fine reverse.

Identification Markers: Two upper-left to lower-right linear marks or streaks left of stars 9, 10, 11, and 12. Upper-left to lower-right adjustment marks on lower-right reverse, especially noticeable on right (facing) cloud and border from 4:30 to 5:30. Dentils very weak over AT of STATES and from I of AMERICA to U in UNITED. The 2 in fraction barely shows.

Provenance: *Howard D. Egolf Collection (Stack's, May 1961), Nearly Very Fine, lot 930, $2,000; Stack's (October 2004), About Very Fine, lot 1367, $51,750; Heritage Auctions inventory (December 2005), PCGS VF 20, $73,500; Bowers and Merena (February 2006), PCGS VF 20, lot 277.*

Additional Notes: None.

Coin Serial Number: 324.

From Ira and Larry Goldberg,
January 2004

1797, O-101.

Low – Higgy Specimen.

Grade: Very Fine obverse, Damaged, Scratched, Fine reverse.

Identification Markers: Light scrape from lower part of star 6 to middle hair ribbon, vertical scratch from lower left of star 9 to a point midway between chin and star 12, and a diagonal scratch left of stars 12 to 15. Digs as follows: two below eye, one on cheek, another just below jaw, two to upper left of star 13 and another to that star's upper right near rim, one near rim to lower right of star 14, and another to upper left of star 15. Short diagonal scratch through the three palm leaves below O in OF, and a vertical scrape to the left of last A in AMERICA.

Provenance: *Lyman H. Low Collection (Edmund Frossard, February 1882), Fine impression, lot 443a, $47; Michael F. Higgy Collection (A. Kosoff, September 1943), Very fine, lot 667, $115; Ira and Larry Goldberg (January 2004), ANACS Net Fine 15, Damaged, lot 2312, $33,375; Superior Galleries (May 2004), ANACS Net Fine 15 (sharpness of Very Fine), Damaged, lot 1451, $41,400.*

Additional Notes: None.

Coin Serial Number: 325.

From Kreisberg, Schulman, Cohen, April 1967

1797, O-101.

10th Anniversary Auction Specimen.

Grade: Very Fine obverse, Fine reverse.

Identification Markers: Mark midway between Liberty's eye and curl over ear, another on mid-cheek left of upper lip. Mark on right-middle torso of eagle where it joins wing. Light rim bruise between UN of UNITED, another over adjacent stand of N. Rim weak over ICA in AMERICA.

Provenance: *10th Anniversary Auction (Kreisberg, Schulman, Cohen, April 1967), Fine, lot 1048.*

Additional Notes: None.

Coin Serial Number: 326.

From Stack's, January 1997

1797, O-101.

Empire State Collection Specimen.

Grade: Very Fine obverse, Fine reverse.

Identification Markers: Mark to upper left of top hair ribbon more or less in line with inner point of star 7. Fine upper-left to lower-right pinscratches from second curl from top extending through hair, above shoulder, into middle chest. Two marks midway between U of UNITED and end of left ribbon. Vertically aligned curved mark left of 2 in fraction. U-shaped mark beneath right (facing) wing (strike-through or photo defect?). Dentils very weak from above E in AMERICA to below left ribbon.

Provenance: *Empire State Collection (Stack's, January 1997), Fine, lot 561, $11,000.*

Additional Notes: None.

Coin Serial Number: 327.

From New Netherlands, June 1970

1797, O-101.

Black Specimen.

Grade: Very Fine obverse, Very Good reverse.

Identification Markers: Mark on Liberty's lower-right neck. Adjustment marks above ER of LIBERTY. Mark on rim to upper right of B. Mark on upper-middle curve of D in UNITED, and two marks on lower part of second S in STATES. Rim worn into tops of RICA of AMERICA and bottom of 2 in fraction. Five or six dark spots on lower-right reverse border (4:00 to 5:30).

Provenance: *Dr. Angus C. Black Collection (New Netherlands, June 1970), Fine, lot 368, $2,000.*

Additional Notes: None.

Coin Serial Number: 328.

From B. Max Mehl,
May 1914

1797, O-101.

Conover Specimen.

Grade: Very Fine obverse, Very Good reverse.

Identification Markers: Moderate mark between rim and upper part of star 2, and another near rim between stars 5 and 6. Mark just below rim above R in LIBERTY. Five or six small marks between lower chin and stars 14 -15. Two to four small marks on upper-left neck below ear lobe. Two moderate, horizontally aligned marks in field between the upper-left part of the eagle's left (facing) leg and wing, another to right of tail. Squiggly linear mark through CA in AMERICA.

Provenance: *Charles H. Conover Collection (Max Mehl, May 1914), Good, lot 323, $18; Bowers and Merena (July 1997), PCGS G-6, lot 167, $9,350.*

Additional Notes: There appears to be the beginnings of a faint crack from the third dentil right of D in UNITED to the top of the laurel leaf, but does not extend through the adjacent leaves to the wing. The coin was therefore classified as O-101 instead of O-101a (see the section "Draped Bust Small Eagle Half Dollar Varieties").

Coin Serial Number: 329.

From Stack's,
January 1989

1797, O-101.

Simon Specimen.

Grade: Very Fine obverse, Very Good reverse.

Identification Markers: Vertical pinscratch right of stars 4 - 6. Short horizontal mark just below second curl from top. Short vertical mark midway between neck curl and shoulder. Mark high between 79 of date. Light rim ding right of star 14. "Lightning bolt" mark (or toning streak) extending from bottom curl halfway to rim. Light vertical streaks below A and M in AMERICA. Mark on lower-middle part of right (facing) wing, and two horizontally aligned marks between lower-left part of wing and palm wreath. Tops of RICA and bottom of 2 in fraction very weak.

Provenance: *Stanley Simon Collection (Stack's, January 1989), Very Good (the head of Fine sharpness), lot 1004, $15,400.*

Additional Notes: None.

Coin Serial Number: 330.

Coin under serial number 331 deleted from study (duplicate).

From Heritage Auctions,
January 2008

1797, O-101.

2008 FUN Specimen.

Grade: Fine obverse, Very Good reverse.

Identification Markers: Moderate spot between bottom hair ribbon and curl. Upper-right to lower-left scratch from rim to right point of star 13. Two vertically aligned spots between eagle's neck and curve of right (facing) wing. Spot adjacent to curve of C in AMERICA. Tops of RICA and bottom of 2 in fraction very weak.

Provenance: *FUN Sale (Heritage Auctions, January 2007), NGC Good 6, lot 954, $34,500; FUN Sale (Heritage Auctions, January 2008), PCGS Good 6, lot 2846, $40,250.*

Additional Notes: None.

Coin Serial Number: 332.

From Heritage Auctions,
June 2004

1797, O-101.

Paulsboro Specimen.

Grade: Fine obverse, Scratched, Very Good reverse, Damaged.

Identification Markers: Moderate spot left of Liberty's mouth. Moderate vertical scratch from lower left of star 9 to bust, diagonal scratch from chin to lower-left part of star 11, another from lower-left part of star 13 into chest. Mark about one-third way between forehead and star 9, another midway between nose and star 10. Diagonal mark from bust to rim at 4:30. About six digs on eagle's left (facing) wing, two just to left of wing, one to left of neck, three small to moderate digs on right (facing) wing immediately adjacent to torso, one to right of neck, moderate dig on middle-left part of right (facing) leg, and small dig on middle of cloud midway between left (facing) leg and left ribbon bow. Border weakness from above F in OF to above U in UNITED.

Provenance: *Bowers and Merena (May 1997), G-4, Pinscratches, lot 1146, $6,875; Paulsboro Collection (Heritage Auctions, June 2004), ANACS Good Details, Scratched, Damaged, Net AG 3, lot 6074, $20,700.*

Additional Notes: None.

Coin Serial Number: 333.

Additional 1797 O-101 Half Dollar Appearances

Images from the following catalogs are not included in the study because poor photo quality makes it virtually impossible to determine a coin's grade or identification markers. Specimens in some of these catalogs may duplicate coins that have been incorporated into the study, while others might represent new appearances. Grades are those listed in the respective catalogs or represent an approximation by this author.

VF or XF. George H. Earle, Jr. Collection (H. Chapman, June 1912), lot 2828.
VF or XF. Robert Coulton Davis Collection (New York Stamp and Coin, January 1890), lot 585.
VF. James A. Stack collection (Stack's, March 1975), lot 315.
VF (obverse plated). A. Kosoff (February 1970), lot 1254.
Fine. John Story Jenks Collection (H. Chapman, December 1921), lot 5914.

1797 Half Dollar Examples
Overton-101a

From American Numismatic Rarities,
March 2004

1797, O-101a, late die state (see Additional Notes below).

Baldenhofer – Norweb Specimen.

Grade: Mint Sate.

Identification Markers: Horizontal adjustment marks through UNIT of UNITED and also AMERICA.

Provenance: *Farish Baldenhofer Collection (Stack's, November 1955), Proof-like surfaces, lot 676; Norweb Collection (Bowers and Merena, November 1988), MS 63 to 65, a prooflike gem, lot 3027, $222,000; Dr. Haig A. Koshkarian Collection (American Numismatic Rarities, March 2004), NGC MS 66, lot 76, $966,000; Stack's (July 2008), NGC MS 66, lot 4261, $1,380,000. (Purchased and resold by Kevin Lipton, John Albarese and Heritage. Subsequently recertified as PCGS 65+ CAC).*

Additional Notes: As indicated in the section of this research entitled "Draped Bust Small Eagle Half Dollar Varieties," "late die state" 1797 O-101a halves are defined, for the purpose of this study, as those showing the crack from the lower-left serif of the first S in STATES that then intersects the crack running from the rim at 9:30 through the laurel wreath to the left (facing) wing.

Coin Serial Number: 400.

From Spink America,
October 1996

1797, O-101a, intermediate die state (see Additional Notes below).

Reed Specimen.

Grade: Mint Sate.

Identification Markers: Vertical adjustment marks through middle of Liberty's portrait, one on forehead above eye, and three or four through TY of LIBERTY and star 9. Lint mark about halfway between tip of nose and stars 10 – 11. Short horizontal linear mark left of eagle's head (aligned with its eye).

Provenance: *Byron Reed Collection (Spink America, October 1996), very choice to gem uncirculated and prooflike, lot 25, $176,000.*

Additional Notes: As indicated in the section of this research entitled "Draped Bust Small Eagle Half Dollar Varieties," "intermediate die state" 1797 O-101a half dollars are defined, for the purpose of this study, as those lacking the crack from the lower-left serif of the first S in STATES that would have intersected the crack from the rim at 9:30.

Coin Serial Number: 401.

From Bowers and Merena, March 1989

1797, O-101a, late die state.

Polis – Jung Specimen.

Grade: Mint Sate.

Identification Markers: Upper-right to lower-left adjustment marks from rim through stars 9 – 13; those from stars 11 – 12 run through Liberty's shoulder. A similarly aligned adjustment mark extends from chin to shoulder, and two more run through breasts and drapery before ending above 97 of date. Mark midway between eagle's neck and left (facing) wing. Milling marks midway between lower tail and right (facing) wing.

Provenance: *Kagin's (January 1975), Prooflike, lot 134; ANA Sale (Kagin's, August 1977), Prooflike, lot 1394, $20,000; Hagle Collection (Bowers and Merena, March 1989), MS 60 or finer, lot 288, $66,550; Superior Galleries (October 1990), PCGS MS 62, lot 3654, $71,500; George N. Polis Collection (Bowers and Merena, June 1991), PCGS MS 62, lot 1366, unsold; Bowers and Merena (August 1998), PCGS MS 63, lot 182, $85,000; Superior Galleries (February 1999), PCGS MS 63, lot 859; RARCOA fixed price list (December 2000), PCGS MS 63, $129,000; James Swan U.S. Type Collection; Oliver Jung Collection (American Numismatic Rarities, July 2004), PCGS MS 63, lot 60, $230,000.*

Additional Notes: Several of the above catalogs, starting with the March 1989 Bowers and Merena sale and continuing with its August 1998 catalog, Superior's February 1999 sale, and American Numismatic Rarities' July 2004 catalog, pedigree this coin to the World's Greatest Collection (F.C.C. Boyd) sold by Numismatic Gallery in its April 1945 sale, lot 62 (an unplated O-101a coin). This seems unlikely, however, for Numismatic Gallery's lot 62 is described as a "very fine" specimen, not "Uncirculated" as is the Polis – Jung specimen. Moreover it sold for only $250, according to the Numismatic Gallery catalog prices realized, while lot 60, a 1796 15 Stars half graded "Uncirculated" realized $575, and lot 61, a 1797 O-101 specimen graded "barely circulated" brought $430. It is also interesting to note that the detailed roster for higher-grade 1797 half dollar examples presented in Kagin's 1977 ANA sale of the 1797 O-101a Mint State piece in question makes no reference to lot 62 in the 1945 Numismatic Gallery sale of the Boyd collection. It does list, however, lot 61, the 1797 O-101 "barely circulated" half from Boyd's collection, and states: "... similar but border dent above Y." The Bowers and Merena 1998 and subsequent catalogers apparently mistook the present 1797 O-101a (serial Number 402) for the unplated piece (lot 62) in the WGC sale.

Coin Serial Number: 402.

From Stack's,
November 1995

1797, O-101a, late die state.

Lelan Rogers Specimen.

Grade: Mint Sate.

Identification Markers: Diagonal mark just to right of neck under Liberty's chin. Mark to left of upper point of middle hair ribbon. Mark in middle of eagle's right (facing) leg.

Provenance: *Lelan Rogers Collection (Stack's, November 1995), Gem Brilliant Uncirculated, lot 1251, $517,000.*

Additional Notes: This piece displays more die cracks than any other high-grade (XF and finer) 1797 O-101a coin in the study. In addition to the heavy obverse crack through star 2 to the curl, it shows a crack from the upper-right point of star 5 that extends into mid-field between star 7 and Liberty's head. The reverse shows some cracks not often apparent on many 1797 O-101a specimens: from the lower-left torso to the diagonal crack between the left (facing) wing and leg; from the rim through the first A in AMERICA and adjacent palm leaves; and another parallel to the rim through the top of the last A. This coin is obviously among the last 1797 O-101a half dollars struck. The Stack's catalog states: "Struck from the same reverse die used to coin the 1796 Half Dollars, here in a much more advanced state, near to total collapse."

Coin Serial Number: 403.

From Bowers and Merena, April 1997

1797, O-101a, intermediate die state.

H.P. Smith – Eliasberg Specimen.

Grade: Mint Sate.

Identification Markers: Relatively short adjustment marks in Liberty's hair below the ear and on the upper shoulder. Small spots between stars 1 – 2 and the lower curls, and two spots in hair to the upper left of shoulder. Two spots to the upper left of the upper-left serif of the second T in STATES.

Provenance: *Harlan P. Smith Collection (S. H. and H. Chapman, May 1906), Very fine, lot 578, $120; Louis E. Eliasberg, Sr. Collection (Bowers and Merena, April 1997), MS 60 or finer, partially prooflike, lot 1675, $104,500.*

Additional Notes: None.

Coin Serial Number: 404.

From Heritage Auctions,
August 2010

1797, O-101a, intermediate to late die state (see Additional Notes).

Granberg – Atwater – Hawn Specimen.

Grade: About Uncirculated.

Identification Markers: Marks on Liberty's cheekbone. Mark in field left of stars 14 – 15. Mark on the upper-left part of the left ribbon bow on the reverse. Light vertical adjustment marks from fraction to last A in AMERICA; a few extend to talons on right (facing) leg.

Provenance: *H.O. Granberg Collection (ANS Exhibition of U.S. Coins, January – February 1914), no grade; William Cutter Atwater Collection (B. Max Mehl, June 1946), Uncirculated, lot 396, $462; Reed Hawn Collection (Stack's, August 1973), Brilliant Uncirculated, lot 8, $13,750; Auction '81 (RARCOA session, July 1981), Uncirculated, lot 132, $54,000; Auction '85 (Superior's session, July 1985), About Uncirculated 55+, lot 750; 2010 ANA Sale (Heritage Auctions, August 2010), PCGS AU 58, lot 3137, $253,000.*

Additional Notes: The crack through the bottoms of ST in STATES extending left to intersect that from the rim at 9:30 is very light, hence the "intermediate to late die state" designation.

Coin Serial Number: 405.

From Heritage Auctions, January 2011

1797, O-101a, late die state.

Ten Eyck – Clarke – 2011 FUN Specimen.

Grade: About Uncirculated, Cleaned, minor reverse Re-engraving.

Identification Markers: Distinctive obverse toning pattern in the form of nearly horizontal and vertical toning streaks. The top of the eagle's right (facing) leg has been neatly separated from the torso by a fine curved cut (such a delineation is absent from even high-end Mint State Draped Bust Small Eagle specimens).

Provenance: *James Ten Eyck Collection (Max Mehl, May 1922), Practically uncirculated, lot 433, $86; T. James Clarke Collection (New Netherlands Coin Co., April 1956), just about Uncirculated, lot 1196; FUN Sale (Heritage Auctions, January 2007), NCS AU Details, Improperly Cleaned, lot 957, $92,000; Bowers and Merena (March 2010), NGC AU Details, Improperly Cleaned, lot 808, unsold; Nashville Sale (Stack's, May 2010), NGC AU Details, Improperly Cleaned, lot 4145, unsold; Bowers and Merena (August 2010), NGC AU Details, Improperly Cleaned, lot 515, $77,625; FUN Sale (Heritage Auctions, January 2011), NGC AU Details, Improperly Cleaned, lot 5542, $54,625.*

Additional Notes: None.

Coin Serial Number: 406.

From Heritage Auctions,
January 2007

1797, O-101a, late die state.

Gardner – 2007 FUN Specimen.

Grade: Extremely Fine, fine obverse Scratches.

Identification Markers: Linear streak or scratch from lower-left point of star 8 to rim, and another from upper-right point of star 8 that runs below L of LIBERTY. Three short upper-left to lower-right scratches in field midway between stars 7 – 8 and Liberty's head. Light diagonal linear mark between eagle's tail and the lower-left part of the right (facing) wing. A small round mark midway between the diagonal mark and palm leaf below wing. Two coelesced dentils below end of left ribbon.

Provenance: *Laurence H. Gardener Collection from the Buffalo and Erie County Historical Society (Stack's, March 2005), Choice Extremely Fine, lot 168, $115,000; Premium Numismatics, Inc. fixed price list, NGC AU 50, Coin World advertisement, April 2006, $155,000; Heritage Auctions (August 2006), NGC AU 50, lot 5225, unsold; FUN Sale (Heritage Auctions, January 2007), NGC AU 50, lot 958, $148,750.*

Additional Notes: None.

Coin Serial Number: 407.

From Mid-American,
March 1989

1797, O-101a, late die state.

Cleneay Specimen.

Grade: Extremely Fine, Bent, Smoothed.

Identification Markers: Rim ding between RT of LIBERTY, and a subtle rim bend at 5:00. Mark above top hair ribbon, and two more to upper left of star 14.

Provenance: *Thomas Cheneay Collection (S.H. and H. Chapman, December 1890), Fine, lot 2600, $70; ANA Mid-Winter Sale (Mid-American Rare Coin Auctions, Inc., March 1989), AU 50, Damaged and Repaired, lot 796.*

Additional Notes: The Mid-American catalog states: "Apparently this coin was bent ... as there is some waviness in the rim at K-5 on the obverse. The repair ... appears in the center of the reverse, where the fields below the eagle's wings have been smoothed out." These impairments are not readily apparent from the photos, but the present author defers to the Mid-American cataloger.

Coin Serial Number: 408.

From Heritage
Auctions, July 2005

1797, O-101a, late die state.

2005 ANA Specimen.

Grade: Extremely Fine, obverse Pinscratches.

Identification Markers: Short upper-right to lower-left mark just below neck curl. Horizontal pinsctatch midway between star 4 and the upper part of the second curl from top, and another from the upper-right point of star 5 through the middle hair ribbon. A minute mark just to the right of the lower-forehead curl, about one-quarter of the way to star 9. A cluster of small marks below the outer stand U of UNITED.

Provenance: *Stack's (March 1998), PCGS XF 40, lot 483, $42,900; Heritage Auctions (May 2003), PCGS XF 45, lot 6696, $62,000; FUN Sale (Heritage Auctions, January 2004), NGC AU 55, lot 2072; ANA Sale (Heritage Auctions, July 2005), NGC AU 55, lot 10204, $103,500; Stack's (November 2008), PCGS AU 53, lot 3495, unsold.*

Additional Notes: None.

Coin Serial Number: 409.

From Superior Galleries, September 1998

1797, O-101a, late die state.

Dr. Clifford E. Smith – Miles Specimen.

Grade: Extremely Fine.

Identification Markers: Squiggly upper-right to lower-left mark (lint mark?) between star 11 and Liberty's chin. Mark midway between inner point of star 7 and upper hair ribbon. Mark or spot near rim between 97 of date. Short horizontal mark on upper-right chest. Minor rim ding above upper right of C in AMERICA.

Provenance: *Dr. Clifford E. Smith and Son Collection (Stack's, May 1955), About Uncirculated, lot 1017, $900; R.L. Miles, Jr. Collection (Stack's, April 1969), Extremely Fine, lot 1207, $4,000; Worrell Collection (Superior Galleries, September 1993), PCGS XF 40, lot 637, $31,900; Superior Galleries (January 1994), PCGS XF 40, lot 1438, $31,350; Superior Galleries (September 1998), NGC AU 55, lot 330, unsold; North America Certified Trading fixed price list (May 2002), PCGS AU 55; John Hamrick Coins fixed price list (December 2002), NGC AU 55, possibly $92,000.*

Additional Notes: None.

Coin Serial Number: 410.

From Stack's,
September 1983

1797, O-101a, intermediate die state (see Additional Notes below).

H.P. Smith – Stickney – Oviedo Specimen.

Grade: Extremely Fine.

Identification Markers: Short horizontal mark on Liberty's cheek. Field mark just to right of upper lip. Slight rim bruise above space between stars 3 – 4, another above space between stars 10 – 11, another above star 12. Mark in center of chest, two more below it at drapery line. Mark just below the horizontal part of the right (facing) wing. Minor rim bruise above upper right of C in AMERICA.

Provenance: *H. P. Smith Collection (S.H. and H. Chapman, May 1906), Fine, lot 579, $60; Mathew A. Stickney Collection (H. Chapman, June 1907), Very fine, lot 930, $110; Auction '79 (Stack's session, July 1979), Extremely Fine, lot 609, $17,000; Dr. George F. Oviedo, Jr. Collection (Stack's, September 1983), Extremely Fine, lot 727.*

Additional Notes: Despite only fair photo quality, the images in the 1906 Chapman and Auction '79 catalogs seem to indicate the start of the crack between the bottoms of ST in STATES. If so, it does not yet intersect the crack from the rim at 9:30.

Coin Serial Number: 411.

From Stack's/American Numismatic Rarities, June 2004

1797, O-101a, late die state.

Frontenac – Genaitis – Friend Specimen.

Grade: Extremely Fine.

Identification Markers: Diamond-shaped spot low between 79 of date. Spot on Liberty's shoulder in line with upper serif of first 7. Mark just to upper right of star 6. Series of spots between upper curve of right (facing) wing and tip of palm leaf. Spot on lower-left part of eagle's neck.

Provenance: *Superior Galleries (February 1991), PCGS XF 40, lot 1632, $41,800; Frontenac Sale (Bowers and Merena, November 1991), PCGS XF 40, lot 3018, $30,800; Bowers and Merena (January 1999), PCGS XF 45, lot 5, $43,700; Richard Genaitis Collection (Heritage Auctions, August 2001), PCGS XF 45, lot 6092, $42,550; Stack's/American Numismatic Rarities (June 2004), PCGS AU 50, lot 1004, $138,000; Premium Numismatics, Inc. fixed price list (September 2004), PCGS AU 50, $155,000; Dale Friend PCGS Set Registry (December 2009), PCGS AU 50.*

Additional Notes: None.

Coin Serial Number: 412.

From Stack's – Bowers,
September 2011

1797, O-101a, late die state.

Lee Miller Specimen.

Grade: Extremely Fine.

Identification Markers: Light upper-right to lower-left linear mark from middle of Liberty's chest through drapery where it terminates above upper-left serif of first 7 in date. Short upper-right to lower-left mark on Liberty's upper-middle chest where it joins field. Arrow point-like mark near rim midway between last S of STATES and O in OF. Upper-left to lower-right mark left of fraction bar.

Provenance: *Lee S. Miller Collection (Stack's, June 1966), strong Very Fine, lot 817, $5,300; Auction '89 (RARCOA session, July 1989), Choice Extremely Fine, lot 201, possibly $28,000; Superior Galleries (February 2006), PCGS VF 30, lot 681, $66,000; Heritage Auctions (August 2006), NGC XF 45, lot 5224, unsold; Stack's – Bowers (September 2011), NGC XF 45, lot 2853, $89,700.*

Additional Notes: None.

Coin Serial Number: 413.

From Stack's, January 2009

1797, O-101a, late die state.

2009 Pre-FUN Sale Specimen.

Grade: Extremely Fine.

Identification Markers: Upper-left to lower-right adjustment marks through the middle part of Liberty's hair, temple, and neck. Small spot just left of the lower hair ribbon, several on the upper part of the left (facing) breast, and a large spot above the right (facing) breast to the left of the space between stars 14 – 15. Spot left of the middle palm leaf, adjacent to the middle-right part of the right (facing) wing, and another on the lower-right feather of the same wing.

Provenance: *Kingswood Coin Auction (August 1999), PCGS XF 45, lot 373, $41,000; Pre-FUN Sale (Stack's, January 2009), PCGS XF 45, lot 401, unsold.*

Additional Notes: None.

Coin Serial Number: 414.

From Stack's,
November 2009

1797, O-101a, intermediate die state.

Uhrich Specimen.

Grade: Extremely Fine, Smoothed obverse fields, Damaged reverse, Cleaned.

Identification Markers: Moderate mark in the middle of Liberty's shoulder close to the hair line, another midway between the ends of the bottom and middle hair ribbons. Several streaks (erasure marks?) below the first S in STATES and the E in UNITED. Several oval-like marks on and around the eagle's torso appear to have been intentionally placed.

Provenance: *Heritage Auctions (March 2007), ANACS XF 40 Details, Rim Filed, Cleaned, Tooled, lot 741, unsold; Rich Uhrich Collection (Stack's, February 2008), NCS AU Details, Damaged, Improperly Cleaned, lot 3184, unsold; Stack's (January 2009), ANACS XF 45 Details, Cleaned, Net VF 35, lot 402, unsold; Bowers and Merena (August 2009), PCGS XF 40, lot 1251, unsold; Stack's (November 2009), PCGS XF 40, lot 1351, unsold.*

Additional Notes: None.

Coin Serial Number: 415.

From Heritage Auctions, February 2012

1797, O-101a, late die state.

February 2012 Long Beach Sale Specimen.

Grade: Extremely Fine, light Scratches.

Identification Markers: Spot about midway between Liberty's chin and star 13. Light horizontal scrape from rim to space between stars 11 and 12. Vertical scratch from the bottom horizontal part of the right (facing) wing, and a light diagonal scratch right of the 2 in the fraction.

Provenance: *May 1991 Auction (Superior Galleries), Very Fine 35, lot 899, $24,750; Long Beach Sale (Heritage Auctions, February 2012), PCGS VF 30, lot 3566, $86,250.*

Additional Notes: None.

Coin Serial Number: 416.

From Heritage Auctions,
January 2011

1797, O-101a, late die state.

Cartwright – Joseph Thomas Specimen.

Grade: Extremely Fine obverse, Very Fine reverse.

Identification Markers: Short horizontal milling mark on upper part of left (facing) breast. Minute horizontal mark midway between star 3 and second curl from top. Minute round mark about midway between eagle's beak and upper curve of right (facing) wing. Spot beneath right (facing) talon on right (facing) leg.

Provenance: *Betty Goff Cartwright Collection (Stack's, October 2004), Choice Extremely Fine, lot 1867, $71,875; ANA Sale (Heritage Auctions, July 2005), PCGS XF 40, lot 10203, $97,750; Premium Numismatics fixed price list (October 2006), PCGS XF 45, $150,000; FUN Sale (Heritage Auctions, January 2007), PCGS XF 45, lot 956, unsold; Heritage Auctions (March 2007), PCGS XF 45, lot 742, $143,750; FUN Sale (Heritage Auctions, January 2011), PCGS XF 45, lot 5541, $138,000.*

Additional Notes: None.

Coin Serial Number: 417.

From Stack's,
January 2008

1797, O-101a, late die state.

Queller Family – Franklinton Specimen.

Grade: Extremely Fine obverse, Very Fine reverse.

Identification Markers: Moderate spot just right of Liberty's chin, another midway between mouth and star 12, and one to the lower left of the first A in AMERICA. Upper-right to lower-left adjustment marks on the central and lower-right reverse.

Provenance: *Queller Family Collection (Stack's, October 2002), Extremely Fine, lot 24, $38,800; 2004 ANA (Heritage, August 2004), NGC VF 30, lot 6160, $71,875; Harry Labstain Rare Coin fixed price list (October 2004), NGC XF 40, $95,000; Drew St. John Sale (American Numismatic Rarities, June 2005), NGC XF 40, lot 7, $86,250; C.L. Lee Sale (American Numismatic Rarities, September 2005), NGC XF 40, lot 389, $80,500; Premium Numismatics, Inc. fixed price list (October 2005), NGC XF 40, $88,750; Bowers and Merena (February 2006), NGC XF 40, lot 276; Superior Galleries (August 2007), NGC XF 40, lot 176; Duncan D. Lee Rare Coins, Inc. fixed price list (September 2007), NGC XF 40, $105,000; Franklinton Collection (Stack's, January 2008), NGC XF 40, lot 426, unsold.*

Additional Notes: None.

Coin Serial Number: 418.

From Stack's,
April 1957

1797, O-101a, late die state.

Guggenheimer Specimen.

Grade: Extremely Fine obverse, Very Fine reverse.

Identification Markers: Mark to the lower left of star 13, another just below the lower-right serif of the Y in LIBERTY. Mark midway between the eagle's tail and the right (facing) wing.

Provenance: *F.S. Guggenheimer Collection (Stack's, January 1953), Very Fine, lot 785, $510; Stack's (April 1957), Very Fine, lot 972.*

Additional Notes: None.

Coin Serial Number: 419.

From Heritage Auctions, October 2006

1797, O-101a, late die state.

October 2006 Dallas Sale Specimen.

Grade: Extremely Fine obverse, Damaged, Very Fine reverse, Damaged, Mount Removed, Re-engraved.

Identification Markers: Vertical cut from outer point of star 14 to the rim at the upper right of star 15. Fine vertical scratch from between ES of STATES through eagle's head. A shorter nearly parallel scratch to the left of the former scratch. Both sides are uniformly peppered with tiny marks (see Additional Notes below). The fraction digits have been re-engraved.

Provenance: *Stack's (May 2004), Very Fine, Tooled, Mount Removed, lot 2427, $27,600; Dallas Sale (Heritage Auctions, October 2006), NCS VF Details, Mount Removed, Damaged, lot 1117, $41,400.*

Additional Notes: The Stack's catalog states: "… this coin exhibit(s) a 'sweated' and porous look with many tiny marks from jostling against other metal goods." This author agrees with the Stack's assessment.

Coin Serial Number: 420.

From Stack's – Bowers,
August 2011

1797, O-101a, late die state.

Yale Clarke Specimen.

Grade: Very Fine, Scratches.

Identification Markers: Horizontal scratch from Liberty's lower lip terminating to right of space between stars 3 and 4, and two or three vertical scratches to the right of stars 3 – 4. Upper-left to lower-right adjustment mark extending from right of the upper curl through the upper-left part of the shoulder. Horizontal scratch from the lower part of the left (facing) wing to the middle part of the right (facing) wing. Moderate round mark just to the upper left of the tip of the palm leaf below the right (facing) wing.

Provenance: *Dr. Yale Clarke Collection (Stack's, October 1975), Very Fine, Scratches, lot 184, $5,500; Heritage (May 2007), ANACS VF 20 Details, Scratched, lot 2127, $34,500; Stack's-Bowers (August 2011), NGC VF Details, Scratches, lot 7339, unsold.*

Additional Notes: None.

Coin Serial Number: 421.

From Superior Galleries,
August 2002

1797, O-101a, late die state.

September 1998 Long Beach Sale Specimen.

Grade: Very Fine, Scratched, Cleaned.

Identification Markers: Diagonal toning streak from the rim through the R in LIBERTY ending in the upper-middle part of Liberty's head. Light scratches in hair and on chest. Light rim ding to the lower left of star 4. Rim ding above AT in STATES. Upper-right to lower-left scratch on eagle's breast, and another from the top of the upper-right ribbon bow to the fraction bar right of the 1.

Provenance: *Macy's Inaugural Auction (June 1954), Extremely Fine, lot 1388, $540; Superior Galleries (August 1991), Very Fine 20, lot 502, $14,850; Long Beach Sale (Heritage Auctions, September 1998), NGC VF 30, lot 6747, $23,000; Superior Galleries (August 2002), Extremely Fine 40, Cleaned, lot 944; J.J. Teaparty fixed price list (August 2002), VF 35 Details, Cleaned, Net VF 30, $33,000.*

Additional Notes: None.

Coin Serial Number: 422.

From Bowers and Merena,
January 1995

1797, O-101a, late die state.

Worrell Specimen.

Grade: Very Fine, Polished, possibly Re-engraved.

Identification Markers: Linear mark on upper-right part of left (facing) breast, and two small round marks to the upper left of the linear mark. Mark on lower drapery above 9 in date, and spot on shoulder above first 7. Mark in the central part of the field between the eagle's tail and right (facing) wing. Mark midway between the upper-right part of the right (facing) wing and the inner palm leaf below F in OF.

Provenance: *Worrell Collection (Superior Galleries, September 1993), Fine 12 Details, Polished, Tooled, lot 638, $9,350; FUN Sale (Bowers and Merena, January 1995), VF 25 Details, Net VG 8, Burnished, Devices Strengthened, lot 1103, $11,000.*

Additional Notes: None.

Coin Serial Number: 423.

From Bowers and Merena, January 1988

1797, O-101a, late die state.

1988 NASC Convention Sale Specimen.

Grade: Very Fine.

Identification Markers: Faint upper-left to lower-right pinscratch from inner point of star 4 running about two-thirds of way to Liberty's portrait. Faint horizontal pinscratch just below eagle's right (facing) wing. Short diagonal pinscratch from upper-left part of left (facing) leg. Mark in middle of right (facing) tail feather. Minute rim ding to lower left of 2 in fraction. Dentils very weak from above I in AMERICA to below right (facing) ribbon. Light vertical pinscratch from apex of first A extending through M.

Provenance: *Paramount (February 1974), VF 25, lot 299, $4,750; Numismatic Association of Southern California Convention (Bowers and Merena, January 1988), VF 20 obverse, VF 30 reverse, lot 257, withdrawn.*

Additional Notes: None.

Coin Serial Number: 424.

From Stack's,
December 1985

1797, O-101a, intermediate die state.

Heller Specimen.

Grade: Very Fine.

Identification Markers: Short diagonal pinscratch just to upper right of star 3, and another from the lower chin pointing to star 15. Mark at juncture of jaw and neck. Scratch from rim to between ST of STATES.

Provenance: *Stack's (May 1979), Very Fine, lot 214; Dennis Heller Collection (New England Rare Coin Auctions, January 1982), Very Fine 25, lot 618, $18,150; Stack's (December 1985), Very Fine, lot 918, $17,600.*

Additional Notes: None.

Coin Serial Number: 425.

From Bowers and Merena,
August 1983

1797, O-101a, late die state.

Hatie Specimen.

Grade: Very Fine, Damaged.

Identification Markers: Distinctive bubbly, rough surfaces, especially on the obverse. Mark under right (facing) wing to the lower left of the first and second vertical feathers. Mark high to the right of the 2 in the fraction.

Provenance: *New Netherlands (November 1956), Very Good, strong claims to Fine, apparent fire exposure, lot 41, $300; Bowers and Ruddy (March 1982), sharpness better than Fine 12, bubbly, rough surfaces, apparent fire exposure, lot 1763; George D. Hatie Collection (Bowers and Merena, August 1983), Fine 15, porous obverse fields, perhaps subjected to fire, lot 721.*

Additional Notes: It is this author's opinion that the coin was in fact exposed to a fire, or at least extreme heat.

Coin Serial Number: 426.

From Bowers and Merena,
May 1993

1797, O-101a, late die state.

Stetson University Specimen.

Grade: Very Fine.

Identification Markers: Fingerprint-like toning pattern in lower-left obverse field. Fine angling scratch from inner point of star 11 to Liberty's mouth. Mark just to the left of the curve of the right (facing) wing.

Provenance: *Stetson University Collection (Bowers and Merena, May 1993), VF 20, lot 279, $15,125; Heritage Auctions (September 1998), NCS VF 20, lot 6746, $18,975.*

Additional Notes: None.

Coin Serial Number: 427.

From Heritage Auctions,
March 2009

1797, O-101a, late die state.

Gainsboro – 2009 FUN Sale Specimen.

Grade: Very Fine.

Identification Markers: Two moderate marks above Liberty's eye. Coalesced dentils over T of LIBERTY. Two tiny marks on chest above left (facing) breast, two more to the lower left of those two, and two on the lower neck above the first two. Mark (or spot) to left of last A in AMERICA.

Provenance: *Stack's (May 1982), strong Fine, lot 1083, $14,000; Gainsboro II Sale (Superior Galleries, February 1997), Fine 15, lot 1801, $15,950; Heritage Auctions (February 2002), PCGS VF 25, lot 5728, $26,450; FUN Sale (Heritage Auctions, January 2009), PCGS VF 25, lot 3835, $63,250; Heritage Internet Auctions (February 2009), PCGS VF 25 CAC, lot 62149, past-auction buy $71,875; Heritage Auctions (March 2009), PCGS VF 25 CAC, lot 1914, $58,650.*

Additional Notes: None.

Coin Serial Number: 428.

From David Lawrence Rare Coin Auctions, October 2006

1797, O-101a, late die state.

Emmons Specimen.

Grade: Very Fine.

Identification Markers: Two marks on Liberty's temple aligned upper right to lower left. Spot just to lower left of eye. Small vertical milling mark to right of eagle's beak. Toning spots between IC of AMERICA.

Provenance: *Dr. Calvert L. Emmons Collection (Stack's, September 1969), Just about Very Fine, lot 613; Bowers and Merena (August 1991), Fine 15, lot 379; Scotsman Auction Co. (July 2004), NGC VF 30, lot 271, $60,950; John B. Hamrick Coins fixed price list (November 2004), NGC VF 30, $67,580; David Lawrence Rare Coin Auctions (October 2006), NGC VF 30, lot 938, $60,375.*

Additional Notes: None.

Coin Serial Number: 429.

From Stack's,
December 1999

1797, O-101a, late die state.

Lambert – Robison – Globus Specimen.

Grade: Very Fine.

Identification Markers: Minor rim ding to upper right of E in LIBERTY. Mark just to upper left of curve of right (facing) wing. Mark midway between beak and end of palm leaf below last S in STATES. Spot on middle of third vertical feather of right (facing) wing. Mark to right of fraction bar.

Provenance: *Major Richard Lambert Collection (S.H. Chapman, October 1910), Very good, lot 269, $40; Ellis and Doris Robison Collection (Stack's, February 1982), Fine, lot 1526, $16,000; Dr. Alfred R. Globus Collection (Stack's, December 1999), Very Fine, lot 1696, $21,850.*

Additional Notes: None.

Coin Serial Number: 430.

From Stack's,
November 1957

1797, O-101a, uncertain die state.

Possibly Cleneay – Empire Specimen.

Grade: Very Fine.

Identification Markers: Horizontal linear marks beneath the eagle's right (facing) wing (they show clearly on the Stack's photo; on the Chapman's photo, however, they show only to a small degree). Photo quality of images in both catalogs makes any other marks virtually indiscernible.

Provenance: *Possibly Thomas Cleneay Collection (S.H. and H. Chapman, December 1890), Fine, lot 2660, $70; Empire Collection (Stack's, November 1957), Very Fine, lot 1269, $600.*

Additional Notes: It cannot be positively stated whether or not these two appearances represent the same coin.

Coin Serial Number: 431.

From Bowers and Merena,
May 1999

1797, O-101a, late die state.

Chesapeake Collection Specimen.

Grade: Very Fine.

Identification Markers: Mark to upper left of top hair ribbon in line with inner point of star 7. Round mark just to left of space between stars 11 – 12 in line with Liberty's lower lip. Two marks between star 14 and chin. Mark to right of fraction bar below twist in ribbon. Minor rim ding to lower left of 2 in fraction.

Provenance: *Chesapeake Collection (Bowers and Merena, May 1999), NGC VF 30, lot 2118, $24,725; Heritage Auctions (September 2004), NGC XF 40, lot 6577, $76,500.*

Additional Notes: None.

Coin Serial Number: 432.

From American Numismatic Rarities,
May 2006

1797, O-101a, late die state.

May 2006 ANR Inventory Specimen.

Grade: Very Fine obverse, Fine reverse.

Identification Markers: Mark to lower left of bottom hair ribbon. Two linear marks trending upper left to lower right between star 3 and third curl from top. Mark on Liberty's upper chest aligned between ear and 9 of date. Mark to left of inner point of star 15. Rim ding between IT of UNITED. Round mark beneath horizontal part of right (facing) wing, and a short, horizontal linear mark to the lower right of it.

Provenance: *American Numismatic Rarities fixed price list (May 2006), NGC VF 30, $77,500.*

Additional Notes: None.

Coin Serial Number: 433.

From Stack's,
November 1967

1797, O-101a, intermediate die state.

McCullough Specimen.

Grade: Very Fine obverse, Fine reverse.

Identification Markers: Couple of toning spots on upper left cheek of Liberty. Mark about midway between mouth and inner point of star 12. Dentils weak between ER of LIBERTY. Large toning spot in middle of right (facing) wing (in line with first A in AMERICA).

Provenance: *Hall Park McCullough Collection (Stack's, November 1967), Fine, lot 396, $2,800.*

Additional Notes: None.

Coin Serial Number: 434.

From the National Numismatic Collection,
Smithsonian Institution

1797, O-101a, intermediate die state.

National Numismatic Collection Specimen.

Grade: Very Fine obverse, Scratched, Fine reverse.

Identification Markers: Fine scratch from inner point of star 7 through Liberty's portrait and star 15 to rim. Moderate toning spot on temple at hairline. Horizontal pinscratch from space between stars 4 and 5 to upper curl, and two diagonal pinscratches from star 2 to hair below second curl from top. Horizontal scratch from bottom of chin to inner point of star 13. Minor rim ding over A of STATES, and three others over IC of AMERICA. Toning spot just under horizontal part of left (facing) wing, another within lower part of E in UNITED, another below first S in STATES, and a cluster to right of laurel leaf between D and S.

Provenance: *From "the cabinet started by Eckfeldt and Dubois back in the 1830s at the Philadelphia Mint, transferred to us ... after 1923" (per Dr. Richard Doty, Curator, National Numismatic Collection, January 26, 2012 email).*

Additional Notes: None.

Coin Serial Number: 434a.

From Superior Galleries,
October 2000

1797, O-101a, intermediate die state.

Davis - Graves - Brilliant Specimen.

Grade: Very Fine obverse, Fine reverse.

Identification Markers: Diagonal scrape between rim and first 7 in date. Minute rim ding left of star 4. Upper-left to lower-right adjustment marks in hair at the upper shoulder. Mark midway between F in OF and first A in AMERICA. Spot just to left of lower-middle inner palm leaf below end of right (facing) wing.

Provenance: *George L. Davis-Henry P. Graves Collection (Stack's, April 1954), Fine to Very Fine, lot 459, $400; Stack's (March 1987), Very Fine, lot 689, $17,600; James D. Brilliant Collection (Bowers and Merena, January 1992), Fine 15, lot 40, $13,750; Superior Galleries (October 2000), NGC VF 25, lot 3263, $23,000; Central States Numismatic Society Sale (Heritage Auctions, April 2012), lot 5114, $54,625.*

Additional Notes: The April 1954 Stack's catalog indicates that the Davis collection lay unopened in a bank vault from his death in 1890 until October, 1953 when his heirs consigned it to auction.

Coin Serial Number: 435.

From Heritage Auctions,
August 1992

1797, O-101a, late die state.

Yarmouth Specimen.

Grade: Very Fine obverse, Fine reverse, Scratches.

Identification Markers: Large spot between Liberty's forehead and star 9, and smaller spots to the right of nose and chin. Scattered minute marks or spots in left obverse field. Short vertical linear marks above R and Y of LIBERTY and star 9. Scattered short light scratches on chest, breasts, and shoulder drapery. Light vertical scratch from middle talon of right (facing) leg to palm leaf below, and a couple more to lower right of latter scratch. What appears to be a very small X is located midway between eagle's neck and curve of right (facing) wing.

Provenance: *Yarmouth Type Collection (Heritage Auctions, August 1992), VG 10, lot 312, $8,800.*

Additional Notes: None.

Coin Serial Number: 436.

From Auction '90,
August 1990

1797, O-101a, late die state.

Auction '90 Specimen.

Grade: Very Fine obverse, Fine reverse, Graffiti.

Identification Markers: Mark on upper part of Liberty's left (facing) breast, another on the lower-middle neck. Upper-right to lower-left scratch on rear cheek – jaw. Horizontal pinscratch from eye through hair. A small X on cloud midway between talons of right (facing) leg and ribbon bow. Another small X to the right of the latter. Faint scratches (including a couple of X marks) on the right (facing) wing. Rim ding over first A of AMERICA.

Provenance: *Auction '90 Sale (Stack's session, August 1990), ANACS Fine 12/12, lot 196; Bowers and Merena (January 1992), PCGS F 12, lot 1207, $11,550.*

Additional Notes: None.

Coin Serial Number: 437.

From Stack's, March 2008

1797, O-101a, intermediate to late die state (see "Additional Notes" below).

Gaziano Specimen.

Grade: Very Fine obverse, Fine reverse.

Identification Markers: Linear mark between star 5 and middle hair ribbon. V-shaped mark in front of Liberty's nose. Two tiny marks on extreme lower-left part of right (facing) wing where it joins juncture of torso and leg.

Provenance: *Dominic Gaziano Collection (Stack's, March 2008), NGC Fine 15, lot 278, $53,475.*

Additional Notes: The crack left of the bottom of the first S in STATES is incomplete.

Coin Serial Number: 438.

From Bowers and Merena, August 1989

1797, O-101a, late die state.

Aspen Specimen.

Grade: Very Fine obverse, Fine reverse.

Identification Markers: Squiggly mark under star 1. Upper-left to lower-right scratch (or streak) on left (facing) breast, another parallel to it (though not as clear) on right (facing) breast. Short horizontal mark below chin, extending from middle of neck. Mark low, midway between eagle's neck and curve of right (facing) wing. Short vertical mark below horizontal part of left (facing) wing. Horizontal scratch from upper end of right (facing) ribbon to rim below last A in AMERICA.

Provenance: *ANA Sale (James Kelly, August 1950), Very Good to About Fine, lot 714, unplated (per following); Dr. Nelson Page Aspen Collection (Bowers and Merena, August 1989), VG 8 to Fine 12, lot 274, $15,400; Anaconda Rare Coins fixed price list (January – February, 2006), NGC VF 20, $76,500.*

Additional Notes: None.

Coin Serial Number: 439.

From Heritage Auctions,
January 2008

1797, O-101a, intermediate die state.

2008 FUN Sale Specimen.

Grade: Very Fine obverse, Fine reverse.

Identification Markers: Two marks on rim above star 10, and mark low between 79 of date. Two moderate vertically aligned spots to right of first curl from top. Diagonal scrape from rim left of first S in STATES. Mark near rim below stem of laurel branch, and another near rim below twist in right (facing) ribbon. Pronounced rim weakness above RICA of AMERICA; rim worn into outer parts of those letters.

Provenance: *Stack's (September 1998), PCGS Fine 12, lot 543, $14,575; FUN Sale (Heritage Auctions, January 2008), PCGS Fine 12, lot 2848, $54,625; Pinnacle Rarities fixed price list (May 2009), PCGS Fine 12, $47,500.*

Additional Notes: None.

Coin Serial Number: 440.

From Stack's,
June 2008

1797, O-101a, intermediate die state.

Husky Specimen.

Grade: Very Fine obverse, Fine reverse.

Identification Markers: Mark to right of star 13. Three milling marks between lower-left part of right (facing) wing extending upper right to lower left to tip of lower, inner palm leaf. Vertical mark between lower-right part of left (facing) wing and left (facing) leg.

Provenance: *Husky Collection (Stack's, June 2008), PCGS VF 20, lot 2015, $69,000.*

Additional Notes: None.

Coin Serial Number: 441.

From Heritage Auctions, July 2009

1797, O-101a, late die state.

Mougey Specimen.

Grade: Very Fine obverse, Scratched, Fine reverse.

Identification Markers: Horizontal scratch from star 4 across Liberty to star 13, and a finer diagonal scratch from star 12 to lower neck. Mark just to upper right of eye, another midway between lower forehead and inner point of star 9, and a nearly horizontal light scratch to the lower left of star 9. Two very short vertical marks from lower-right neck curl to lower neck. Short horizontal fine scratch from middle-right eagle's neck, curving slightly upward toward beak. Short diagonal mark from horizontal part of right (facing) wing to field.

Provenance: *Peter Mougey Collection (Thomas Elder, September 1910), Very good, lot 425, $41; Joel Rettew Rare Coin Galleries fixed price list (Winter, 1976), Fine, $6,750; Heritage Auctions (August 1995), Fine 12, Obverse Scratch, lot 5170, $12,650; William H. La Belle Collection (American Numismatic Rarities, July 2005), PCGS Fine 15, lot 1148, $46,000; Dick Osburn fixed price list (October 2005), PCGS Fine 15 (Osburn VF 20+, obverse scratch), $59,000; Heritage Auctions (February 2006), PCGS Fine 15, lot 1146, $48,875; Stack's (November 2007), PCGS Fine 15, lot 1077, $57,500; Heritage Auctions (January 2009), PCGS Fine 15, lot 3834, unsold; Heritage Auctions (July 2009), PCGS Fine 15, lot 1112, $51,750.*

Additional Notes: None.

Coin Serial Number: 442.

From Mayflower Coin Auctions, December 1967

1797, O-101a, late die state.

December 1967 Sale Specimen.

Grade: Very Fine obverse, Fine reverse.

Identification Markers: Upper-right to lower-left adjustment marks from stars 10 and 11 extending through right obverse field. Mark midway between star 8 and Liberty's head, another beneath L in LIBERTY and closer to head. Weak dentils below U of UNITED. RICA of AMERICA and adjacent dentils very weak. Poor photo quality makes all markers problematical.

Provenance: *Mayflower Coin Auctions, Inc. (December 1967), Very Fine, lot 734.*

Additional Notes: Photo quality makes it difficult to determine whether or not this coin duplicates another mid-grade 1797 O-101a, late die state half dollar in the study.

Coin Serial Number: 443.

From Superior Galleries,
September 2006

1797, O-101a, intermediate die state.

2011 Central States Numismatic Society Sale Specimen.

Grade: Very Fine obverse, Fine reverse.

Identification Markers: Light scratch from rim extending through space between stars 2 and 3. Mark adjacent to rim below star 1. Upper-left to lower-right mark in field below jaw, midway between neck and point of chin. Broad, U-shaped lint mark between TE of STATES. Fine linear streak between UN in UNITED. Horizontal milling marks in middle of right (facing) leg.

Provenance: *Pre-Long Beach (Superior Galleries, September 2006), NGC VF 25, lot 1119; Central States Numismatic Society (Heritage Auctions, April 2011), NGC VF 25, lot 5139, $57,500.*

Additional Notes: None.

Coin Serial Number: 444.

From RARCOA,
August 1987

1797, O-101a, intermediate die state.

Auction '87 Sale Specimen.

Grade: Very Fine obverse, Fine reverse.

Identification Markers: Short upper-left to lower-right scratch on drapery below left (facing) breast, and a finer vertical scratch on upper part of breast. Mark just to the right of the middle of the last 7 in date. Two marks between the drapery and rim, below the left (facing) breast. Numerous tiny spots on chest, neck, face, and in right obverse field. Rim ding above T of LIBERTY. Very weak dentils between E of AMERICA and right of fraction. Prominent dig or scrape just to the right of F in OF.

Provenance: *Auction '87 (RARCOA's session, August 1987), Fine, lot 1106.*

Additional Notes: None.

Coin Serial Number: 445.

From Stack's – Bowers,
November 2012

1797, O-101a, late die state.

November 2012 Baltimore Auction Specimen.

Grade: Fine obverse, Very Good reverse.

Identification Markers: Moderate dark spots in hair and on cheek. Horizontal pinscratch through eagle's lower torso and left (facing) wing to laurel wreath.

Provenance: *Baltimore Auction (Stack's-Bowers, November 2012), PCGS Very Good 8, lot 3140, $46,000.*

Additional Notes: None.

Coin Serial Number: 445a.

From Stack's,
June 1952

1797, O-101a, late die state.

Golding Specimen.

Grade: Very Fine obverse, Fine reverse.

Identification Markers: Very weak dentils from above LIBERTY to about star 13. Two to three short upper-right to lower-left marks on rim below and to right of fraction (planchet defects?). Bottom part of 2 in fraction appears to be missing, and what might be an area of tooling/smoothing runs from near rim (between diagonal marks and fraction) between the two ribbon ends. Rim appears to be worn into tops of letters RICA. Photo quality makes all markers, except diagonal marks on lower reverse rim, problematical.

Provenance: *David Golding Collection (Stack's, June 1952), About Very Fine, lot 33, $300.*

Additional Notes: The Stack's catalog states: "Die imperfection at bottom of reverse." This author concurs with Stack's assessment. Moreover, were it not for this imperfection as a pedigree marker, this coin would have been placed in "Additional 1797 O-101a Appearances" because of poor photo quality.

Coin Serial Number: 446.

From Superior Galleries,
May 1989

1797, O-101a, late die state.

Casterline and Brooks Hall Specimen.

Grade: Very Fine obverse, Fine reverse.

Identification Markers: Two short horizontal pinscratches on Liberty's lower neck, one on chest, and one in drapery at shoulder. Two moderate marks between second curl from top and lower ribbon end. Spot in hair near temple. Pinscratch between rim and stars 2 – 3. Vertical pinscratch from lower point of star 9 to upper point of star 15. Vertical adjustment marks on rim over TY of LIBERTY and star 9. Mark just to left of first A in AMERICA. Mark between serif of last A and stem-end of laurel wreath. Pinscratch from rim to laurel leaf between NI in UNITED.

Provenance: *Fred J. Casterline and Brooks Hall Collections (Superior Galleries, May 1989), Good 5, lot 2671.*

Additional Notes: None.

Coin Serial Number: 446a.

From Heritage Auctions,
March 2004

1797, O-101a, late die state.

Fairchild Family – Walser PCGS Registry Set Specimen.

Grade: Fine.

Identification Markers: Vertical adjustment marks in Liberty's hair and back of neck to lower left of ear. Vertical streaks in right obverse field. Two vertically aligned spots in hair to lower left of ear. X-shaped mark (adjustment mark?) extending from field below lower hair ribbon through two top curls. Light, short horizontal scratch on upper-right part of eagle's torso, and a diagonal one on left part of torso. Lower-right reverse border worn nearly smooth, including tops of CA in AMERICA and lower part of 2 in fraction. Mark right of 2, below twist in ribbon.

Provenance: *Superior Galleries (January 1990), VG 8, lot 3421, $11,000; Stack's fixed price list (1991), Very Good, nearly Fine, number 115, $14,750; Stack's (December 1991), strong Very Good, virtually Fine, lot 1794, unsold; Stack's fixed price list (Fall 1992), Very Good, nearly Fine, number 529, $14,500; Heritage Auctions (August 2000), PCGS Fine 12, lot 5971, $17,250; Fairchild Family Trust Collection (Ira and Larry Goldberg, May 2001), PCGS Fine 12, lot 695, $16,675; Bowers and Merena (July 2002), PCGS Fine 12, lot 284, $19,550; J.J. Teaparty fixed price list (August 2002), PCGS Fine 12, $24,250; MGS/NSI fixed price list (March 2003), PCGS Fine 12, $24,500; Heritage Auctions (March 2003), PCGS Fine 12, lot 5801, $36,800; William Walser PCGS Registry Set (May 2005), PCGS Fine 12.*

Additional Notes: None.

Coin Serial Number: 447.

From Stack's,
August 1976

1797, O-101a, uncertain die state.

1976 ANA Sale Specimen.

Grade: Fine.

Identification Markers: Diamond-shaped mark in drapery just to the upper right of the last 7 in date. Mark or spot to right of last 7, midway between rim and drapery. Rim bruise over right side of M in AMERICA. Rim appears to be worn into tops of ICA. Photo quality prevents discernment of other pedigree markers.

Provenance: *Stack's (May 1956), Fine to Very Fine, lot 819, $600; ANA Sale (Stack's, August 1976), Fine, lot 1088, $6,250.*

Additional Notes: None.

Coin Serial Number: 448.

From Stack's,
May 1956

1797, O-101a, late die state.

Regal Specimen.

Grade: Probably Fine (photo quality makes it difficult to determine whether Fine or Very Fine).

Identification Markers: Moderate mark just above obverse die crack, about two-thirds of the way to the right of the upper part of star 2, near the third curl from the top. Minor rim ding above the right part of E in AMERICA.

Provenance: *Regal Collection, Part II (Stack's, May 1956), Fine, lot 496, $400.*

Additional Notes: Were it not for the distinctive obverse identification mark, this coin would have been placed in the "Additional 1797 O-101a Appearances" section because of poor photo quality.

Coin Serial Number: 449.

From Harry Labstain Rare Coins, September 2011

1797, O-101a, late die state.

HLRC September 2011 Inventory Specimen.

Grade: Fine obverse, Very Good Reverse.

Identification Markers: Short horizontal scratch in field just to upper right of nose tip extending about halfway to inner point of star 11. Mark just to lower left of inner point of star 12. Mark immediately left of lower point of star 7. Dark rim mark above space between UN of UNITED. A moderate mark just to lower-left part of lower stand of N, and another on the lower diagonal of N. Short upper-left to lower right milling mark just left of stem of palm branch. Moderate horizontal scrape on upper-left part of right (facing) wing. Rim very weak from R of AMERICA to fraction. Short vertical mark near rim midway top serif of F in OF and first A in AMERICA.

Provenance: *Harry Labstain Rare Coins fixed price list (September 2011), PCGS Fine 15, $50,000.*

Additional Notes: None.

Coin Serial Number: 449a.

From Heritage Auctions,
October 2000

1797, O-101a, late die state.

October 2000 Long Beach Sale Specimen.

Grade: Very Good, Plugged, Re-engraved.

Identification Markers: 1 in date re-engraved; outline of plug partially shows. Minute mark or spot just to lower left of lower hair ribbon point. Second T of STATES re-engraved (its stand wider than that of first T). Dentils worn from ICA of AMERICA to U of UNITED.

Provenance: *Long Beach Sale (Heritage Auctions, October 2000), VG 8, Cleaned, Holed, Plugged, lot 6802, $8,913.*

Additional Notes: Photo quality prevents identification of other pedigree markers. The Heritage catalog states: "... holed and plugged through the lower obverse, and the 1 in the date and the second T in STATES have been re-engraved over the plug." This author concurs with that assessment.

Coin Serial Number: 450.

From Superior Galleries,
August 1991

1797, O-101a, late die state.

Norweb Specimen.

Grade: Very Good obverse, Damaged, Good reverse, Graffiti.

Identification Markers: Moderate punch mark at the right base of T in LIBERTY. Mark to lower left of star 8. Vertical pinscratch just to right of Liberty's eye-nose-mouth-chin, and diagonal pinscratch from between stars 12 – 13 into mid-field right of mouth. An X scratched into lower part of right (facing) wing. Rim worn into ICA of AMERICA and 2 of fraction.

Provenance: *Purchased by Albert Fairchild Holden prior to 1913 (per Bowers and Merena, November 1988); Norweb Collection, Part III (Bowers and Merena, November 1988), G-3, AG-2, lot 3028, $8,250; Auction '89 (Stack's session, July 1989), Good, close to Very Good, lot 1712, $7,150; Superior Galleries (August 1991), Good 4 obverse, About Good 3 reverse, lot 503, $5,775.*

Additional Notes: None.

Coin Serial Number: 451.

From Bowers and Merena,
August 2001

1797, O-101a, late die state.

August 2001 Rarities Sale Specimen.

Grade: Very Good obverse, Good reverse, reverse Scratched.

Identification Markers: Small spot or mark midway between rim and lower-right point of star 1. Two tiny marks just right of Liberty's mouth. Rim ding above star 11. Pinscratch runs from right side of O in OF diagonally through eagle to juncture of left (facing) leg and torso, and another extends from upper part of left (facing) wing through eagle and lower palm wreath to border at about 4:30; these give the appearance of a large X.

Provenance: *Rarities Sale (Bowers and Merena, August 2001), AG 3, "The obverse nearly qualifies at the VG-8 grade level," lot 181, $9,488.*

Additional Notes: None.

Coin Serial Number: 452.

From Heritage Auctions,
April 2006

1797, O-101a, late die state.

2006 Central States Sale Specimen.

Grade: Good, Bent, Damaged, Scratched.

Identification Markers: Worn smooth from stars 12 to 14 through Liberty's chin, neck, and upper chest; bottoms of date digits, and dentils above stars 7 – 8 and LIB. Small punch marks above stars 6 and 8, above B of LIBERTY, on star 14, and on shoulder and neck. Heavy lower-left to upper-right scratch from rim between stars 1 and 2 through lower hair. Worn smooth at ICA of AMERICA and adjacent wreath, and from ED of UNITED through wreath and adjacent lower wing. Punch mark above first T of STATES, on upper part of left (facing) wing, and on lower-right border.

Provenance: *Stack's (April 1976), Good to Very Good, Dents, Nicks, Bends, lot 612, $2,100; Bowers and Ruddy (February 1977), AG, Bent, Surface Marks, lot 1229, $2,600; Central States Numismatic Society Sale (Heritage Auctions, April 2006), NCS VG Details, Bent, Damaged, lot 1924, $20,700.*

Additional Notes: None.

Coin Serial Number: 453.

From Heritage Auctions,
September 2003

1797, O-101a, intermediate die state.

September 2003 Long Beach Sale Specimen.

Grade: Good obverse, Scratches, About Good reverse, Pockmarked.

Identification Markers: Vertical scratch traverses Liberty's portrait right of ear lobe. Another runs from tip of nose to drapery below right (facing) breast. Short vertical pinscratch between 79 of date, and another between 97. Numerous pockmarks uniformly scattered over reverse. Outer parts of UNI in UNITED, ATE of STATES, all of AMERICA, and 2 in fraction worn smooth. Short upper-left to lower-right scratch on lower palm wreath at about 4:00.

Provenance: *Long Beach Sale (Heritage Auctions, September 2003), Good 4, Repaired, lot 6954, $10,925.*

Additional Notes: None.

Coin Serial Number: 454.

From Superior Galleries,
May 2003

1797, O-101a, late die state.

2003 Pre-FUN Sale Specimen.

Grade: Good obverse, About Good reverse, reverse Scratched.

Identification Markers: Short, light vertical pinscratch just right of Liberty's forehead and upper part of nose. Moderate dark spot midway between eagle's tail and lower part of right (facing) wing. Long, faint scratch runs from wreath near N in UNITED though left (facing) cloud and tail to lower part of right (facing) wing.

Provenance: *Pre-FUN Sale (Superior Galleries, January 2003), NGC About Good 3, lot 691, $13,225; Superior Galleries (May 2003), NGC About Good 3, lot 2532.*

Additional Notes: None.

Coin Serial Number: 455.

From New England
Rare Coin Auctions,
November 1980

1797, O-101a, late die state.

Carnegie Specimen.

Grade: Good obverse, About Good reverse.

Identification Markers: Short linear mark or streak near rim from under star 1 extending two-thirds of way to base of 1 in date. Fine mark or streak from bust below star 15 to rim. Light spot to right of chin, about one-third of way to star 12. Right (facing) wing worn smooth, as are letters ICA in AMERICA and 2 in fraction.

Provenance: *David K. Carnegie Sale (New England Rare Coin Auctions, November 1980), Almost Good 3, lot 728, $10,615.*

Additional Notes: None.

Coin Serial Number: 456.

From Superior Galleries,
June 1998

1797, O-101a, intermediate die state.

June 1998 Auction Specimen.

Grade: Good obverse, Rims Filed, About Good reverse, Rims Filed, Re-engraved Fraction.

Identification Markers: Mark on shoulder drapery above right serif of first 7 in date. Rim mark above I in LIBERTY. Right (facing) wing of eagle worn smooth. Fraction boldly, and uncharacteristically re-engraved. Photo quality only fair.

Provenance: *June Auction (Superior Galleries, June 1998), About Good 3, Re-engraved, lot 1180, $6,875.*

Additional Notes: The Superior catalog states: "… the obverse has been reingraved (sic) and reworked, including the adding of radial lines to the worn down stars and numerous other attempts of strengthening the device detail." Photo quality prevents the discernment of these. Only the re-engraved fraction and rim filings are obvious.

Coin Serial Number: 457.

From Stack's – Bowers,
August 2011

1797, O-101a, intermediate die state.

Bloomfield – 2011 ANA Sale Specimen.

Grade: Good obverse, Fair reverse.

Identification Markers: Faint vertical streak or pinscratch from Liberty's ear lobe to lower neck. Two minute marks immediately to right of star 7. Most of fraction worn smooth, as are letters UN of UNITED and ICA of AMERICA. Eagle's head and left (facing) wing outlined, but its other features smooth. Most leaves on laurel wreath show, and about two-thirds of palm leaves. Short horizontal scratch just left of a lower, inner palm leaf. Two minute marks aligned horizontally to right of eagle's mouth, another below mouth.

Provenance: *R.M. Smythe (November 2000), Good/About Good, lot 1889, $8,250; Paul Bloomfield Collection (Bonhams, May 2010), PCGS Good 4, lot 1421, $37,440; Northeast Numismatics, Inc. fixed price list (June – September 2010), PCGS Good 4, $41,500; 2011 ANA Sale (Stack's – Bowers, August 2011), PCGS AG 3, lot 7341, $20,700.*

Additional Notes: None.

Coin Serial Number: 458.

From Superior Galleries,
September 2003

1797, O-101a, late die state.

September 2003 Pre-Long Beach Sale Specimen.

Grade: Good obverse, Fair reverse, Plugged, probably Whizzed.

Identification Markers: Mark in form of an inverted C on drapery line above last 7 in date. Rim worn into outer parts of right-border stars. Outline of plug on lower reverse near rim at 6:00. Vertical grooves to the lower right of eagle. Only letters TED and ST show at left border; rim worn into tops of letters along right border.

Provenance: *Long Beach Sale (Superior Galleries, September 2003), Fair 2 obverse, About Good 3 reverse, Cleaned, Plugged, lot 1648; First American Numismatics, Inc. fixed price list (December 2003), AG 3, $9,750; The Coin Depot fixed price list (March 2006), Good to VG, $21,950.*

Additional Notes: None.

Coin Serial Number: 459.

From Bowers and Merena,
September 1986

1797, O-101a, late die state.

Ingle Specimen.

Grade: Good obverse, Rough Surface, Fair reverse.

Identification Markers: Left obverse field very rough. Spot left of Liberty's mouth, larger one just left of star 11. Mark on drapery line above right serif of last 7 in date. Two moderate marks on lower reverse. Right (facing) side of eagle worn smooth, as is adjacent lower and middle palm wreath. Photo quality only fair.

Provenance: *Charles W. Ingle Collection (Bowers and Merena, September 1986), ANACS certificate Good 4 obverse, About Good 3 reverse, Tooled surfaces, lot 1959, $6,380.*

Additional Notes: Tooling not readily evident from photos.

Coin Serial Number: 460.

From Stack's,
October 1971

1797, O-101a, uncertain die state (photo quality prevents definitive attribution).

Shapero Specimen.

Grade: Good obverse, probably Fair reverse (photo quality makes it difficult to determine whether Fair or About Good), Plugged, Graffiti reverse.

Identification Markers: Outline of plug shows at star 13, and even more clearly at corresponding reverse border at 3:00. Short vertical scratch on Liberty's neck and upper chest (aligned with upper-left serif of last 7 in date). Inverted W (or right-side-up M) to lower right of eagle.

Provenance: *Collections of Nate S. Shapero and the Nate S. and Ruth B. Shapero Foundation (Stack's, October 1971), Good obverse, Fair reverse, Plugged, lot 62, $750.*

Additional Notes: None.

Coin Serial Number: 461.

From Stack's,
November 1995

1797, O-101a, late die state.

2004 Palm Beach Sale Specimen.

Grade: About Good obverse, Fair reverse.

Identification Markers: Two horizontally aligned marks centrally located on Liberty's portrait, and one visible directly below the right-most above mark. Mark between laurel wreath and eagle, aligned with base of T in UNITED. Only part of eagle fully visible is its head.

Provenance: *Bowers and Merena, (August 1995), AG 3/Fair 2, lot 131, $5,775; Stack's (November 1995), About Good, lot 1252, $6,270; Palm Beach Sale (Heritage Auctions, November 2004), PCGS Fair 2, lot 7355, $20,701.*

Additional Notes: None.

Coin Serial Number: 462.

Additional 1797 O-101a Half Dollar Appearances

Images from the following catalogs are not included in the study because poor photo quality makes it virtually impossible to determine a coin's grade or identification markers. Specimens in some of these catalogs may duplicate coins that have been incorporated into the study, while others might represent new appearances. Grades are those listed in the respective catalogs or represent an approximation by this author.

VF. George O. Walton Collection (Stack's, October 1963), lot 857.
VF. George H. Hall Collection (Stack's, May 1945), lot 1002.
VF (obverse plated). ANA Sale (Steve Ivy, August 1982), lot 2305.
VF. John Cobb (April 1964), lot 716.
VF. Superior (June 1988), lot 3053.
VF. R.E. Cox, Jr. Collection (Stack's, April 1962), lot 1758.
VF. George H. Earle, Jr. Collection (H. Chapman, June 1912), lot 2827.
Fine-VF. Malcolm N. Jackson Collection (United States Coin Co., May 1913), lot 636.
Fine-VF. Charles Gregory Collection (S.H. Champan, June 1916), lot 2525.
Fine+. ANA Sale (RARCOA, August 1970), lot 871.
Fine. James Kelly (April 1957), lot 1019.
VG 10, PCGS. Bowers and Merena (August 1998), lot 183.
VG. RARCOA (May 1969), lot 140.
VG, Initials near face. Schulman Coin & Mint (December 1973), lot 682.
Good 5 obverse, About Good reverse. Superior Galleries (February 1978), lot 397.

1797 Half Dollar Examples
Overton-102

From American Numismatic Rarities, August 2004

1797, O-102.

Allison Park Specimen.

Grade: Mint State.

Identification Markers: Diamond-shaped spot midway between star 5 and middle hair ribbon. Spot on middle part of Liberty's upper neck. Spot between ME of AMERICA.

Provenance: *Superior Galleries (May 1999), NGC MS 61, lot 2173, unsold; 2003 ANA (Bowers and Merena, July 2003), NGC MS 61, lot 1383; David Lawrence Rare Coins fixed price list (November – December 2003), NGC MS 61, $128,500; Allison Park Collection (American Numismatic Rarities, August 2004), NGC MS 61, lot 420, unsold.*

Additional Notes: None.

Coin Serial Number: 500.

From Bowers and Ruddy,
May 1974

1797, O-102.

Terrell – Austin Specimen.

Grade: About Uncirculated.

Identification Markers: Spot near rim to lower left of 1 in date, and four more below 97. Light mark below star 1. Mark or spot low between stars 9 – 10, another on tip of lower hair ribbon. Toning area right of star 14.

Provenance: *Charles Jay Collection (Stack's, October 1967), XF or better, lot 153, $5,000; John Cobb (May 1968), Choice AU, lot 1187; Terrell Collection (American Auction Association, May 1973), AU, lot 58, $16,000; Bowers and Ruddy (May 1974), AU, lot 679, $13,500.*

Additional Notes: None.

Coin Serial Number: 501.

From Heritage Auctions, July 2004

1797, O-102.

Willamette Specimen.

Grade: Extremely Fine, Microporosity.

Identification Markers: Two spots on upper chest above left (facing) breast, and one on drapery below same breast. Upper-right to lower-left adjustment marks at right obverse border. Mark to right of F in OF, in line with tip of palm leaf.

Provenance: *Auction '85 (Stack's session, July 1985), VF, lot 1701; Willamette Collection (Heritage Auctions, July 2004), ANACS AU Details, Net XF 40, Environmental Damage, lot 7851, $71,300; Superior Galleries (January 2005), XF 40, lot 280.*

Additional Notes: While not readily apparent from the images, both sides exhibit light porosity.

Coin Serial Number: 502.

From Heritage Auctions, July 2008

1797, O-102.

Bayside Specimen.

Grade: Very Fine.

Identification Markers: Two diagonal marks on upper chest above left (facing) breast. Short toning streak just below star 9. Toning spot above first T in STATES, another near rim between S and O in OF. Minute spot midway between beak and tip of palm leaf.

Provenance: *Bayside Collection (Heritage Auctions, July 2008), PCGS VF 35, lot 1671, $97,750.*

Additional Notes: None.

Coin Serial Number: 503.

From Ira and Larry Goldberg,
February 2003

1797, O-102.

Arnel – Benson Specimen.

Grade: Very Fine.

Identification Markers: Spot just above stand of B in LIBERTY, another to lower-right of star 4, and three or four smaller ones between star 3 and third curl from top. Mark on forehead to upper left of eye, and another on cheek right of ear. Short upper-left to lower-right pinscratch on eagle's lower neck.

Provenance: *Robert A. Arnel Collection (Stack's, January 1967), Very Fine, lot 65, $3,800; Stack's (May 1974), Very Fine, lot 209, $8,750; Heritage Auctions (July 1997), PCGS VF 30, lot 6334, $24,150; Superior Galleries (February 1998), PCGS VF 30, lot 2164, unsold; Superior Galleries (August 2002), PCGS VF 30, lot 1661, $32,200; Benson Collection, Part 3 (Ira and Larry Goldberg, February 2003), PCGS VF 30, lot 515, $33,925; Heritage Auctions (July 2003), PCGS VF 30, lot 7336, $36,915.*

Additional Notes: None.

Coin Serial Number: 504.

From Heritage Auctions,
August 2006

1797, O-102.

Chief Paduke Specimen.

Grade: Very Fine, light reverse Scratches.

Identification Markers: Light, short horizontal scratch just to upper left of star 15, another to lower right of chin. Short upper-left to lower-right scratch to right of eagle's neck, and a longer vertical one from tip of palm leaf to concave curve of wing. Several faint scratches below right (facing) wing. Light vertical marks (adjustment marks?) in lower-right reverse quadrant.

Provenance: *Chief Paduke Collection (Heritage Auctions, August 2006), PCGS VF 25, lot 5223, $51,750.*

Additional Notes: None.

Coin Serial Number: 505.

From A. Kosoff,
May 1968

1797, O-102.

Shufford Specimen.

Grade: Probably Very Fine, (poor photo quality prevents determination as to Very Fine or Extremely Fine).

Identification Markers: What appears to be a planchet depression is located on the rim between stars 14 and 15, and another on rim between AM of AMERICA. Possible minor rim ding between U of UNITED and ribbon end. Photo quality prevents identification of any other pedigree markers.

Provenance: *Alex Shufford Collection (A. Kosoff, May 1968), not quite Extremely Fine, lot 1095, $3,850.*

Additional Notes: The Kosoff catalog states: "A planchet break at the edge between the last 2 stars." Were it not for this prominent identification marker, this piece would have been placed in the "Additional 1797 O-102 Half Dollar Appearances" section because of poor photo quality.

Coin Serial Number: 506.

From Ira and Larry Goldberg,
February 2007

1797, O-102.

Edmonton – Rudolph Specimen.

Grade: Very Fine, obverse Scratches.

Identification Markers: Horizontal scratch on Liberty's lower neck. Upper-right to lower-left scratch traversing upper cleavage, and a vertical streak through right side of star 14 to rim below star 15. Upper-right to lower-left mark right of eagle's beak, and a spot to its upper right. Mark to lower right of D in UNITED, and two more below bottom serif of first S in STATES.

Provenance: *Stack's (June 1975), borderline VF, lot 463, $5,800; Edmonton Sale (Bowers and Merena, March 1993), PCGS VF 20, lot 1226, unsold; Heritage Auctions (June 2006), NGC VF 30, lot 1589, unsold; Ira and Larry Goldberg (February 2007), NGC VF 30, lot 1428, $71,875; Scott Rudolph Collection (Heritage Auctions, January 2009), NGC VF 30, lot 3836, $60,375; Harry Labstain Rare Coins fixed price list (March 2009), NGC VF 30, $72,500; J.J. Teaparty fixed price list (March 2009), PCGS VF 25, $75,000.*

Additional Notes: None.

Coin Serial Number: 507.

From Stack's,
April 1967

1797, O-102.

Copeland Specimen.

Grade: Very Fine.

Identification Markers: Two marks between Liberty's nose and star 11, another about midway between chin and star 14. Mark midway between rim and stem of laurel wreath (to left of last A in AMERICA).

Provenance: *RARCOA (April 1963), Very Fine to Extremely Fine, lot 1044, $3,625; Bernard L. Copeland Collection (Stack's, April 1967), very strong Fine, a hairsbreadth from Very Fine, lot 852, $3,600.*

Additional Notes: None.

Coin Serial Number: 508.

From Stack's,
May 1974

1797, O-102.

May 1974 Stack's Sale U.S. Type Coins Specimen.

Grade: Very Fine.

Identification Markers: Mark right of nose bridge, about one-third of way to inner point of star 10. Mark under tip of palm leaf, in line with eagle's beak.

Provenance: *United States Type Coins Consignment (Stack's, May 1974), Very Fine, lot 209, $8,750.*

Additional Notes: None.

Coin Serial Number: 509.

From Stack's,
March 1959

1797, O-102.

Pelletreau Specimen.

Grade: Very Fine obverse, Fine reverse.

Identification Markers: Planchet clip to right of stars 13, 14, 15 on obverse and over letter E of AMERICA and adjacent spaces on reverse. Vertical pinscratch or streak from outer point of star 4 to rim at the lower left of star 3. Moderate mark just below Liberty's forehead curl. Two vertical pinscratch-like marks extending from bottom of last S in STATES into field above right (facing) wing (possibly photo imperfections?).

Provenance: *Stack's (May 1937) lot 371 (per Stack's, March 1959); Robert H. Pelletreau Collection (Stack's, March 1959), Very Good, lot 726, $370.*

Additional Notes: None.

Coin Serial Number: 510.

From Heritage Auctions,
August 2011

1797, O-102.

2011 ANA Sale Specimen.

Grade: Very Fine obverse, Graffiti, Fine reverse.

Identification Markers: X-like mark moderately scratched in field between Liberty's neck and stars 13 – 15. Tear-drop-like mark below eye. Upper-left to lower-right pinscratch (or streak) from middle of left (facing) wing to left (facing) leg. Mark midway between neck and upper curve of right (facing) wing. Spot on reverse rim at 6:00. Rim ding between NI in UNITED.

Provenance: *Stack's (November 1968), Fine, "X" scratch right obverse field, lot 716, $2,150; ANA Sale (Heritage Auctions, August 2011), PCGS Fine 15, lot 7137, $54,625.*

Additional Notes: Reverse very nearly VF, except that left (facing) wing not completely separated from torso.

Coin Serial Number: 511.

From Stack's,
December 1993

1797, O-102.

Cowden Specimen.

Grade: Very Fine obverse, Fine reverse.

Identification Markers: Mark under space between stars 7 – 8. Light rim ding over star 10. Several tiny marks or spots between forehead – nose bridge and stars 9 – 10. Light planchet flaw on edge over ER of AMERICA. Mark in field just to upper right of juncture of torso with right (facing) wing.

Provenance: *William B. Cowden Type Collection (Stack's, December 1993), Choice Fine, lot 1002.*

Additional Notes: None.

Coin Serial Number: 512.

From Heritage Auctions,
June 2008

1797, O-102.

Glenwood Specimen.

Grade: Very Fine obverse, Fine reverse.

Identification Markers: Mark below right serif of L in LIBERTY. Faint upper-right to lower-left adjustment marks confined to rim above TY and stars 9 – 14. Faint vertical pinscratch bisects eagle from head to upper-left part of right (facing) leg, and horizontal pinscratch from middle of left (facing) tail to tip of palm leaf below right (facing) wing. Mark midway between top right of 2 in fraction and ribbon end. Base of 2 worn away.

Provenance: *Stack's (May 1973), Fine, with claims to Very Fine, lot 253, $3,800; Bowers and Merena (September – October 1996), F 12, lot 2011, $4,620; Glenwood Collection (Heritage Auctions, June 2008), PCGS Fine 15, lot 962, $54,625.*

Additional Notes: None.

Coin Serial Number: 513.

From Bowers and Merena, June 2010

1797, O-102.

June 2010 Baltimore Auction Specimen.

Grade: Very Fine obverse, Smoothed, Polished, Fine reverse, Polished.

Identification Markers: Small spots on Liberty's cheek bone and jaw. Mark to left of second curl from top, in line with end of bottom hair ribbon, and another below base of L in LIBERTY. Mark to lower-right base of last 7 in date. Two short horizontal pinscratches extend from right side of eagle's neck. Upper-right to lower-left pinscratch from palm leaf tip below right (facing) wing extend about one-half way to tail. Tops of RICA in AMERICA very weak, as is base of 2 in fraction. Two marks right of U in UNITED, aligned with tip of palm wreath stem.

Provenance: *Baltimore Auction (Bowers and Merena, June 2010), NGC Fine Details, Repaired, Polished, lot 2193, $25,415.*

Additional Notes: The Bowers and Merena catalog states: "Smoothing … in right obverse field" and "glossy texture due to polishing."

Coin Serial Number: 514.

From "a Texas Collector"

1797, O-102.

A Texas Collector Specimen.

Grade: Very Fine obverse, Fine reverse.

Identification Markers: Faint upper-left to lower-right pinscratch traverses Liberty's neck, and an upper-right to lower-left one is visible in the upper hair. Mark on Liberty's lower-right jaw. Mark in field just to upper right of eyebrow. Spot on lower-left part of eagle's torso. Rim ding above last A in AMERICA.

Provenance: *In a Texas collection since late 1970s (per present owner of coin).*

Additional Notes: None.

Coin Serial Number: 515.

From Stack's, March 1994

1797, O-102.

1990 G.N.A. Sale Specimen.

Grade: Very Fine obverse, Dig, Fine reverse.

Identification Markers: Vertical pinscratch from Liberty's cheek bone to upper neck. Moderate dig in field adjacent to upper part of chest, in line with inner point of star 14. Mark to right of lower base of last 7 in date. Rim mark left of star 4, another above space between LI in LIBERTY. Rim bruise to upper right of second T in STATES.

Provenance: *Georgia Numismatic Association Sale (Mid-American Rare Coin Auctions, May 1990), PCGS Fine 15, lot 485, $18,150; Stack's (March 1994), Fine, lot 858.*

Additional Notes: None.

Coin Serial Number: 516.

From Bowers and Merena,
January 1996

1797, O-102.

Shahbabian Specimen.

Grade: Very Fine obverse, Fine reverse, Plugged, Scratched reverse.

Identification Markers: Moderate mark to upper right of star 2. Light mark on middle part of jaw, another midway between star 6 and upper hair ribbon. Several small marks in right obverse field. Upper-left to lower-right scratch from laurel leaf below second T in STATES through eagle's upper neck. Two horizontal streaks from rim to laurel wreath (between D in UNITED and first S in STATES).

Provenance: *Set Shahbabian Collection (Bowers and Merena, January 1996), Net VG 8, sharpness of Fine 12, Holed and Plugged at 12:00 obverse, lot 1470, $13,200.*

Additional Notes: The plug and any re-engraving are not readily discernible in the photos.

Coin Serial Number: 517.

From B. Max Mehl,
April 1949

1797, O-102.

Manning – Charles Green Specimen.

Grade: Very Fine obverse, Scratched, Fine reverse.

Identification Markers: Diagonal pinscratch from Liberty's lips toward star 13, ending with upside-down diamond scratch prior to reaching star 13 (resembles a pipe in Liberty's mouth). A moderate mark on mid-cheek. Dark spot in back of hair, in line with ear lobe and hair ribbon knot. Short vertical mark midway between the tip of the third inner palm leaf from top and the upper-right part of the right (facing) wing. Diagonal streak or scratch on eagle's upper torso.

Provenance: *Probably Ex: Harold P. Newlin Collection (John Haseltine, April 1883), lot 140 (unplated), described as "Hair lines all distinct. A good specimen, but has a small pipe scratched in the mouth of Liberty, $32;" probably Ex: Charles Steigerwalt fixed price lists (November 1902 and October 1903, unplated), described as "A pipe has been lightly scratched in field from mouth; otherwise a very good piece, with bold date;" B.W. Smith Collection (B. Max Mehl, May 1915), strictly very good, nearly fine, lot 772, $25; James Manning Collection (B. Max Mehl, May 1921), very good, parts approaching fine, lot 522, $38; Dr. Charles Green Collection (B. Max Mehl, April 1949), extremely fine, lot 2735, $340.*

Additional Notes: None.

Coin Serial Number: 518.

From Stack's,
June 1989

1797, O-102.

Southern Gentleman Specimen.

Grade: Very Fine obverse, Fine reverse.

Identification Markers: Minute mark midway between inner point of star 7 and top hair ribbon. Linear mark or streak just right of D in UNITED, running from rim to top of laurel leaf. Vertical pinscratch on eagle's lower-middle torso. Horizontal adjustment marks from rim through CA of AMERICA, lower palm wreath, and clouds. These are intersected by vertical adjustment marks from rim through fraction, the lower-right ribbon, lower palm wreath, and right (facing) cloud.

Provenance: *A Southern Gentleman's Collection (Stack's, June 1989), Fine, lot 1751, $11,000.*

Additional Notes: None.

Coin Serial Number: 519.

From Princeton University,
May 2006

1797, O-102.

Princeton University Specimen.

Grade: Very Fine obverse, Fine reverse.

Identification Markers: Round mark to upper right of star 2. Toning areas within date and lower curls. Upper-right to lower-left mark in field just below eagle's mouth. Mark below lower serif of first S in STATES.

Provenance: *Charles A. Cass (Princeton University class of 1902) Collection, bequeathed to the university numismatic collection at his death in 1958 (per Alan Stahl, Curator of Numismatics, Princeton University, May 25, 2006 email).*

Additional Notes: None.

Coin Serial Number: 520.

From Bowers and
Ruddy, October 1976

1797, O-102.

1976 Western States Convention Sale Specimen.

Grade: Very Fine obverse, Fine reverse.

Identification Markers: Mark just right of Liberty's forehead. Series of small marks (staple scratches?) extending vertically from left of the curve of the eagle's right (facing) wing to the upper-inner palm leaf. Minor rim bruise to the right of F in OF, another to the right of 2 in fraction, and one above the space between IT of UNITED.

Provenance: *Western States Convention (Bowers and Ruddy, October 1976), Fine, lot 1624, $5,250.*

Additional Notes: None.

Coin Serial Number: 521.

Reverse unplated

From S.H. Chapman, June 1916
Obverse initials, as seen in Chapman (June 1916) catalog

Heritage Auctions, May 2012
Repaired obverse, as seen in Heritage (May 2012) catalog

1797, O-102.

Gregory Specimen.

Grade: Very Fine obverse, Repaired, Fine reverse, Repaired.

Identification Markers: The Chapman catalog obverse photo displays three initials on Liberty's portrait – what appears to be a small script s, a large A and a large H. A linear mark under star 8 and L is located midway to Liberty's head. There is a small rim ding above star 8, and another above T. The Heritage obverse photo shows all initials removed. The linear mark and the rim ding over T are still visible, but the NGC holder obscures the rim ding over star 8.

Provenance: *Charles Gregory Collection (S.H. Chapman, June 1916), "Three large initials … otherwise good," lot 2526, $12; Long Beach Sale (Heritage Auctions, May-June 2012), NGC VF Details, Repaired, lot 3757, $28,750.*

Additional Notes: The Chapman catalog also states: "three (initials) on reverse with date 1844."

Coin Serial Number: 521a.

From Stack's,
June 1985

1797, O-102.

March 2005 *Coins* magazine Plate coin.

Grade: Very Fine obverse, Fine reverse.

Identification Markers: Two vertically aligned marks to right of inner point of star 3. Spot adjacent to inner point of star 9. Light smudge on cheek midway between ear and nose. Short horizontal mark just left of neck curl. Upper-right to lower-left adjustment marks in central reverse, most noticeable in fields between neck and curve of right (facing) wing, neck and curve of left (facing) wing, and between left (facing) leg and bottom of left (facing) wing. Mark between inner berry on laurel branch and cloud, in line with I of UNITED. Two marks between last A of AMERICA and ribbon end.

Provenance: *Stack's (June 1985), Very Good, lot 498; Plate coin, Coins magazine (March 2005).*

Additional Notes: None.

Coin Serial Number: 522.

From Heritage Auctions,
January 2007

1797, O-102.

2007 FUN Sale Specimen.

Grade: Fine.

Identification Markers: Light, upper-right to lower-left streaks (toning streaks or erasure marks?) in obverse fields. Short, faint pinscratches on drapery above second 7 in date. Short diagonal mark on eagle's middle-left torso very near juncture with left (facing) wing.

Provenance: *FUN Sale (Heritage Auctions, January 2007), NCS Fine Details, Scratched, lot 955, $43,125.*

Additional Notes: The present author cataloged this coin, and felt, along with four other Heritage catalogers, that this piece should not be in a "problem" holder as the pinscratches are very minor.

Coin Serial Number: 523.

From Stack's,
September 1968

1797, O-102.

Lovi Specimen.

Grade: Very Fine obverse, Fine reverse, Plugged, reverse Re-engraved.

Identification Markers: Plug to right of last 7 in date. Vertical scratch or streak from rim extending along the left side of the stand in R of LIBERTY. Small spot to lower left of O in OF, both of which letters are re-engraved. Rim ding over U in UNITED, another above right serif of T.

Provenance: *Probably B.W. Smith Collection (B. Max Mehl, May 1915), Fine, lot 773, $17; Art Lovi Collection (Stack's, September 1968), Fine, Plugged, lot 57, $1,100.*

Additional Notes: None.

Coin Serial Number: 524.

From Heritage Auctions, September 2004

1797, O-102.

September 2004 Long Beach Sale Specimen.

Grade: Fine, Plugged, Re-engraved.

Identification Markers: Plugged at 12:00 obverse at the letter E and left side of R in LIBERTY, that are then re-engraved, as is the reverse fraction. Re-engraved letters and numerals are of a different style than seen on original examples. Mark near rim between stars 11 – 12. Short horizontal scratch above eagle's beak, another between F in OF and first A in AMERICA, which extends into the palm branch.

Provenance: *Auction '86 (Stack's session, July 1986), Fine, Plugged, lot 178, $, $10,450; Long Beach Sale (Heritage Auctions, September 2004), NCS Fine Details, Plugged, lot 6576, $18,400.*

Additional Notes: None.

Coin Serial Number: 525.

From American Auction Association,
November 1973

1797, O-102.

Rothert Sale Specimen.

Grade: Fine, obverse Graffiti.

Identification Markers: The numeral 4 is visible on the upper part of the left (facing) breast, in line with the final 7 in the date. A dark toning streak extends from the rim above E in AMERICA, through R, the palm branch and the bow knot to the curve of the U in UNITED. A lighter diagonal streak runs from the rim through C, intersecting the darker one in the palm branch before extending through the field midway between the right (facing) wing and tail. Three shorter horizontal streaks are visible in the upper reverse.

Provenance: *Matt Rothert Sale (American Auction Association, November 1973), About Fine, lot 843, $3,300.*

Additional Notes: None.

Coin Serial Number: 526.

From "an Upstate New York Collector"

1797, O-102.

An Upstate New York Collector's Specimen.

Grade: Fine.

Identification Markers: Moderate mark midway between star 3 and third curl from the top. Horizontal pinscratch from bottom of neck curl into hair, in line with inner point of star 3. Minor rim ding above first T of STATES, and another above space between AM in AMERICA. Faint vertical staple scratch through right (facing) wing.

Provenance: *Northeast Numismatics, Inc to an Upstate New York collector, April 1996, ANACS Fine 12.*

Additional Notes: None.

Coin Serial Number: 527.

From Bowers and Merena,
January 1992

1797, O-102.

Brilliant Specimen.

Grade: Fine.

Identification Markers: Mark left of space between stars 9 – 10. Mark on shoulder, above first 7 in date. Light pinscratch from nose tip to lower part of star 11. Three light pinscratches extend from tail and upper part of right (facing) leg into field.

Provenance: *Leo Young (April 1957), Fine – VF, lot 1325; Bowers and Ruddy (November 1976), About Fine, lot 561, $5,600; FUN Sale (New England Rare Coin Auctions, January 1982), VG 10, lot 617, $11,000; James D. Brilliant Collection (Bowers and Merena, January 1992), VG 10, lot 41, $15,400; Premium Numismatics fixed price list (October 2005), NGC Fine 12, $44,000.*

Additional Notes: None.

Coin Serial Number: 528.

From Heritage Auctions, October 2010

1797, O-102.

Silliphant Specimen.

Grade: Very Fine obverse, Very Good reverse, Scratched.

Identification Markers: Upper-left to lower-right adjustment marks in Liberty's lower-middle hair, confined between shoulder and ear. Light vertical streaks in field running from TY in LIBERTY to the right side of mouth. Prominent, deep scratches in lower and lower-right reverse. Neck, upper-left torso and adjacent wing worn smooth.

Provenance: *New England Rare Coin Auctions (July 1976), VG 10, Reverse Scratches, lot 1009, $4,200; Sterling Silliphant Collection (Heritage Auctions, July 1988), Fine 15/15, Reverse Scratches, lot 679, $9,250; Mid-American Auctions (January 1989), Fine 12, Scratches, lot 462, $9,900; Heritage Auctions (May 2008), NCS Fine Details, Scratched, lot 495, $23,000; Diotte Collection (Heritage Auctions, October 2010), NCS Fine Details, Scratched, lot 3641, $25,300.*

Additional Notes: None.

Coin Serial Number: 529.

From Heritage Auctions, April 2009

1797, O-102.

Reiver Specimen.

Grade: Very Good.

Identification Markers: Round mark just right of nose tip, and two marks on rim to right of star 12. Round mark just to upper left of star 15, and another above right (facing) breast. Squiggly scratch near rim below lower-right ribbon. Lower reverse rim very weak and nearly worn into bottom of 2 in fraction. Vertical pinscratch from U in UNITED to lowest berry.

Provenance: *Julian Leidman (May 1987); Overton plate coin, Early Half Dollar Die Varieties; Jules Reiver Collection (Heritage Auctions, January 2006), NGC VG 10, lot 22515, $46,000; Joseph C. Thomas Collection (Heritage Auctions, April 2009), NCS VG 10, lot 2389, $37,375.*

Additional Notes: None.

Coin Serial Number: 530.

From Stack's,
May 1998

1797, O-102.

May 1998 Sale Specimen.

Grade: Very Good.

Identification Markers: Mark just left of inner point of star 11. Mark adjacent to lower-right base of 2 in fraction. Mark just below space between uppermost laurel and palm leaves. Two marks below end of the right ribbon. Two horizontally aligned spots to lower right of right (facing) leg. Photo quality makes most of these marks problematical.

Provenance: *Stack's (May 1998), PCGS VG 10, lot 552, $12,650.*

Additional Notes: None.

Coin Serial Number: 531.

From Stack's – Bowers, August 2011

1797, O-102.

2011 ANA Sale Specimen.

Grade: Very Good.

Identification Markers: Vertical pinscratch in field right of Liberty's neck. Vertical cut from rim through right part of star 10 to top of star 11. Dark, moderate toning spot left of star 15, and a smaller one on drapery above 9 in date. Dark toning area below bust to right of final 7. Dark toning area on left clouds, end of left (facing) wing, on lowest inner laurel leaf, and in adjacent fields. Bottom of 2 in fraction worn nearly smooth.

Provenance: *ANA Sale (Stack's – Bowers, August 2011), NGC VG 8, lot 7340, unsold.*

Additional Notes: None.

Coin Serial Number: 532.

From Heritage Auctions,
January 2013

1797, O-102.

Sale of the 70's Specimen.

Grade: Good obverse, Polished, About Good reverse, Polished, Repaired.

Identification Markers: Upper-right to lower-left pinscratch on Liberty's neck. Diagonal mark in hair in line with inner point of star 3 and 1 in date. Squiggly scratch from rim to upper-right point of star 11. Numerous other finer pinscratches and hairlines over both sides. Central part of eagle virtually smooth, as are the outer part of U in UNITED, the bottom of 2 in fraction, and the last A in AMERICA. Rim ding above T in UNITED. Small repair (in the form of removed metal) under the right (facing) wing.

Provenance: *Kreisberg and Schulman (March 1965), About Very Good, lot 309; Sale of the 70's (Kagins, November 1973), good to very good, lot 436, $2,200; Bowers and Merena (September 1992), Good 4, Lightly Polished and Burnished, lot 1336, $6,160; Early American History Auctions (circa May 2007), PCI Good 4, Repaired, lot number unknown; Dick Osburn Rare Coins fixed price list (October 2007), PCGS Genuine (Osburn Good 4), $34,750; 2013 FUN Sale (Heritage Auctions, January, 2013), NGC Good Details, reverse Repaired.*

Additional Notes: None.

Coin Serial Number: 533.

Additional 1797 O-102 Half Dollar Appearances

Images from the following catalogs are not included in the study because poor photo quality makes it virtually impossible to determine a coin's grade or identification markers. Specimens in some of these catalogs may duplicate coins that have been incorporated into the study, while others might represent new appearances. Grades are those listed in the respective catalogs or represent an approximation by this author.

XF. Leo Young (April 1961), lot 1826.
VF. Estate of George C. Clawson Collection (Stack's, April 1970), lot 1005.
Fine. W.F. Dunham Collection (B. Max Mehl, June 1941), lot 675.
Fine. Million Dollar Sale I (Harmer, Rooke, November 1969), lot 1084.

THE RESEARCH FINDINGS

The previous section listed information on the date, variety, grade, etc. of 270 Draped Bust Small Eagle half dollars. The author has a high degree of confidence that 256 of these are distinct specimens, i.e., the probability that any are duplicates is extremely small. A somewhat lower level of confidence, however, is given to 14 of the listed coins, i.e., it is possible that some duplicate other examples in the study. This results from substandard photo quality of the 14 appearances that makes plate matching imprecise and open to question. These coins are identified under "Additional Notes" in the previous section.

The possible duplications notwithstanding, the following tabular summary of the 1796-1797 half dollar census and concomitant discussion are based on the 270-piece enumeration. The author feels that the 14 possible duplicates, representing only 5% of the census, are unlikely to significantly distort the overall research findings.

The 1796-1797 Half Dollar Census Summarized

The 270 Draped Bust Small Eagle half dollars in the census are summarized in Table 3 by Overton variety, grade, and impairments. The latter are defined, for the purpose of this study, as whizzing/harsh cleaning, "improper" cleaning, polishing, corroded/porous surfaces, long or deep scratches, cuts, digs, smoothed surfaces, counterstamps, initials, graffiti, re-engraved design elements, bent coins, mount removal, plugs, and other repairs that materially affect the appearance of the coin.

***Table 3* — 1796-1797 Half Dollars by Variety, Grade, and Impairments**

	1796 15 Stars	1796 16 Stars	1797 O-101	1797 O-101a	1797 O-102	Total
MS	9 (2)	3	2	5	1	20 (2)
AU	9 (2)	2 (1)	1	2 (1)	1	15 (4)
XF	6 (2)	4 (1)	4	10 (5)	1 (1)	25 (9)
VF	24 (9)	20 (2)	16 (6)	16 (5)	7 (2)	83 (24)
Fine	18 (6)	15 (6)	5 (2)	19 (4)	20 (9)	77 (27)
VG	4 (4)	12 (5)	5 (1)	3 (1)	4 (1)	28 (12)
Good	1	1	0	3 (3)	0	5 (3)
AG	2 (2)	2 (1)	0	4 (3)	1 (1)	9 (7)
Fair	1	1 (1)	0	5 (3)	0	7 (4)
Poor	0	1	0	0	0	1
Total	74 (27)	61 (17)	33 (9)	67 (25)	35 (14)	270 (92)

Source: Research by author
(n) = Number of coins with one or more major impairments

The above data reveal the following findings. First, the number of 1796-dated and 1797-dated coins in the census is the same (135 1796 pieces and 135 1797 examples). Whether this survival rate of each date reflects that the original mintage of each was equal or approximately so is problematic. It is possible that fewer 1796s were coined, but more were saved as the first year of issue, as often occurs with a new coin design type. The relatively high number of 1796 15 Star pieces, especially in XF and finer grades, lends some credence to this notion. On the other hand, the census data would also seem to indicate that, even if fewer 1796s were minted, the disparity between the two dates is probably less than that estimated by Overton/Parsley (934 1796s and 2,984 1797s).

Second, while the 1796 16 Stars issue (O-102) is considered by many numismatists to be the scarcest of the four known varieties, the census data indicate that the early die state of the 1797 O-101 variety with 33 pieces and the 1797 O-102 variety with 35 examples are much scarcer.

Third, the grade distribution of 1796-1797 half dollars in Table 3 refutes the generally held notion of many numismatists that most surviving examples are in low grade. Indeed, 60 of the 270 coins in the census (nearly 23%) are XF or finer. Moreover, 160 specimens (over 59%) fall into the VF and Fine grade categories. Only 50 pieces (about 18%) grade VG or less.

The 92 coins in Table 3 that exhibit one or more major impairments represent 34% of the 1796-1797 half dollars in the census. The most frequently occurring impairments are deep or noticeable scratches on 31 specimens, plugs on 14 pieces, damage on 13 coins, re-engraving on 17 examples, smoothing on 13 specimens, and "improper" cleaning on 11 pieces (coins that exhibit plugs, re-engraving, or cleaning might well be underreported in the study as these particular impairments are often difficult to discern from photo images). Isolated pinscratches, light hairlines, and shallow scratches are not designated as problems on VF and lower-grade coins in the study, but are listed as impairments on Mint State, AU, and XF pieces.

Interpretation of Findings

The relatively high number of Mint State, AU, and XF 1796-1797 half dollars documented in the study census might be attributed, at least in part, to their "parental" association with the Bank of the United States. As indicated earlier, all three deliveries of these coins were made to the Bank. The minuscule mintage may have been recognized early on by its board directors and employees in the various branches who might have acquired some specimens and passed them on as family heirlooms. These eventually may have been sold to the growing number of coin collectors and dealers in the mid 19th century.

Another possible explanation for the large number of high-grade 1796-1797 survivors is that they (along with other early half dollars) resided in the Bank's vaults for a number of years, or even decades. This might have resulted from their use for backing the Bank's paper notes, and/or because the large mintage of 1795 halves may have temporarily obviated the need for additional half dollars in the channels of commerce.

Some 1796-1797 half dollars (along with other American coins) might have been acquired by visitors from European countries who visited America in the late 18th and early 19th centuries. These coins were undoubtedly Mint State specimens if obtained directly from the Mint. Upon the visitors' return to Europe, they may have been held as souvenirs or family heirlooms for untold periods of time until they eventually found their way back to America, and into the hands of American collectors and dealers.

The large number of surviving Draped Bust Small Eagle halves in VF and Fine grades might be explained by their being pulled from circulation in the first few decades of the 19th century by astute individuals who recognized that they were seen less frequently than other half dollars of the era, and therefore were likely from a very small original mintage. Like their high-grade counterparts, they may have later been sold to the increasing base of coin collectors and dealers.

The recognition that 1796-1797 half dollars were encountered less frequently than other contemporary halves might also help to explain the relatively small number of low-grade (Poor to VG) examples in the study census. Perhaps these pieces spent a greater period of their circulation-life in the more remote areas of the country (i.e., the frontier) where there may have been less likelihood of them being pulled from circulation by individuals having a heightened sense of their low mintage. They therefore continued to become more heavily worn until removed from circulation at a later time (this theory is based on the arguable assumption that the recognition of low mintage and potential scarcity was more likely in urban areas such as Philadelphia, Boston, and New York than in frontier areas).

An alternative explanation of the small number of VG and lower-grade 1796-1797 half dollar examples in the census is that they did not command the prices of higher-grade specimens, so may not have warranted photographs, especially in the late 19th and early 20th centuries when coin photography was still in an early stage of development. If this theory is correct, a greater number of surviving low-grade specimens have apparently been omitted from the present study. A few numismatists responding to the author's February 2005 article in the John Reich Journal expressed this very viewpoint.

While the above notion may have been relevant with respect to 19th and early 20th century auctions, why haven't a greater number of low-grade 1796-1797 half dollars made auction appearances over the past few years, considering their significant increases in value? Even the few AG and Fair examples having sold in recent auctions have realized five-figure prices!

The present author subscribes to the theory that most Draped Bust Small Eagle half dollars were pulled from circulation before they wore to VG and lower levels of preservation, thereby accounting for the relatively few coins that have survived in those grades. Whatever the reason for the sparse number in low grades, it is instructive to note that the tentative census of 1794 dollars in Martin Logies' (2010) treatise displays the same general pattern. He documented a mere five specimens out of a total of 134 dollars of 1794 in grades below Fine (with another three reported to possibly exist).

One final issue regarding the 1796-1797 half dollar census needs to be addressed--that of the frequency (or infrequency) of appearance of some specimens at auction or in fixed price lists. Perusal of the pedigree chain for each coin shows that many pieces display infrequent (or even solitary) appearances. Coin Serial Number 122, for example, a 1796 15 Stars half, reveals only one appearance--an Auction '89 sale. Another 1796 15 Stars specimen (Serial Number 153) likewise has made only one appearance--a November 2009 fixed price list.

Infrequent auction or fixed price list appearances might be attributed to the following. Perhaps coins such as these were held for generations as family heirlooms or as novelties. Or perhaps they appeared in earlier auctions but were not plated (many, if not most, auction appearances of 1796-1797 halves in the 19th, and to some degree in the early 20th century, were not plated). Or maybe they traded primarily via private treaty, or were obtained from a "want list" submitted to a dealer. And some pieces might have resided (and possibly still reside) in "strong hands" (this author is aware of several holders of early scarce/rare coins who have held them for decades without any intention to sell in their lifetime). Then again, some Draped Bust Small Eagle half dollars may have appeared in catalogs not available to the author. Whatever the explanation, it is again significant that many 1794 dollars in Logies' reference display similar patterns of infrequent auction or fixed price list appearances, which probably can be attributed to circumstances similar to those mentioned for 1796-1797 half dollars.

The author wishes to emphasize that the above interpretations of 1796-1797 half dollar census findings are strictly conjectural, and should not be taken or passed on as fact (as so often happens in numismatic research). Indeed, readers of this study may offer perfectly legitimate alternative explanations of the survival rate of Draped Bust Small Eagle half dollars in the various levels of preservation, as well as their frequency of appearance at auction or in fixed price lists.

SUMMARY AND CONCLUSION

This study has documented 270 1796-1797 half dollars, 256 of which the author is highly confident are distinct specimens. He makes no claim that this enumeration represents the extant population of the series. Some examples, for various reasons, may never be documented. They might be buried in some remote location, repose in a shipwreck, lie under the floorboards of an old barn, or reside in a family drawer or bank safe deposit box.

What percent of the extant Draped Bust Small Eagle half dollars might this study have accounted for? Heritage Senior Cataloger and Researcher Mark Borckardt estimates that early U.S. coins generally have a 10% survival rate, a figure with which the present author tends to agree. Applying this survival rate to the original mintage of 3,918 1796-1797 halves, about 392 specimens should, theoretically, still exist. Based on this assumption, the 270-piece census in the study accounts for nearly 69% of the extant population.

How many more 1796-1797 half dollars might be uncovered through further research? And how many more years of examining auction catalogs and fixed price lists, and soliciting information from private collectors, would it take to significantly increase the census of extant specimens? Answers to these questions can only be guessed at, but are certainly relevant in the serious study of any scarce/rare coin series.

Some light (albeit very limited) might be shed on these questions from the following observations. The author's February 2005 *John Reich Journal* article showed 216 Draped Bust Small Eagle half dollars. His special write-up of the four 1796-1797 half dollar varieties in the Bayside New York Collection for the July-August 2008 Heritage ANA sale recorded 246 specimens, an increase of 30 pieces over a three-and-one-half year period. On the other hand, only 15 coins (five of which were from institutional cabinets) have been added to the census in the three-year period from November 2009 to November 2012. In other words, the number of "new discoveries" appears to be decreasing. At this rate, it could be years, if not decades, before significant increases are made to the 1796-1797 half dollar census.

At this point, more definitive statements can be made about the grade distribution of surviving Small Eagle halves than about their survival rate or the time it will take to add more pieces to the census. As mentioned previously, the author based his assessment of the grade of each coin in the census on his experience in examining hundreds of auction-sale and fixed price list images, as well as in describing actual coins while cataloging for Heritage Auctions. While these assessments often differed from grades assigned by auction houses, coin dealers, or third-party certification services, he believes that overall the grade distribution of documented specimens comes close to representing that of the extant population.

INVITATION FOR READER RESPONSE

Readers are invited to respond to this study. In particular, images, descriptions, and pedigrees of 1796-1797 half dollars that have been omitted from the study would be greatly appreciated. Correspondence should be sent to:

Jon P. Amato

PO Box 5535

Albany, NY 12205

or to

JonA@HA.com

Additionally, Heritage Auctions has set up a special page at www.HA.com/JonAmato for readers to view "new 1796-1797 half dollar discoveries" and for other information about 1796-1797 half dollars.

REFERENCES

Adams, John W., *United States Numismatic Literature, Volume I, Nineteenth Century Auction Catalogs*, 1982.

Adams, John W., *United States Numismatic Literature, Volume II*, Twentieth Century Auction Catalogs, 1990.

Amato, Jon P., "An Analysis of 1796-97 Draped Bust Half Dollars," *The Numismatist*, September 2001, pp. 1015-1019, 1088-1091.

Amato, Jon P., "Surviving Draped Bust Half Dollars And Their Grade Distribution," *John Reich Journal*, Vol. 16/Issue 2, February 2005, pp. 12-17.

Amato, Jon P., "A Numismatic Overview of the Draped Bust Half Dollars of 1796-1797 as Illustrated by the Jules Reiver Collection," in *Heritage Auctions' January 2006 Jules Reiver Sale*, Volume III, pp. 107-128.

Amato, Jon P., "A Numismatic Review of the Draped Bust Half Dollars of 1796-1797 as Illustrated by the Bayside, NY Collection of Early Half Dollars," in *Heritage Auctions' ANA Sale* (July 2008) pp. 156-172.

Amato, Jon P., "Breakup of the 1796-1797 Half Dollar Reverse A," *John Reich Journal*, Vol. 22/ Issue 1, May 2012, pp 36-40.

Balulescu, Lano, "The 1796-97 Half Dollars," www.abacoin.com, October 18, 2000.

Bowers and Merena, *The Louis E. Eliasberg, Sr. Collection*, April 1997.

Bowers, Q. David, *Silver Dollars and Trade Dollars of the U.S.*, Vol. 1, 1993.

Bowers, Q. David, *Louis E. Eliasberg, Sr.: King of Coins*, 1996

Bowers, Q. David, *A Guide Book of United States Type Coins*, 2005.

Breen, Walter, An *Encyclopedia of U.S. and Colonial Coins*, 1988.

Brunk, Gregory, *Merchant and Privately Countermarked Coins*, 2003.

Camper, Randy, "Draped Bust Small Eagle Half Dollars: Introducing an Early Numismatic Mystery," *Coin World*, September 3, 2001.

Carlson, Carl, "Tracker: An Introduction to Pedigree Research in the field of Rare American Coins, Carl Carlson and Michael Hodder (eds.), *ANA Centennial Anthology*, 1981, pp. 349-364.

Carothers, Neil, *Fractional Money*, 1930

Cowen, David, *The Origins and Economic Impact of the First Bank of the United States, 1791-1797.*

"Echoes From a Coin Dealer's Sanctum," (author unknown), *The Numismatist,* August 1892, pp. 20-21.

Evans, Dorinda, *The Genius of Gilbert Stuart*, Chapter 5: "The Years in Philadelphia," 1999.

Gengerke, Martin, *American Numismatic Auctions*, 1990.

Goldsborough, Reid, "The Case for Anne Willing Bingham," *Coins*, May 2001, p. 156.

Goldsborough, Reid, "Anne Willing Bingham: The Evidence," http://home.comcast.net/reidgold/draped_busts/debate.html (2010).

Henry, Red, "The Girl on the Bust Coins: Anne Willing Bingham of Philadelphia," http://www.nsdr.org/march2001.htm, December 31, 2002.

Hilt, Robert, *Die Varieties of Early U.S. Coins,* 1980.

Jones, Bill, "Stuart and the Phillie Socialite," *The Numismatist,* June 1996, pp. 684-685.

Julian, Robert, "The Nation's First Halves," *Coins,* March 2000, pp. 34-36.

Kaplan, Edward S., *The Bank of the United States and the American Economy,* 1999.

Lange, David, "Forming a Type Set of Half Dollars," *The Numismatist,* April 1990.

Logies, Martin, *The Flowing Hair Silver Dollars of 1794,* 2010.

Mason, E. L., Mason's *Coin Collectors' Herald,* Vol. 1, June 1879, No. 2.

Mason, George C., *The Life and Works of Gilbert Stuart,* 1879.

Moulton, Karl, *U.S. Numismatic Auction Catalogs, 1990-2000,* 2001.

Overton, Al, *Early Half Dollar Die Varieties,* (Don Parsley, Ed.), 1990, 2005.

Pareick, Jesse, "An Interesting 1796 Bust Half Dollar, " *John Reich Collector's Journal,* December 1996, pp. 28-33.

Snowden, James Ross, *A Description of the Medals of Washington...,* 1861.

Stuart, Jane, "Stuart Portraits of Washington," *Scribner's Monthly,* July 1876, pp. 367-374; "Anecdotes of Gilbert Stuart, " *Scribner's Monthly,* July 1877, pp. 376-382.

Taxay, Don, *The U.S. Mint and Coinage,* 1966.

U.S. Mint Records, National Archives, Philadelphia, Record Group 104.
Bullion Journals, 1794-1831
Bullion Ledgers, 1794-1802
Mint Warrants for Payments Through 1817
Waste Books, 1794-1833

Wells, Jim, "Strokes of Genius: Gilbert Stuart's Brushes with Numismatics," *The Numismatist,* September 2011, pp. 40-46.

ABOUT THE AUTHOR

Jon Amato spent most of his professional life in fields outside of numismatics. He earned a bachelor's degree from Arizona State University and a master's from the State University of New York at Buffalo, both in the field of environmental geography, and a doctorate in economic geography from the University of Toronto. He taught for 20 years in the Departments of Geography and Planning at Buffalo State College and the State University of New York at Albany, and published several works on environmental impacts and planning, agricultural land use analysis, and regional land use planning.

The author also spent 12 years working as a professional economic developer, first with the Arizona Department of Commerce and then with the New York State Department of Economic Development. In Arizona he provided technical assistance to non-metro communities for retaining and attracting businesses. In New York he managed a statewide technical and financial assistance education program to help small- and medium-size manufacturing companies improve their productivity and competitiveness, and served as liaison between the New York State Departments of Economic Development and Environmental Conservation. He also managed a $2 million grant program to assist 17 New York communities in their efforts at economic revitalization. His economic development publications ranged from "The Economic Challenges Facing Rural Arizona" and the "Quality of Life and Economic Development in Rural Arizona" to "Manufacturing Competitiveness and Pollution Prevention in New York" and "Economic Development Technical Assistance Programs Relating to Environmental Compliance/Pollution Prevention."

Amato developed a keen interest in numismatic research in the early 1990s, and by the end of the decade was focusing on the half dollars of 1796-1797. This led to his first numismatic publication entitled "An analysis of 1796-97 Draped Bust Half Dollars," appearing in the September 2001 issue of *The Numismatist.* He presented follow-up reports on research into this coinage series at ANA World's Fair of Money Numismatic Theatres in New York on August 3, 2002 and in Baltimore on July 31, 2003. The feedback received on these endeavors proved invaluable for his ongoing research on Draped Bust Small Eagle halves and ultimately for the publication of this book.

The author joined the U.S coin cataloging staff at Heritage Auctions in Dallas in March 2004. This position gave him the unparalleled opportunity to personally inspect and catalog about 50 Draped Bust Small Eagle half dollars, including those of the Jules Reiver and Bayside New York collections, each of which was noteworthy for having included all four Overton varieties of this fascinating coinage series. This rarely accomplished feat resulted in the author's special write-ups in the catalog for each collection.

Other numismatic works the author has published or co-authored include: "Surviving 1796-97 Draped Bust Half Dollars and Their Grade Distribution," *John Reich Journal*, February 2005; *The Coinage of Augustus Saint-Gaudens as Illustrated by the Philip H. Morse Collection* (with James L. Halperin, Mark Van Winkle, and Gregory Rohan); "Jules Reiver's 1796-1797 Draped Bust Half Dollar Varieties," *John Reich Journal*, April 2007; "The Bayside New York Collection of 1796-1797 Half Dollar Varieties," *John Reich Journal*, November 2008; and "American Indian

Treaty Payments," *The Numismatist*, November 2010. The latter article was awarded Large Club Publications *Best Article* by the Numismatic Literary Guild, August 2011.

The author is a thirty-year member of the American Numismatic Association. He also belongs to the American Numismatic Society, the Central States Numismatic Society, the John Reich Collectors Society, the Liberty Seated Collectors Club, and the Numismatic Bibliomania Society.

Amato went into semi-retirement in April 2010. He still catalogs part-time for Heritage Auctions, and looks forward to other numismatic research projects, and perhaps those in geography and economic development as well.

Weeknights

A Dierbergs School of Cooking Publication

Dierbergs Markets, Inc.
16690 Swingley Ridge Road
Chesterfield, Missouri 63017

This cookbook is a collection of recipes, which has been developed and tested by Dierbergs Home Economists.

ISBN: 978-0-9749955-1-9
First Printing 2007

Cover photograph: Fresh Tomato Pizza Recipe on page 19

Acknowledgements

Director of Marketing and Advertising
John Muckerman

Managing Editor
Gena Bast

Food Editor
Barb Ridenhour

Cookbook Project Manager
Janice Martin

Copywriters
Gena Bast, Therese Lewis

Art Director/Designer
Mike Parker

Dierbergs School of Cooking Managers
Loretta Evans, Ginger Gall, Jennifer Kassel, Nancy Lorenz, Pam Pahl

Photography
Michelle Havens, Group 360 Communications
Dave Casper, Group 360 Communications (pages 4, 5)
Steve Adams, Steve Adams Studio (pages 23, 96)

Food Stylists
Carol Ziemann
Linda Behrends (pages 22, 46, 52)

Food Styling Assistant
Janice Martin

Prop Stylist, Dierbergs Test Kitchen Manager
Karen Hurych

Nutrition Analysis
Trish Farano, D.T.R., Dierbergs Markets
Sherri Hoyt, R.D., Missouri Baptist Medical Center

Recipe Editing
Patty Tomaselli

Contributors
Jack and Mary Billings, Cathy Chipley, Suzanne Corbett, Jan Ford

TABLE OF

contents

Introduction 5

Nutrition Information 7

FROM THE OVEN 8

FROM THE STOVETOP 24

FROM THE SLOW COOKER 42

FROM THE SOUP POT 52

FROM THE GARDEN 64

FROM THE SWEET SHOPPE 82

Recipe Standards 91

Dicing and Chopping 91

Equivalents 92

Minimum Safe Internal Temperatures 92

To Freeze or Not To Freeze 92

Index 94

From left to right: Susan and Greg Dierberg, Bob and Sharon Dierberg, Brian Dierberg, Laura and Dr. Jeff Padousis.

I'd like to thank you for picking up our cookbook, *Weeknights*. When our family gets together for dinner, we find ourselves catching up, laughing, and making a lasting memory. I wish you and your family many happy meals together.

Sincere regards,

Bob Dierberg

Introduction

There are so many benefits to gathering the family around the dinner table for a home-cooked meal. Dinner is a great time for families to connect, to share stories and deepen relationships. At Dierbergs, we want to be an inspiration for creating family meals, with recipes that come together easily and become a tradition at your dinner table for years to come.

Dierbergs School of Cooking first series cookbook, *Entrées*, was so well received, it was clear we were on the right path, serving a purpose in the kitchens of our customers. *Weeknights*, the second in Dierbergs' series cookbooks, provides recipes for quick family meals that are simply delicious and satisfying. The recipes are perfect for those who want to cook and desire to expand their weeknight repertoire.

When you want really good food in a hurry, these recipes are perfect. Want a pizza? Try our Fresh Tomato Pizza (page 19). Craving Chinese? How about Beef and Broccoli Stir-Fry (page 33). We recognize that weeknights can be hectic, so we have highlighted many recipes that can be on your table in 30 minutes or less.

Weeknight family meals. Simply delicious and satisfying.
Gather your family around the dinner table. Let Dierbergs help.

LAURA'S Weeknight Tip

Laura Dierberg Padousis shares creative weeknight suggestions such as time-saving kitchen tips and ideas to round out your meal. Look for her helpful information throughout this cookbook.

prep time 15 minutes

In this cookbook, you'll find extra helpful tips. Look for this graphic on each entrée recipe to quickly determine the recipes which work best with your schedule.

You'll find the Eat Hearty logo, indicating foods meeting heart healthier criteria, on more than half of the entrées (see more information on page 7).

Nutrition Information

Dierbergs Markets along with Missouri Baptist Medical Center, a member of BJC HealthCare, proudly sponsor *Eat Hearty®*, an informational program aimed at helping you choose a heart-healthy eating plan. In *Weeknights*, you'll find heart-healthy recipes identified by the red heart logo shown with the nutrition analysis.

Criteria Used for Calculating Nutrition Information

- Whenever a choice is given, the following are used: The first ingredient; the lesser amount of an ingredient; the larger number of servings.
- Ingredients without specific amounts listed, such as "optional" or "toppings," have not been included in the analysis.
- The nutrition information provided in *Weeknights* was calculated using *Nutritionist Pro*, a nutrition analysis program developed by First DataBank, Inc. for the Hearst Corporation. The information is believed to be reliable and correct.
- The nutrition professionals compiling the information have made every effort to present the most accurate information available, but have undertaken no independent examination, investigation or verification of information provided by original sources. Therefore, Dierbergs assumes no liability and denies any responsibility for incorrect information resulting from the use of the nutrition information provided in *Weeknights*.

Ingredients Used in Nutrition Calculation

- Certain ingredients are considered "standard" for nutrition analysis. They include large eggs, 2% milk, lean ground beef and canned broth. Other ingredient selections were based on information from the USDA and/or readily available brands.
- If a recipe specifies reduced-fat/reduced-sodium products in the ingredient list, these products were used for nutrition analysis.
- Some recipes meet *Eat Hearty* criteria without modification. You may wish to make additional substitutions to further reduce the fat/sodium content of these recipes.

Recipe Criteria

Recipes that have a red heart logo in this cookbook must not exceed the following guidelines per serving:

3 g fat/480 mg sodium*

Beverages (alcoholic beverages have not been considered)
Appetizers
Soups served as an appetizer
Vegetable side dishes
Breads and rolls

5 g fat/720 mg sodium*

Meat salads
Starch side dishes
Salads (vegetable/pasta/fruit)
Desserts
Breakfast breads and muffins

10 g fat/960 mg sodium*

Main dishes
Combination entrées such as spaghetti and meatballs
Entrée soups
Entrée sandwiches

**Sodium levels are a suggested level only. If you are following a sodium-restricted diet, please consult your physician or dietitian for specific recommendations.*

FROM THE

oven

Steak and Potato Pot Pie 10

Meat Loaf Italiano 11

French Onion Beef Sandwiches 12

Open-Faced Tuna Melt 13

Wasabi-Encrusted Tilapia 15

Almond-Encrusted Cod 15

Easy Weeknight Lasagna 16

Light and Easy Chicken Enchiladas 17

Mexican Flatbread Pizza 19

Fresh Tomato Pizza 19

Sausage-Stuffed Spaghetti Pie 20

Maple Harvest Cornbread 21

Quick Herb Muffins 21

Honey Wheat Knots 23

Steak and Potato Pot Pie
Recipe on page 10

Steak and Potato Pot Pie

Forget everything you remember about pot pies. This one is packed with hearty chunks of beef, potatoes, and savory gravy – so good it tastes like it took hours to prepare.

- 1 beef sirloin steak (about 1 pound), partially frozen
- 1 tablespoon vegetable oil
- 3/4 cup chopped onion
- 3/4 cup chopped carrot
- 1 clove garlic, minced
- 1 teaspoon Italian herb seasoning
- 1 can (14 ounces) beef broth
- 1 can (8 ounces) tomato sauce
- 4 1/2 cups peeled and cubed potatoes (about 2 pounds)
- 1 tablespoon cornstarch, dissolved in 2 tablespoons cold water
- 1/2 cup frozen peas
- 1 refrigerated pie crust (1/2 of 15-ounce package)

prep time 30 minutes

Trim any visible fat from beef; cut into bite-size pieces. In large skillet, heat oil over medium-high heat. Add half of the beef; cook stirring occasionally until beef is browned, about 2 to 3 minutes. Remove beef from skillet; set aside. Repeat procedure with remaining beef.

In same skillet, combine cooked beef, onion, and carrot; cook stirring occasionally until onion begins to brown, about 2 to 3 minutes. Stir in garlic and Italian seasoning. Add broth, tomato sauce, and potatoes; bring to a boil. Reduce heat, cover, and simmer until potatoes are tender, about 12 to 15 minutes. Stir in cornstarch mixture until evenly blended. Remove from heat; stir in peas. Divide mixture evenly among six 10-ounce custard cups.

On lightly floured surface, roll pie crust into 12-inch circle. Cut rounds to fit top of custard cups, rerolling dough as needed. Place 1 crust over top of each custard cup. Pierce crust several times. Place on foil-lined baking sheet. Bake in 375°F. oven until crust is golden brown, about 20 to 25 minutes.

Makes 6 servings

MAKE-AHEAD TIP Assemble pot pies the day before; cover and refrigerate. To bake, remove cover and increase baking time by 5 minutes as needed.

Photogragh on page 8

technique savvy

Slicing Raw Meat

Ever wonder how to get super-thin slices of meat or chicken for a recipe? It's really quite simple. When a dish calls for very thin slices of meat or chicken, partially freeze it first. Place the meat in a single layer, cover it with plastic, and put it in the freezer until it's very firm, but not frozen solid. Depending on the size of the pieces and the freezer temperature, this usually takes about 20 to 30 minutes. Then using a sharp knife, carefully cut the meat very thinly across the grain. Now you're ready to cook!

Per serving

Calories 377
Fat 14 g
Cholesterol 31 mg
Sodium 646 mg
Carbohydrate 47 g
Fiber 4 g

Meat Loaf Italiano

Dierbergs Staff Home Economist Jennifer Kassel combines two of her family's favorite comfort foods, pizza and meat loaf, into one satisfying entrée. Place the ingredients in a plastic bag and let the kids help mix it up.

- 1 pound lean ground round
- 1 pound lean ground pork
- 2 eggs, slightly beaten
- 1 1/2 cups pizza sauce (divided)
- 1 cup fresh bread crumbs, OR 3/4 cup dry
- 1/2 cup grated parmesan cheese
- 1/2 cup diced onion
- 1 clove garlic, minced
- 1 1/2 teaspoons Italian herb seasoning
- 1 teaspoon salt
- 1/2 teaspoon ground black pepper
- 4 ounces (1 cup) provel cheese ropes

prep time 15 minutes

Crumble beef and pork into large mixing bowl. Add eggs, 1/2 cup of the pizza sauce, bread crumbs, parmesan, onion, garlic, Italian seasoning, salt, and pepper. Mix gently until combined. (If desired, place ingredients in large reclosable plastic bag; squeeze to mix.)

Line 9 x 5-inch loaf pan with foil; fill with meat mixture. Bake in 375°F. oven for 45 minutes. Remove from oven. Drain off any fat. Turn onto parchment-lined baking sheet. Top with remaining 1 cup pizza sauce and provel cheese. Return to oven; bake until cheese melts and begins to brown, and internal temperature is 165°F., about 10 to 15 minutes. Let stand 10 minutes before slicing.

Makes 6-8 servings

MAKE-AHEAD TIP Line loaf pan with foil as directed; then line with plastic wrap. Fill pan with meat mixture; cover and freeze until solid. Remove meat loaf from pan. Place wrapped meat loaf in freezer-weight reclosable plastic bag. To bake, remove foil and plastic wrap; place frozen meat loaf in foil-lined loaf pan. Increase baking time by about 20 minutes.

LAURA'S Weeknight Tip

When it's meatloaf night, you just have to have mashed potatoes! Pick up your favorite ready-made potatoes from Dierbergs Deli, or from the meat or dairy departments. Keep the Italian flavors going with Zucchini Roma (recipe on page 75) on the side.

ingredient savvy

Meat Loaf Mix

Meat loaf is the quintessential blue-plate special and everyone has their own version of the recipe. Traditionally made with ground beef, meat loaf is even more delicious when you include some fresh ground pork in the mix. Pork adds both body and richness to the flavor and helps keep the meat loaf moist during baking. Substitute fresh ground pork for up to half the amount of ground meat called for in your favorite recipe.

Per serving

Calories 271
Fat 12 g
Cholesterol 130 mg
Sodium 958 mg
Carbohydrate 10 g
Fiber 1 g

French Onion Beef Sandwiches

Savory roast beef, sweet caramelized onions, gooey cheese...are you hungry yet? Dip this hearty sandwich into a bowl of au jus for a stick-to-your-ribs supper.

- 1 tablespoon butter
- 2 large onions, sliced
- 1 teaspoon brown sugar
- 1/3 cup dry white wine or beef broth
- 1/2 teaspoon seasoned pepper
- 1 loaf (8 ounces) Dierbergs French baguette, cut in half lengthwise
- 3/4 pound sliced Deli roast beef
- 4 ounces sliced gruyére, swiss, or fontina cheese
- 1 package (0.6 to 1.0 ounce) au jus gravy mix, prepared according to package directions

prep time **30** minutes

In large skillet, melt butter over medium-high heat. Add onions and brown sugar; cover and cook until onions wilt. Uncover and cook stirring frequently until onions are golden brown, about 20 minutes. Stir in wine and seasoned pepper; cook stirring frequently until liquid evaporates, about 3 minutes.

Place bottom half of bread cut-side up on sheet of foil. Top with beef, caramelized onions, cheese, and top half of bread. Wrap in foil; place on baking sheet. Bake in 400°F. oven until warm, about 10 minutes. Cut into pieces; serve with au jus gravy.

Makes 4-6 servings

ingredient savvy

Say "Cheese"

Wherever you go in the world, it's easy to find a cheese you'll love.

Gruyére (groo-YEHR) is perhaps Switzerland's most famous cheese. Made in 100-pound wheels, then aged for 10 to 12 months, gruyére has a pale yellow color, medium-size holes, and a rich, sweet, nutty flavor. It's also made in France and other countries.

Swiss cheese refers to the family of cheeses with pale yellow flesh, a nutty flavor, and large eyes or holes.

Semi-firm yet creamy, fontina is one of Italy's most popular cheeses. It is pale yellow, has a mild, slightly nutty flavor, and melts to creamy perfection. Fontina is also made in Denmark, France, and the United States.

Per serving

Calories 314
Fat 11 g
Cholesterol 52 mg
Sodium 1223 mg
Carbohydrate 28 g
Fiber 1 g

Open-Faced Tuna Melt

A blue-plate special gets dressed up for dinner. A dash of Old Bay seasoning wakes up the flavor of this hot and toasty classic.

1/2 cup light mayonnaise
1 tablespoon Dijon-style mustard
1 teaspoon Old Bay or Cajun/Creole seasoning
2 cans (6 ounces each) water-packed solid white albacore tuna, drained and flaked
1/3 cup sliced green onion
1 can (2.25 ounces) sliced ripe olives, drained
6 slices Dierbergs soft Italian or sourdough bread, lightly toasted
3 slices havarti or other white cheese, cut in half

In medium bowl, combine mayonnaise, mustard, and seasoning. Add tuna, green onion, and olives; gently stir until combined.

Place toasted bread on foil-lined baking sheet. Divide tuna mixture evenly among bread slices. Place 1 cheese slice on each sandwich. Broil 6 inches from heat source until cheese is melted and bubbly, about 2 to 3 minutes.

Makes 4-6 servings

LAURA'S Weeknight Tip *You can keep everything on-hand that you'll need to make this hot, cheesy sandwich. Try it on an English muffin half or small pre-baked pizza crust for a change of pace. Serve yellow bell pepper strips with ranch dip on the side.*

ingredient savvy

Albacore Tuna

There are many varieties of tuna in the world, and all are members of the mackerel family. Tuna has a richly flavored, firm-textured flesh that cooks up flaky and tender. Albacore is the highest in fat of all varieties. It has a light pinkish-white to tan color, a mild flavor, and is the only variety that can be labeled *white*.

Canned tuna is available in three grades: *solid or fancy*, which contains large pieces; *chunk*, which is smaller pieces; and *flaked*, usually tiny pieces. Tuna is a great source of Omega-3 fatty acids, which are beneficial to heart health.

Per serving

Calories 290
Fat 16 g
Cholesterol 44 mg
Sodium 840 mg
Carbohydrate 18 g
Fiber 1 g

Almond-Encrusted Cod

Wasabi-Encrusted Tilapia

With a flavor similar to horseradish, wasabi adds a punch of flavor to crispy-coated fish fillets. It's just the thing to wake up a weeknight meal!

- 1 1/2 pounds tilapia fillets (or orange roughy, grouper, or salmon)
- 1 teaspoon wasabi powder
- 1 teaspoon water
- 1/3 cup light mayonnaise
- 1 clove garlic, minced
- 1/2 cup fresh bread crumbs
- 2 teaspoons vegetable oil
- 1/2 teaspoon Old Bay seasoning

ready in 25 minutes

Place fish in shallow baking dish that has been lightly coated with no-stick cooking spray.

In small bowl, dissolve wasabi powder in water; let stand 5 minutes. Stir in mayonnaise and garlic. Spread over fish.

In small bowl, combine bread crumbs, oil, and seasoning. Sprinkle over top of fish. Bake in 400°F. oven until fish flakes easily with fork and internal temperature is 145°F., about 10 minutes per inch of thickness.

Makes 6 servings

TIP Wasabi powder heat varies by brand. This recipe was tested with Sushi Chef brand wasabi.

Per serving

Calories 116
Fat 7 g
Cholesterol 4 mg
Sodium 211 mg
Carbohydrate 5 g
Fiber <1 g

Almond-Encrusted Cod

Almonds and panko (Japanese bread crumbs) make a crispy, crunchy coating for tender, flaky cod. Add a squeeze of fresh lemon to bring out the flavors.

- 1/2 cup slivered almonds, toasted
- 1/4 cup panko bread crumbs
- 1 teaspoon lemon pepper seasoning
- 1/4 cup egg substitute
- 4 frozen cod loins (about 1 pound), thawed

ready in 30 minutes

Place almonds in work bowl of food processor fitted with steel knife blade; pulse until finely chopped. In shallow dish, combine chopped almonds, panko crumbs, and lemon pepper. Place egg substitute in second shallow dish. Dip fish into egg, then coat with crumbs. Place on foil-lined baking sheet. Bake in 425°F. oven until fish flakes easily with fork and internal temperature is 145°F., about 15 minutes (about 10 minutes per inch of thickness).

Makes 4 servings

Per serving

Calories 211
Fat 9 g
Cholesterol 48 mg
Sodium 181 mg
Carbohydrate 6 g
Fiber 2 g

Easy Weeknight Lasagna

Lasagna – it's not just for weekends anymore. Loretta Evans, Dierbergs Staff Home Economist, has a delicious version that is just the right size for a family dinner, and it's ready in no time.

ingredient savvy

No-Boil Noodles

Second only to sliced bread, no-boil noodles just might be the greatest thing ever! No more waiting until the weekend to enjoy lasagna and other baked pasta dishes that take a whole afternoon to prepare. When using no-boil noodles in recipes, be sure that the top layer of noodles is covered in sauce so it doesn't dry out during baking.

- 1 1/2 cups light spaghetti sauce (divided)
- 1 container (15 ounces) light ricotta cheese
- 1 package (10 ounces) frozen spinach, thawed and well drained
- 1/4 cup egg substitute, OR 1 egg, slightly beaten
- 1 teaspoon dried basil
- 1 clove garlic, minced
- 6 no-boil lasagna noodles
- 4 ounces (1 cup) finely shredded Italian cheese blend (divided)

prep time 15 minutes

Lightly coat 8-inch square baking pan with no-stick cooking spray. Spread 2 tablespoons of the spaghetti sauce on bottom of pan.

In medium bowl, combine ricotta cheese, spinach, egg substitute, basil, and garlic. Place 2 lasagna noodles over sauce in pan. Top with half of the ricotta cheese mixture and sprinkle with 1/4 cup of the shredded cheese. Top with 2 more noodles, the remaining ricotta cheese mixture, and another 1/4 cup shredded cheese. Top with remaining 2 noodles and pour remaining spaghetti sauce over top. Sprinkle with remaining 1/2 cup shredded cheese.

Cover and bake in 350°F. oven for 30 minutes; remove cover and bake until cheese is lightly browned, about 10 to 15 minutes. Let stand 10 to 15 minutes before cutting into squares.

Makes 6 servings

Laura's Weeknight Tip *If you're bored with garlic bread, serve sliced French bread with small dishes of olive oil for dipping. Plain extra virgin olive oil has a lot of flavor. Or try one of the seasoned olive oils specially made for dipping.*

Per serving

Calories 235
Fat 8 g
Cholesterol 47 mg
Sodium 473 mg
Carbohydrate 23 g
Fiber 3 g

Light and Easy Chicken Enchiladas

When you're in the mood for Mexican food, these easy, cheesy, lightened-up enchiladas are just the thing. They have plenty of flavor without the extra calories.

1 teaspoon vegetable oil
1 pound boneless, skinless chicken breast halves, cut into bite-size pieces
1/2 cup finely chopped onion
1 can (10 3/4 ounces) low-fat cream of celery soup
1 can (4.5 ounces) chopped green chiles, drained
1 carton (8 ounces) light dairy sour cream
8 large fat-free tortillas (8-inch diameter)
1 can (10 ounces) enchilada sauce
4 ounces (1 cup) shredded 2% milk colby/monterey jack cheese

prep time **20** minutes

In large nonstick skillet, heat oil over medium-high heat. Add chicken and onion; cook stirring frequently until chicken is no longer pink, about 4 to 5 minutes. Stir in soup, green chiles, and sour cream.

Spoon 1/2 cup filling down center of each tortilla; roll tortillas around filling. Place tortillas, seam-side down, in 9 x 13-inch baking dish that has been lightly coated with no-stick cooking spray. Pour enchilada sauce over top; sprinkle with cheese. Cover and bake in 375°F. oven until bubbly around edges and center is hot, about 25 to 30 minutes.

Makes 4-6 servings

TIP Enchiladas can be made, covered, and refrigerated overnight. Increase baking time by about 15 minutes.

LAURA'S Weeknight Tip *Let everyone snack on grape tomatoes while the enchiladas bake. A package of black beans and rice mix is an easy way to finish the meal when you're pressed for time.*

technique savvy

Chicken Tonight or Any Night

If chicken is frequently on the menu at your house, here's a great time-saving idea. Take advantage of sales and stock up on boneless, skinless chicken breast halves. Cut them into bite-size pieces or strips as you would use them in your favorite recipes. Then place the amount you need for a recipe in a freezer-weight reclosable plastic bag. Seal the bag, label, and freeze. Now you're one step ahead for making weeknight casseroles, stir-fries, soups, and all sorts of dishes.

Per serving

Calories 364
Fat 10 g
Cholesterol 52 mg
Sodium 964 mg
Carbohydrate 44 g
Fiber 2 g

Fresh Tomato Pizza

Mexican Flatbread Pizza

These tasty south-of-the-border-style pizzas are ready in less time than it takes to cruise through your favorite fast-food place. Add your favorite toppings and you're all set!

1 pound lean ground beef
1 package (1.25 ounces) reduced-sodium taco seasoning
1/2 cup water
3 sheets flatbread, OR 4 large flour tortillas (8-inch diameter)
Vegetable oil
1/2 cup salsa
1 package (8 ounces) shredded Mexican cheese blend
Shredded iceberg lettuce, diced tomato, salsa, dairy sour cream

ready in 20 minutes

Heat medium skillet over medium-high heat. Crumble ground beef into skillet; cook stirring occasionally until browned, about 5 to 6 minutes. Drain off any fat. Stir in taco seasoning and water. Cook until liquid is absorbed, about 2 to 3 minutes.

Place flatbread on baking sheet; lightly brush with oil. Bake in 400°F. oven until lightly browned, about 5 minutes. Spread about 2 to 3 tablespoons salsa over each toasted flatbread. Sprinkle 1/4 cup of the cheese over each. Top with meat and remaining cheese. Bake until cheese melts, about 3 minutes. Cut into serving-size pieces. Top with lettuce, tomato, salsa, and sour cream.

Makes 4-6 servings

Per serving

Calories 368
Fat 18 g
Cholesterol 71 mg
Sodium 1019 mg
Carbohydrate 24 g
Fiber 2 g

Fresh Tomato Pizza

All it takes are a few simple ingredients to give pizza a bold, fresh flavor. Purchase pre-baked pizza crust to make this extra easy.

1 pre-baked thin pizza crust (12-inch diameter)
2 cups seeded and chopped tomatoes, or halved grape tomatoes
1 package (8 ounces) shredded Italian cheese blend (divided)
2 cloves garlic, minced
Coarse salt and freshly ground black pepper to taste
1 package (3/4 ounce) fresh basil, thinly sliced into shreds (about 1/2 cup)

ready in 25 minutes

Place crust on pizza pan or baking sheet. In medium bowl, combine tomatoes, 1 cup of the cheese, and garlic; toss until well mixed. Arrange over crust. Season with salt and pepper. Top with remaining cheese. Bake in 450°F. oven until cheese melts, about 10 to 12 minutes. Sprinkle basil over cooked pizza.

Makes 6 servings

Per serving

Calories 274
Fat 13 g
Cholesterol 27 mg
Sodium 546 mg
Carbohydrate 27 g
Fiber 2 g

Sausage-Stuffed Spaghetti Pie

Here's a whole new way to love spaghetti. Serve a wedge of this savory pie with your favorite red sauce, some breadsticks, and a crisp salad.

- 1 package (16 ounces) spaghetti
- 1 cup ricotta cheese
- 1/2 cup grated parmesan cheese
- 2 eggs, slightly beaten
- 1 clove garlic, minced
- 1/2 teaspoon dried basil
- 1/2 teaspoon dried oregano
- 1 pound bulk Italian sausage
- 1 cup chopped green bell pepper
- 1 cup chopped onion
- 1 package (8 ounces) finely shredded mozzarella cheese (divided)
- 1 jar (25 to 30 ounces) spaghetti sauce

prep time 25 minutes

In large pot of rapidly boiling water, cook spaghetti according to package directions. Rinse with cold water; drain well. In large bowl, combine cooked spaghetti, ricotta cheese, parmesan, eggs, garlic, basil, and oregano. Toss until well combined and spaghetti is coated; set aside.

In large skillet, cook sausage over medium-high heat stirring frequently for 3 to 4 minutes. Add bell pepper and onion; cook stirring frequently until sausage is no longer pink, about 4 to 5 minutes. Drain off any fat.

Press half of the spaghetti mixture in bottom of 9-inch springform pan that has been lightly coated with no-stick cooking spray. Top with 1/2 cup of the mozzarella, the sausage mixture, and another 1/2 cup mozzarella. Press remaining spaghetti mixture on top. Top with remaining 1 cup mozzarella.

Bake in 350°F. oven until heated through and cheese is lightly browned on top, about 30 to 35 minutes. Let stand until set, about 10 to 15 minutes.

Pour spaghetti sauce into medium microwave-safe bowl. Microwave (high) for 5 to 6 minutes, stirring once, until heated through. Remove sides of springform pan. Cut spaghetti pie into wedges; top each serving with spaghetti sauce.

Makes 8 servings

technique savvy

To Rinse or Not to Rinse

When asked whether or not to rinse pasta after cooking, the answer is decidedly yes and no. The correct answer depends on how you will use it. When you're making pasta for salads, rinse the cooked pasta with cool water to remove the excess starch. Drain it well and toss with just a bit of oil to keep the pieces separate.

Don't rinse pasta if you will serve it hot. The starch will help the sauce cling better and that's what we like. If pasta has cooled too much, simply rinse it gently with hot water, drain well, add sauce, and enjoy!

Per serving

Calories 637
Fat 27 g
Cholesterol 126 mg
Sodium 1001 mg
Carbohydrate 63 g
Fiber 5 g

Maple Harvest Cornbread

Just about any bowl of soup or pot of chili tastes better with a square of warm cornbread alongside. Pumpkin and Maple Butter make this version moist, sweet, and delicious.

- 1 package (6.5 to 8.5 ounces) cornbread mix
- 1 egg
- 1/2 cup pure pumpkin
- 1/4 cup milk
- 1/4 cup real maple syrup
- Maple Butter (optional)

ready in 30 minutes

In medium bowl, stir cornbread mix to break up lumps; set aside. In 2-cup glass measure, stir together egg, pumpkin, milk, and syrup until well blended. Stir into cornbread mix until just blended. Pour into 8-inch square baking pan that has been lightly coated with no-stick cooking spray. Bake in 375°F. oven until wooden pick inserted in center comes out clean, about 18 to 20 minutes. If desired, serve with Maple Butter.

Makes 9 servings

Per serving without Maple Butter

Calories 125
Fat 3 g
Cholesterol 25 mg
Sodium 240 mg
Carbohydrate 22 g
Fiber 2 g

Maple Butter

- 1/4 cup butter, softened
- 1 tablespoon real maple syrup

In small bowl, stir together butter and syrup until combined.

Makes 1/4 cup

Quick Herb Muffins

Food historian, cookbook author, and Certified Culinary Professional Suzanne Corbett blends her love of history into every class she teaches at Dierbergs School of Cooking. These tender, herb-scented muffins are one of her favorite recipes.

- 2 cups self-rising flour
- 1 carton (8 ounces) dairy sour cream
- 1 cup butter, melted
- 2 tablespoons fresh thyme
- 1 tablespoon minced fresh chives

ready in 20 minutes

In medium bowl, stir together flour, sour cream, melted butter, and herbs until just blended. Lightly coat mini-muffin cups with no-stick cooking spray or line with paper muffin cups. Spoon batter into muffin cups, filling to top. Bake in 375°F. oven until lightly browned, about 12 to 15 minutes.

Makes about 36 mini-muffins

TIP If desired, substitute the following for the 2 cups self-rising flour: 2 cups sifted all-purpose flour, 3 teaspoons baking powder, and 1/4 teaspoon salt.

Per 2 mini muffins

Calories 172
Fat 14 g
Cholesterol 34 mg
Sodium 185 mg
Carbohydrate 11 g
Fiber <1 g

Honey Wheat Knots

Hot roll mix makes these warm, soft, homemade rolls easy to make and hard to resist. We know you can't eat just one!

- 1 package (16 ounces) hot roll mix
- 1 cup hot (120° to 130°F.) water
- 2 tablespoons butter, softened
- 1 egg, slightly beaten
- 3 tablespoons wheat germ
- 3 tablespoons honey
- Honey Butter Glaze

Prepare dough according to package directions, stirring in wheat germ and honey along with water, butter, and egg. Turn dough out onto lightly floured surface; set mixing bowl aside. Knead as directed on package, sprinkling with additional flour as needed to reduce stickiness. Cover dough with mixing bowl; let rest for 5 minutes.

Divide dough into 16 equal-size pieces. 1 Roll each piece of dough into 9-inch rope; 2 gently tie into knot. Place on parchment-lined baking sheets. Cover and let rise in warm place until doubled in size, about 30 minutes.

Bake in 375°F. oven until golden brown, about 12 to 15 minutes. Brush Honey Butter Glaze over warm rolls.

Makes 16 rolls

Honey Butter Glaze

- 2 tablespoons butter, softened
- 2 tablespoons honey

In small bowl, combine butter and honey. Microwave (high) for 30 seconds; stir to combine.

Makes 1/4 cup

HEART-HEALTHY TIP Omit Honey Butter Glaze.

Per roll Calories 139; Fat 3 g; Cholesterol 17 mg; Sodium 194 mg; Carbohydrate 24 g; Fiber <1 g

technique savvy

Step-by-Step Instructions

Per roll

Calories 160
Fat 4 g
Cholesterol 21 mg
Sodium 194 mg
Carbohydrate 26 g
Fiber <1 g

FROM THE

stovetop

Mediterranean Chicken Orzo 26

Chicken Piccata Penne 27

Skillet Turkey Tetrazzini 29

Hoisin Pork Medallions with Asparagus 30

Pork Tenderloin Diane 31

Asian Lettuce Wraps 32

Beef and Broccoli Stir-Fry 33

Bistro Beef Medallions 34

Weeknight Beef Stroganoff 36

Monterey Wild Mushroom Risotto 37

Baja Fish Tacos 39

Savory Salmon Cakes 40

Piquant Garlic Shrimp 41

Mediterranean Chicken Orzo
Recipe on page 26

technique savvy

Step-by-Step Instructions

Mediterranean Chicken Orzo

One pan is all you need to create this quick chicken dinner filled with sun-drenched Mediterranean flavors. Add a crisp salad and you're set.

- 1 can (2.25 ounces) sliced kalamata or ripe olives, drained
- 1/3 cup chopped oil-packed sun-dried tomatoes, plus 1 tablespoon sun-dried tomato oil
- 1 tablespoon balsamic vinegar
- 1 teaspoon dried basil (divided)
- 1 pound chicken tenders
- 1 can (14 ounces) reduced-sodium chicken broth
- 1 cup orzo or rosamarina pasta
- 2 ounces (1/2 cup) crumbled feta cheese

In medium bowl, toss together olives, sun-dried tomatoes, vinegar, and 1/2 teaspoon of the basil; set aside.

1 If desired, remove tendons from chicken.

In large nonstick skillet, heat the 1 tablespoon sun-dried tomato oil over high heat. Add chicken and sprinkle remaining 1/2 teaspoon basil over top; cook until browned on one side, about 2 minutes. Turn tenders and push to one side of skillet. Add broth and orzo; bring to a boil. Reduce heat, cover, and simmer until liquid is absorbed, about 12 minutes.

Remove chicken from skillet. Stir half of the olive mixture into orzo. Spoon orzo mixture onto 4 individual serving plates; top with chicken, feta, and remaining olive mixture.

Makes 4 servings

LAURA'S Weeknight Tip *Partner this colorful chicken entrée with some crusty cheese bread. While the chicken cooks, slice a baguette and lightly butter one side of each slice. Sprinkle with a little asiago or parmesan cheese and some Italian seasoning, if you like. Then bake until the cheese melts.*

Photograph on page 24

Per serving

Calories 419
Fat 16 g
Cholesterol 55 mg
Sodium 586 mg
Carbohydrate 40 g
Fiber 2 g

Chicken Piccata Penne

Chicken and pasta never had it so good! Crisp white wine, tangy lemon juice, and capers give the light sauce plenty of fresh Italian flavor.

1 tablespoon olive oil
1 1/2 pounds boneless, skinless chicken breast halves, cut into bite-size pieces
2 cloves garlic, minced
1/3 cup flour
1 can (14 ounces) chicken broth
1/4 cup fresh lemon juice
1/4 cup dry white wine
1/4 cup capers, rinsed and drained
2 teaspoons Italian herb seasoning
1 box (16 ounces) penne pasta, cooked according to package directions
1/3 cup chopped fresh parsley

ready in 25 minutes

In large skillet, heat olive oil over medium-high heat. Add chicken and garlic; cook stirring occasionally until no longer pink, about 4 to 5 minutes.

Stir in flour; cook stirring occasionally for 1 minute. Whisk in broth, lemon juice, and wine; cook until mixture thickens, about 1 minute. Stir in capers and Italian seasoning. Add cooked pasta; toss until well mixed. Sprinkle parsley over top.

Makes 8 servings

LAURA'S Weeknight Tip

This delicious recipe is so simple to make. Asparagus Gremolata (recipe on page 78) with its lemony-garlic topping is all you need to make a terrific meal.

technique savvy

Precooking Pasta

Love pasta but hate to wait? Here's a time-saving trick: Cook enough pasta for two meals at the same time. Eat some tonight and save the rest for tomorrow.

Cook pasta just until it is *al dente*, which means it is tender yet firm. Then drain the pasta well. Place tomorrow's portion in a reclosable plastic bag and add 1 tablespoon olive or vegetable oil; seal bag and refrigerate. To reheat, place pasta in a colander over the sink, run hot water over it, and it's ready for your favorite sauce.

Per serving

Calories 319
Fat 3 g
Cholesterol 33 mg
Sodium 328 mg
Carbohydrate 48 g
Fiber 2 g

Skillet Turkey Tetrazzini

Serve up turkey leftovers in style! We've streamlined the time-honored casserole into a stovetop skillet sensation that's ready in minutes. It's also delicious with chicken.

- 2 tablespoons butter
- 1 package (8 ounces) sliced cremini mushrooms
- 2 cloves garlic, minced
- 1 can (14 ounces) chicken broth
- 1 cup water
- 1 tablespoon dry sherry
- 8 ounces spaghetti, broken in half
- 2 cups cooked turkey, cubed
- 2 cups half-and-half, at room temperature
- 1 cup frozen peas
- 1/2 cup grated parmesan cheese (divided)
- 1 tablespoon minced fresh parsley
- Freshly ground black pepper to taste

ready in 25 minutes

In large skillet, melt butter over medium-high heat. Add mushrooms and garlic; cook stirring occasionally until mushrooms are lightly browned, about 4 minutes. Add broth, water, and sherry; bring to a boil. Stir in spaghetti. Reduce heat, cover, and simmer until most of the liquid is absorbed, about 10 minutes.

Stir in turkey, half-and-half, and peas. Cook stirring occasionally until pasta is tender and sauce is slightly thickened, about 5 minutes. Remove from heat; stir in half of the parmesan, parsley, and pepper. Serve with remaining parmesan.

Makes 4-6 servings

HEART-HEALTHY TIP Use fat-free half-and-half.

Per serving Calories 373; Fat 9 g; Cholesterol 53 mg; Sodium 512 mg; Carbohydrate 42 g; Fiber 3 g

LAURA'S Weeknight Tip *Pop a loaf of Dierbergs Bakery ready-to-bake whole wheat bread into the oven while you finish the Tetrazzini. Serve this family-style, right from the skillet along with the hot, crusty bread.*

ingredient savvy

Sherry

Sherry, like Madeira, Marsala, and Port, is a fortified wine which has a dash of brandy or another spirit added during fermentation. Available at every level of quality, sherry is usually a pale golden color and may be dry or sweet.

Dry sherry has a mild nutty flavor and is ideal for meat and poultry recipes, as well as Asian dishes. Cream sherry is much sweeter and fuller in flavor, and is best used in desserts.

Store sherry tightly capped at room temperature. Avoid products labeled cooking sherry, which contain a fair amount of salt.

Per serving

Calories 425
Fat 19 g
Cholesterol 82 mg
Sodium 464 mg
Carbohydrate 37 g
Fiber 3 g

Hoisin Pork Medallions with Asparagus

Tender pork and crisp asparagus spears are a delectable combination. Hoisin sauce adds a rich sweetness to this flavorful dish.

- 1 pork tenderloin (about 1 1/4 pounds)
- 1 to 2 teaspoons coarsely ground black pepper
- 1/4 cup hoisin sauce
- 2 tablespoons honey
- 2 tablespoons dry sherry (optional)
- 2 tablespoons soy sauce
- 1 tablespoon vegetable oil
- 1 pound asparagus, trimmed and cut into bite-size pieces (about 3 cups)
- 2 cloves garlic, minced
- 1 teaspoon minced fresh ginger root
- 1/4 cup water

ready in 30 minutes

Trim fat and silver skin from tenderloin. Cut pork into 1-inch-thick medallions; flatten slightly with heel of hand. Place in shallow dish; season medallions with pepper. In 1-cup glass measure, combine hoisin sauce, honey, sherry, and soy sauce. Pour about 1/4 cup of the marinade over pork; reserve remaining marinade for stir-fry. Let pork stand for 15 minutes. Drain pork; discard marinade.

In large nonstick skillet, heat oil over medium-high heat. Add pork; cook until no longer pink, about 3 to 4 minutes per side. Transfer meat to platter; cover to keep warm.

In same skillet, combine asparagus, garlic, and ginger; stir-fry until crisp-tender, about 4 minutes. Stir in reserved 1/4 cup marinade and water; cook for 1 minute. Serve with pork.

Makes 4 servings

TIP See Removing Silver Skin information on page 31.

LAURA'S Weeknight Tip *For a nice change of pace, pick up a package of jasmine rice and follow the cooking directions. The aroma will remind you of popcorn and the mild nutty flavor is the perfect accompaniment to Asian dishes. Fortune cookies are fun for dessert!*

ingredient savvy

Asian Sauces

Hoisin sauce is to Asian cuisine as ketchup is to American dining. This thick, sweet, and spicy – but not hot – reddish brown sauce is made from soybeans, garlic, and various spices. It adds wonderful flavor to meat and chicken dishes.

Oyster sauce is a combination of oysters, brine, and soy sauce. Opposite of what you might think, it actually has a very subtle flavor that adds a richness to dishes.

Plum sauce is an Asian classic with a bit of a sweet and sour flavor. Often served with duck, it is also known as duck sauce.

Tightly covered in their original glass jars, these sauces will keep indefinitely in the refrigerator.

Per serving

Calories 271
Fat 8 g
Cholesterol 85 mg
Sodium 780 mg
Carbohydrate 19 g
Fiber 2 g

Pork Tenderloin Diane

Impress that special someone or the whole family any night of the week. And there are no reservations required!

- 1 pork tenderloin (about 1 1/4 pounds)
- 2 teaspoons lemon pepper seasoning
- 1 tablespoon butter
- 1/4 cup brandy or chicken broth
- 1 tablespoon fresh lemon juice
- 1 tablespoon Worcestershire sauce
- 2 teaspoons Dijon-style mustard
- 1/4 cup heavy whipping cream
- Chopped fresh parsley (optional)

ready in 25 minutes

Trim fat and silver skin from tenderloin. Cut pork into 1-inch-thick medallions; flatten slightly with heel of hand. Season medallions with lemon pepper.

In large skillet, melt butter over medium-high heat. Add medallions; cook until no longer pink, about 3 to 4 minutes per side. Transfer meat to platter; cover to keep warm.

In same skillet, combine brandy, lemon juice, Worcestershire, and mustard; stir to scrape browned bits from bottom of pan. Stir in whipping cream; cook over medium heat until heated through, about 1 to 2 minutes. Serve sauce over pork. If desired, garnish with parsley.

Makes 4 servings

LAURA'S Weeknight Tip *Keep some convenient side dishes on hand and you're ready for anything! The ready-to-cook green beans from the produce section are a real time-saver and cooking directions are right on the package. One of the long grain and wild rice blends rounds this meal out nicely.*

technique savvy

Removing Silver Skin

Silver skin is a thin, translucent membrane that covers pork tenderloin. It is best to remove and discard it before cooking to make the meat more tender and prevent it from curling. Use a sharp knife to loosen the silver skin and gently scrape it away; or grasp it with a paper towel and pull it from the tenderloin.

Per serving

Calories 218
Fat 10 g
Cholesterol 90 mg
Sodium 357 mg
Carbohydrate 2 g
Fiber 0 g

Asian Lettuce Wraps

Serve up a little midweek fun with this hands-on wrap. Fill cool, crisp lettuce leaves with savory pork filling spiked with plum sauce and fresh ginger. Roll them up and watch them disappear!

- 1 pound lean ground pork
- 2 cloves garlic, minced
- 1/8 teaspoon salt
- 1 jar (9.2 ounces) plum sauce (Kikkoman)
- 1 can (8 ounces) water chestnuts, coarsely chopped
- 1/4 cup diced red bell pepper
- 1/4 cup sliced green onion
- 1 tablespoon minced fresh ginger root
- 1 teaspoon dark sesame oil
- Iceberg lettuce leaves

ready in 30 minutes

Heat wok or large skillet over medium-high heat. Add pork, garlic, and salt; stir-fry until pork is no longer pink, about 7 minutes. Drain any excess fat. Add plum sauce, water chestnuts, bell pepper, green onion, ginger root, and sesame oil. Cook stirring often until pork is evenly coated with sauce and mixture is heated through, about 1 to 2 minutes.

To serve, spoon generous 1/4 cup warm pork mixture into lettuce leaves. Roll up to enclose filling. Serve immediately.

Makes 4-6 servings

TIP For crisp lettuce cups, core lettuce head and run hot tap water onto the opening. Immediately plunge lettuce head into large bowl of ice water. Lettuce leaves will separate easily.

LAURA'S Weeknight Tip *This is a great dinner when you want something light and really quick. Place the pork mixture on the table alongside a bowl of lettuce leaves and let everyone make their own wraps.*

ingredient savvy

Ginger Root

Sweet and slightly peppery, fresh ginger is a tan, knobby root found in the Produce Department. Just break off a piece the size you need. If you buy extra, use the edge of a spoon to scrape off the peel, then mince the entire piece. Place in a small freezer-weight plastic bag. Roll the bag up to form a log; secure with a rubber band. Freeze for up to 6 months. Slice off frozen rounds as needed.

Dried ginger has a very different flavor and is not interchangeable in recipes specifying fresh ginger.

Per serving

Calories 189
Fat 3 g
Cholesterol 43 mg
Sodium 326 mg
Carbohydrate 22 g
Fiber 1 g

Beef and Broccoli Stir-Fry

The heady aroma of fresh ginger and garlic will get everyone to the table almost as fast as you can make this colorful entrée. Try it with pork or chicken, too.

- 1 beef flank steak (about 1 pound), partially frozen
- 1 tablespoon cornstarch
- 1 tablespoon lite soy sauce
- 2 teaspoons vegetable oil
- 1 tablespoon minced fresh ginger root
- 3 cloves garlic, minced
- 1/2 pound broccoli, cut into bite-size pieces (about 2 cups)
- 1 package (8 ounces) sliced mushrooms
- 1/4 cup oyster sauce
- 1/4 cup thinly sliced green onion
- Hot cooked rice

ready in 30 minutes

Cut beef diagonally across the grain into very thin slices; cut into 2-inch pieces. In medium bowl, stir together meat, cornstarch, and soy sauce.

In wok or large skillet, heat oil over medium-high heat. Add meat mixture, ginger, and garlic; stir-fry until meat is browned, about 3 to 4 minutes. Add broccoli, mushrooms, and oyster sauce. Cover and cook stirring occasionally until broccoli is crisp-tender, about 3 to 4 minutes. Stir in green onion. Serve over hot cooked rice.

Makes 4 servings

TIP See Slicing Raw Meat information on page 10 and Asian Sauce information on page 30.

VARIATIONS

Pork and Broccoli Stir-Fry Substitute 1 pound pork tenderloin, trimmed of fat and silver skin, and cut into bite-size strips, for the flank steak.

Per serving without rice Calories 211; Fat 6 g; Cholesterol 68 mg; Sodium 910 mg; Carbohydrate 14 g; Fiber 2 g

Chicken and Broccoli Stir-Fry Substitute 1 pound chicken tenders, cut into bite-size pieces, for the flank steak.

Per serving without rice Calories 169; Fat 4 g; Cholesterol 43 mg; Sodium 901 mg; Carbohydrate 14 g; Fiber 2 g

technique savvy

Stir-Fry

Create a quick and colorful stir-fry meal from almost anything you have on hand. Just follow these tips:

- Chop, slice, and measure everything before you begin cooking.
- Cut foods of similar texture into the same-size pieces for even cooking.
- Use a wok or large skillet to allow room for stirring foods as they cook.
- Choose peanut or vegetable oil for cooking, not olive oil or butter.
- Start with ingredients that need the longest cooking time, like carrots or broccoli. Next, add more tender vegetables and meats. Add sauce ingredients last for a splash of flavor.

Per serving without rice

Calories 256
Fat 10 g
Cholesterol 43 mg
Sodium 920 mg
Carbohydrate 14 g
Fiber 2 g

Bistro Beef Medallions

Special occasions don't just happen on the weekend. A quick and savory pan sauce, caramelized onions, and crumbled blue cheese transform this budget-friendly cut of beef into a restaurant-style entrée in just minutes.

- 1 pound beef petite shoulder tender medallions
- 1 teaspoon Montreal steak seasoning
- 1 teaspoon herbes de Provence
- 1 tablespoon olive oil
- 1 large sweet onion (Maui, Vidalia, red), halved and thinly sliced
- 1 tablespoon honey
- 1/2 cup dry red wine
- Gorgonzola or blue cheese crumbles (optional)

ready in 30 minutes

Season beef medallions with steak seasoning and herbes de Provence. In medium skillet, heat olive oil over medium-high heat. Add medallions; cook until lightly browned, about 3 to 4 minutes per side. Transfer meat to platter; cover to keep warm.

In same skillet, combine onions and honey; cover and cook until onions wilt. Uncover and cook stirring frequently until onions are golden brown, about 5 minutes. Stir in wine; cook stirring frequently until liquid evaporates, about 3 minutes.

To serve, spoon caramelized onions over beef medallions. If desired, top with gorgonzola.

Makes 4 servings

LAURA'S Weeknight Tip *Cut baby potatoes in half and put them on a foil-lined jellyroll pan. Drizzle them with a little olive oil and season with salt and pepper. They will caramelize and roast in just 20 minutes in a hot oven (400°F.). Add steamed or microwaved broccoli (directions on page 71) and you have an easy, but dressed-up weeknight dinner.*

ingredient savvy

Beef Petite Shoulder Tender

Once reserved for trendy, upscale restaurants, beef petite shoulder tender is now readily available in Dierbergs Meat Department. Known in the trade as *teres major*, it is second in tenderness only to beef tenderloin. This lean, flavorful roast averages 1/2 to 3/4 pound.

It can be roasted or grilled whole, or cut into medallions before cooking – just like beef tenderloin! You'll love the reasonable price, too! The secret to perfect petite shoulder tender is to cook it just to medium doneness. Use a meat thermometer and stop cooking when it registers 145°F.

Per serving without cheese crumbles

Calories 256
Fat 10 g
Cholesterol 64 mg
Sodium 233 mg
Carbohydrate 12 g
Fiber 1 g

Weeknight Beef Stroganoff

From the simple to the sublime, no one knows entrées like Dierbergs Staff Home Economist Nancy Lorenz. Here she combines tender beef, hearty mushrooms, and a rich, creamy sauce for perfect weeknight fare.

1 beef sirloin steak (about 1 pound), partially frozen
1 tablespoon vegetable oil
Salt and ground black pepper to taste
1 package (8 ounces) sliced mushrooms
1/2 cup diced onion
1 clove garlic, minced
2 tablespoons flour
1 cup beef broth
1 tablespoon Dijon-style mustard
1/2 cup light dairy sour cream
Hot buttered noodles

Trim any visible fat from beef; slice into thin strips. In large skillet, heat oil over medium-high heat. Add half of the beef and season with salt and pepper; cook stirring occasionally until beef is browned, about 2 to 3 minutes. Remove beef from skillet; set aside. Repeat procedure with remaining beef.

In same skillet, cook mushrooms, onion, and garlic stirring occasionally until lightly browned, about 3 to 4 minutes. Stir in flour. Add broth and mustard; bring to a boil and cook stirring frequently until thickened, about 2 to 3 minutes. Stir in cooked beef along with any accumulated juices and sour cream; cook until heated through. Serve over hot buttered noodles.

Makes 4 servings

TIP See Slicing Raw Meat information on page 10.

VARIATION

Weeknight Chicken Stroganoff Substitute 1 pound chicken tenders, cut into bite-size pieces, for the sirloin steak; and chicken broth for the beef broth. Cook chicken in batches stirring occasionally until browned, about 3 to 4 minutes.

Per serving without noodles Calories 180; Fat 6 g; Cholesterol 50 mg; Sodium 395 mg; Carbohydrate 10 g; Fiber 1 g

ingredient savvy

Mushrooms

Mushrooms add a rich earthiness to so many dishes. To keep them fresh and flavorful, transfer mushrooms to a paper bag or loosely covered container and store in the refrigerator for up to 3 days. Since they soak up water very quickly, wipe mushrooms clean with a damp paper towel to preserve their texture. A sturdy egg slicer makes quick work of getting them recipe-ready. Or purchase pre-sliced mushrooms for added convenience.

Per serving without noodles

Calories 211
Fat 9 g
Cholesterol 62 mg
Sodium 384 mg
Carbohydrate 10 g
Fiber 1 g

Monterey Wild Mushroom Risotto

This satisfying meatless entrée of hearty mushrooms has deep, rich flavor. Adding the broth gradually and gently stirring creates risotto's famous creamy consistency.

- 2 cans (14 ounces each) reduced-sodium chicken broth, OR 1 can (14 ounces) vegetable broth plus 1 3/4 cups water
- 1/2 teaspoon herbes de Provence
- 2 tablespoons olive oil
- 1 package (8 ounces) sliced cremini mushrooms
- 1/2 cup chopped onion
- 1 cup arborio rice
- 1/2 cup dry white wine
- 4 ounces (1 cup) shredded monterey jack cheese

ready in 30 minutes

In medium saucepan, heat broth and herbes de Provence over medium heat until hot but not boiling.

In large saucepan, heat oil over medium heat. Add mushrooms and onion; cook stirring frequently for 2 minutes. Add rice; cook stirring frequently for 2 minutes. Add wine; cook until absorbed. Add 1 cup hot broth mixture; cook stirring frequently until broth is absorbed. Add remaining broth mixture, 1 cup at a time, cooking and stirring frequently until liquid is absorbed before adding additional broth.

When rice is tender and very creamy, stir in cheese. Serve immediately.

Makes 4-6 servings

TIP See Mushroom information on page 36.

LAURA'S Weeknight Tip *Sometimes you want a meatless meal and this one is rich and hearty. Add bright color to your plate with some steamed baby carrots (directions on page 76) tossed with a little butter and honey. Cook the carrots in just a few minutes while you finish the Risotto.*

ingredient savvy

Arborio Rice

Arborio is the variety of rice used to make risotto. Grown in Italy, arborio's short, fat rounded kernels have a high starch content that becomes thick and creamy when cooked. The more familiar long grain rice cooks to a light, fluffy consistency with kernels that stay separate.

When making classic risotto, choose arborio, which is the right rice, and add a little patience to guarantee success. Add the liquid little by little and stir often to give risotto that rich, creamy texture that made it famous.

Per serving

Calories 255
Fat 10 g
Cholesterol 17 mg
Sodium 419 mg
Carbohydrate 28 g
Fiber 1 g

Baja Fish Tacos

Here's a fun way to serve fish! Soft tacos filled with chunks of mild, flaky tilapia will become a family favorite. Top them with a colorful and refreshing citrus salsa and cool cilantro cream, or with a generous spoonful of traditional tomato salsa.

1 1/2 to 2 pounds tilapia fillets
2 tablespoons vegetable oil (divided)
2 teaspoons ground cumin
2 teaspoons chili powder
2 teaspoons coarsely ground black pepper
1 1/2 teaspoons coarse salt
Cilantro Cream
12 large flour tortillas (8-inch diameter), warmed
Shredded iceberg lettuce
Avocado Salsa

Lightly brush both sides of fillets with 1 tablespoon of the oil. In small bowl, combine cumin, chili powder, pepper, and salt; rub on both sides of fillets. In large nonstick skillet, heat remaining 1 tablespoon oil over medium-high heat. Add fish; cook in batches until fish is lightly browned and flakes easily with fork, about 3 minutes per side. Flake into large chunks.

To assemble, spread Cilantro Cream on warm tortillas; top with lettuce, fish, and Avocado Salsa.

Makes 6 servings

Cilantro Cream

1/4 cup light mayonnaise
1/4 cup light dairy sour cream
2 tablespoons lime juice
2 tablespoons chopped fresh cilantro

In small bowl, stir together all ingredients.

Makes 1/2 cup

Per tablespoon Calories 48; Fat 4 g; Cholesterol 7 mg; Sodium 89 mg; Carbohydrate 2 g; Fiber <1 g

Avocado Salsa

2 medium oranges
2 small avocados, pitted, peeled, and diced
1/2 cup diced red onion
2 cloves garlic, minced
Grated peel and juice of 2 limes
2 tablespoons olive oil
1 tablespoon chopped fresh cilantro
1/2 teaspoon ground cumin
1/4 teaspoon coarse salt

To section orange, use sharp knife to cut off both ends. Place orange on flat end. Cut away peel, following curve of fruit and removing all white pith. Holding fruit over medium bowl to catch juice, cut between orange and membrane; twist knife to loosen sections and lift out. Coarsely chop segments and place in bowl. Add remaining ingredients. Gently stir to combine.

Makes 1 1/2 cups

Per 1/4 cup Calories 190; Fat 15 g; Cholesterol 0 mg; Sodium 82 mg; Carbohydrate 15 g; Fiber 7 g

technique savvy

Thawing Tilapia

Keeping versatile ingredients on hand can be a real time-saver for busy weeknight meals. Individually wrapped and frozen tilapia fillets are a great choice for many recipes.

For quick – and safe – thawing, remove just the number of frozen fillets you need. Place the wrapped fillets in a large bowl and add cold water to cover, changing the water every 30 minutes, until the fish is thawed.

Per serving with Cilantro Cream and Avocado Salsa

Calories 569
Fat 27 g
Cholesterol 7 mg
Sodium 934 mg
Carbohydrate 67 g
Fiber 10 g

Savory Salmon Cakes

These light and luscious salmon cakes are a modern take on an old favorite. Serve them with a squeeze of lemon juice to brighten the flavor.

- 1 egg, slightly beaten
- 1/2 cup saltine cracker crumbs (about 10 to 15 crackers)
- 1/2 cup mayonnaise
- 1/4 cup finely chopped red bell pepper
- 1/4 cup finely chopped onion
- 1 teaspoon minced fresh parsley
- 1 tablespoon Cajun/Creole seasoning
- 2 cans (6 ounces each) skinless, boneless pink salmon, drained
- 2 tablespoons vegetable oil

ready in 25 minutes

In large bowl, combine egg, cracker crumbs, mayonnaise, bell pepper, onion, parsley, and seasoning. Add salmon; stir until evenly moistened. Let mixture stand for 10 minutes. Shape salmon mixture into 6 cakes.

In large skillet, heat oil over medium-high heat. Add salmon cakes, flattening slightly with back of pancake turner. Cook until golden brown, about 3 to 4 minutes per side. Drain on paper towels.

Makes 6 servings

VARIATION

Savory Crab Cakes Substitute 2 cans (6.5 ounces each) white crab meat, drained and flaked, for the salmon.

Per serving Calories 250; Fat 21 g; Cholesterol 99 mg; Sodium 580 mg; Carbohydrate 5 g; Fiber <1 g.

ingredient savvy

Convenient Crumbs

It's important to use the type of crumb specified in the recipe for best results.

Fresh bread crumbs have a light, airy, and coarse texture. Collect pieces of leftover not-so-fresh bread in your freezer. When you need crumbs, tear the bread into pieces and toss into the food processor.

Panko are Japanese dried bread crumbs that have a coarse texture and make an especially light, crispy crust.

Crackers and cereals make great crumbs, too. Just toss them into the food processor, or place them in a freezer-weight plastic bag and crush with a rolling pin.

Keep crumbs on hand in an airtight container in the freezer.

Per serving

Calories 260
Fat 22 g
Cholesterol 59 mg
Sodium 514 mg
Carbohydrate 5 g
Fiber <1 g

Piquant Garlic Shrimp

Dierbergs Staff Home Economist Pam Pahl always seems to have the perfect blend of short cuts and secret ingredients to put together a terrific main dish in minutes. A generous splash of Caribbean-style pepper sauce does the trick here.

- 1 pound jumbo (16 to 20 count) shrimp
- 1 1/2 cups water
- 1 tablespoon butter
- 1 tablespoon olive oil
- 2 to 3 cloves garlic, minced
- 3 tablespoons Pickapeppa sauce
- 2 tablespoons fresh lime juice
- 1 1/2 teaspoons honey
- 1/2 teaspoon salt
- 2 tablespoons fresh thyme leaves
- Hot cooked yellow rice

ready in 30 minutes

Peel and devein shrimp, reserving shells and leaving tails intact; set shrimp aside. In 2-cup glass measure, combine water and reserved shrimp shells. Microwave (high) for 2 to 3 minutes or until water comes to a boil. Strain and discard shells; set shrimp stock aside.

In large skillet, melt butter over medium heat. Add olive oil and garlic; cook until fragrant, about 1 minute. Stir in shrimp stock, Pickapeppa sauce, lime juice, honey, and salt; simmer for 5 minutes. Stir in shrimp and thyme; cook turning halfway through cooking time until shrimp are pink and opaque, about 2 to 3 minutes. Serve over hot cooked rice.

Makes 4 servings

Laura's Weeknight Tip *You can make this recipe in a moment's notice if you keep a bag of Dierbergs frozen shrimp on hand. For a quick thaw method, place the sealed bag of frozen shrimp in a large bowl of cold water and let it stand for about 30 minutes.*

ingredient savvy

Pickapeppa Sauce

There are dozens of hot pepper sauces on the shelf, but Pickapeppa is something special. This sweet and lightly spiced sauce, made with mangoes, tomatoes, and just a splash of hot pepper sauce, is a Caribbean favorite. Its unique flavor is similar to Worcestershire sauce with *a little something extra* that adds just the right finishing touch to all sorts of dishes. Splash it on shrimp, into a pot of baked beans or gumbo, or over grilled meat, fish, and chicken. Look for Pickapeppa sauce near the other hot sauces in the condiment aisle.

Per serving without rice

Calories 145
Fat 8 g
Cholesterol 116 mg
Sodium 473 mg
Carbohydrate 7 g
Fiber <1 g

FROM THE

slow cooker

Hearty Beef Burgundy 44

Barbecued Beef Sandwiches 45

Teriyaki Pulled Pork 47

Chicken Paprikash 48

Southwest Black Bean Soup 49

Vegetable Beef Barley Soup 51

Hearty Beef Burgundy
Recipe on page 44

Hearty Beef Burgundy

This rich and flavorful stew has been a favorite of Dierbergs' customers for many years. Spoon it over hot mashed potatoes for an easy and comforting meal.

- 1 tablespoon vegetable oil
- 2 to 2 1/2 pounds beef stew meat
- 1 can (10 3/4 ounces) condensed golden mushroom soup
- 3/4 cup Burgundy or other dry red wine
- 1 package (8 ounces) mushrooms, quartered
- 4 medium carrots, sliced
- 2 ribs celery, sliced
- 1 medium onion, cut into wedges
- 1 envelope (1 ounce) dry onion soup mix
- Hot mashed potatoes

prep time 15 minutes

In large skillet, heat oil over medium-high heat. Add meat; cook stirring occasionally until browned on all sides, about 5 minutes. Place meat in 4-quart slow cooker that has been lightly coated with no-stick cooking spray. Add remaining ingredients except mashed potatoes. Cook until meat is tender, about 6 to 8 hours on low heat setting, or for 4 to 5 hours on high heat setting. Serve over mashed potatoes.

Makes 8 servings

LAURA'S Weeknight Tip *Line your slow cooker with a plastic liner made especially for slow cookers. You'll find them in the plastic bag aisle and they make cleanup really quick and easy.*

Photograph on page 42

ingredient savvy

Cooking With Wine

Confused about which wines to cook with? It's fairly simple. If you can drink it, you can cook with it. For savory dishes, choose dry (not sweet) wines. Dry white wines include Chardonnay, Pinot Grigio, and Sauvignon Blanc. Dry red wines include Cabernet Sauvignon, Chianti, Merlot, Shiraz, Pinot Noir, and Burgundy. Avoid products labeled cooking wine. They contain salt, which can alter the flavor of the recipe.

Per serving without mashed potatoes

Calories 213
Fat 8 g
Cholesterol 39 mg
Sodium 603 mg
Carbohydrate 12 g
Fiber 2 g

Barbecued Beef Sandwiches

Take a break from Sloppy Joes. Pile this savory, slow-simmered beef onto toasted buns. Then serve with a crisp pickle for hot and hearty sandwiches the whole family will love.

- 1 tablespoon vegetable oil
- 1 beef arm roast (about 2 to 3 pounds), trimmed
- 2 cups ketchup
- 1 cup salsa
- 1/2 cup chopped onion
- 2 tablespoons brown sugar
- 2 tablespoons apple cider vinegar
- 2 tablespoons Worcestershire sauce
- 2 cloves garlic, minced
- 1/2 teaspoon chili powder
- 1/2 teaspoon dry mustard
- 1/4 teaspoon ground black pepper
- 8 sandwich buns, toasted

prep time **20** minutes

In large skillet, heat oil over medium-high heat. Add meat; cook turning occasionally until browned on all sides, about 5 minutes. Place meat in 4-quart slow cooker that has been lightly coated with no-stick cooking spray. Add remaining ingredients except sandwich buns. Cook until meat begins to fall apart, about 6 to 8 hours on low heat setting, or for 4 to 5 hours on high heat setting.

Remove meat; cover and let stand 10 minutes. Use two forks to shred beef. Return shredded meat along with any accumulated juices to sauce in slow cooker; stir to combine. Serve on toasted sandwich buns.

Makes 8 servings

TIP See Step-by-Step Instructions on shredding meat on page 47.

LAURA'S Weeknight Tip *Make this the star of a kids' night meal. Spoon the beef onto dollar rolls or into mini pita pockets for kid-size sandwiches. Serve it with macaroni and cheese and their favorite fresh fruit.*

ingredient savvy

Meat for Stewing

They may not be the most tender cuts on the butcher block, but beef arm roast, chuck roast, and stew meat are all great choices for creating deep, rich, flavorful stews.

There's one at the right price for any budget. Cubes of stew meat come already trimmed for convenience. Arm and chuck roasts are sold whole and are less expensive, but need to be trimmed and cut into cubes. Use them interchangeably in your favorite stew recipe.

Braising, which means cooking low and slow, breaks down the tough, connective tissue and makes the meat melt-in-your-mouth tender. These cuts are perfect for a slow cooker.

Per serving

Calories 300
Fat 5 g
Cholesterol 30 mg
Sodium 920 mg
Carbohydrate 45 g
Fiber 2 g

Teriyaki Pulled Pork

Start this roast in the morning, then forget about it until dinner time. Serve it on Kaiser rolls for a terrific sandwich.

- 2 teaspoons olive oil
- 1 boneless pork loin roast (about 2 1/2 to 3 pounds)
- 3/4 cup teriyaki baste and glaze
- 3/4 cup beef broth
- 1 tablespoon cornstarch, dissolved in 2 tablespoons water
- 4 green onions, thinly sliced (optional)

prep time 10 minutes

In large skillet, heat oil over medium-high heat. Add pork; cook turning occasionally until browned on all sides, about 5 minutes. Place pork in 4-quart slow cooker that has been lightly coated with no-stick cooking spray. Pour teriyaki baste and glaze and broth over pork. Cook until meat is tender, about 6 to 8 hours on low heat setting, or for 4 to 5 hours on high heat setting.

Remove meat; cover and let stand 10 minutes. **1** Use two forks to shred pork. Stir cornstarch mixture into hot liquid in slow cooker. Cook on high heat setting stirring occasionally until slightly thickened, about 10 minutes. Return shredded meat along with any accumulated juices to slow cooker; stir to combine. If desired, serve with green onion sprinkled over top.

Makes 8-10 servings

LAURA'S Weeknight Tip *This recipe makes plenty, so you can freeze the extras for a second meal. Serve it the next time wrapped up in warm flour tortillas or iceberg lettuce leaves (see Asian Lettuce Wraps TIP on page 32).*

technique savvy

Step-by-Step Instructions

Per serving

Calories 174
Fat 6 g
Cholesterol 48 mg
Sodium 594 mg
Carbohydrate 7 g
Fiber 0 g

Chicken Paprikash

While you were out, your slow cooker streamlined this creamy Hungarian classic. Serve it over egg noodles for a delicious weeknight splurge.

technique savvy

Slow Cooker Saves The Day

The slow cooker can be an indispensable tool for home-cooked meals without the fuss.

Choose recipes designed for slow, moist heat cooking – soups, stews, roasts, and braised meats.

Slow cookers work best when they're half to two-thirds full.

Cut foods into same-size pieces for even cooking.

Use plastic liners specially made for slow cookers to minimize clean-up.

Brown meats and poultry in a skillet right before adding to the slow cooker for a richer flavor.

Never start with frozen food in the slow cooker.

Per serving without noodles

Calories 181
Fat 7 g
Cholesterol 54 mg
Sodium 400 mg
Carbohydrate 10 g
Fiber 2 g

2 pounds boneless, skinless chicken breast halves or thighs, cut into bite-size strips
1/3 cup flour
1 can (14 ounces) chicken broth
1 cup chopped green bell pepper
1 cup chopped red bell pepper
1 package (8 ounces) sliced mushrooms
2 cloves garlic, minced
3 tablespoons Hungarian sweet paprika
1 teaspoon ground black pepper
1/2 teaspoon salt
1 cup (8 ounces) dairy sour cream
Hot buttered noodles

prep time 15 minutes

In 4-quart slow cooker that has been lightly coated with no-stick cooking spray, combine chicken and flour; toss until well mixed. Add remaining ingredients except sour cream and noodles; stir to combine. Cook 6 to 8 hours on low heat setting, or for 4 to 5 hours on high heat setting.

Just before serving, heat sour cream in microwave (high) for 45 seconds; stir into paprikash. Spoon over buttered noodles.

Makes 6-8 servings

LAURA'S Weeknight Tip *Frozen puff pastry shells are a fun way to serve this chicken stew. Bake them according to the directions on the package, and then fill them with Paprikash.*

Southwest Black Bean Soup

No need to soak the beans for this hearty soup from Staff Home Economist Ginger Gall. Just toss everything into the slow cooker and let it simmer all day. Add a basket of cornbread or tortilla chips, and dinner is ready.

1 package (16 ounces) dry black beans
3 cans (14 ounces each) vegetable broth
1 can (14.5 ounces) petite diced tomatoes with chipotles
1 cup diced carrot
3/4 cup diced celery
3/4 cup diced onion
1/2 cup diced red bell pepper
1 tablespoon minced garlic
1 tablespoon ground cumin
2 tablespoons fresh lime juice
Coarse salt and freshly ground black pepper to taste
Dairy sour cream (optional)
Thinly sliced green onion (optional)
Chopped fresh cilantro (optional)

prep time 20 minutes

Rinse and sort beans. In 6-quart slow cooker, combine beans, broth, tomatoes, carrot, celery, onion, bell pepper, garlic, and cumin; stir to combine. Cook until beans are very tender, about 7 to 8 hours on high heat setting.

Transfer 2 cups bean mixture to work bowl of food processor fitted with steel knife blade or blender container; process until smooth. Return to slow cooker. Stir in lime juice, salt, and pepper. Ladle into serving bowls; top with sour cream, green onion, and cilantro, if desired.

Makes 6-8 servings

technique savvy

Cooking Dry Beans

Available in a rainbow of colors, dry beans are a pantry staple no cook should be without. They're hearty, satisfying, and versatile, not to mention a great source of protein, vitamins A and C, and fiber.

Most dry beans need to be covered with cold water and soaked overnight. To quick-soak, put beans in a large pot with water to cover and bring to a boil. Remove from heat, cover, and let stand for 1 to 2 hours before cooking. After soaking, drain the beans and discard the soaking liquid. One pound of dry beans equals about 6 cups cooked beans.

Per serving

Calories 243
Fat 1 g
Cholesterol 0 mg
Sodium 816 mg
Carbohydrate 46 g
Fiber 10 g

Vegetable Beef Barley Soup

Few things are as comforting as a bowl of homemade soup. Barley gives this one an old-fashioned, satisfying flavor.

- 1 pound beef stew meat, cut into bite-size pieces
- 2 cans (14.5 ounces each) petite diced tomatoes
- 2 cans (14 ounces each) beef broth
- 1 package (16 ounces) frozen mixed vegetables (corn, peas, carrots, lima beans)
- 1/2 cup chopped onion
- 1/4 cup medium barley
- 1 teaspoon dried thyme
- 1 bay leaf

prep time 10 minutes

In 6-quart slow cooker, combine all ingredients. Cook until meat and barley are tender, about 8 hours on low heat setting, or for 4 to 5 hours on high heat setting. Remove bay leaf before serving.

Makes 6-8 servings

TIP For extra flavor, use tomatoes seasoned with chipotles, Italian herbs, or Mexican seasonings.

LAURA'S Weeknight Tip *Get the soup ingredients ready the night before. Then in the morning, just toss everything together in the slow cooker and dinner is on the way. Keep a package of corn muffin mix in the pantry, and bake it while you set the table for dinner.*

ingredient savvy

Barley

Barley adds a nutty, wholesome flavor and nutritious fiber to soups and stews, and is used in many types of cereal. Pearl barley is husked and polished, and comes in coarse, medium, and fine grains. Scotch barley has more of the bran left on it, while quick-cooking has been processed to make it cook faster.

Cook 1 cup of barley in 3 cups water for a firm but chewy texture. Use 4 cups water for a softer texture. Drain off any water that the grains don't absorb. Barley partners especially well with full-flavored foods like beef, lamb, and root vegetables.

Per serving

Calories 139
Fat 3 g
Cholesterol 19 mg
Sodium 516 mg
Carbohydrate 17 g
Fiber 3 g

FROM THE

soup pot

Asian Meatball Soup 54

Easy Oven Meatballs 54

Tortellini Minestrone Soup 55

French Onion Soup 57

Chicken Orzo Soup 58

Chicken and Broccoli Cheese Soup 59

Loaded Potato Soup 61

Hearty Veggie Chili Bowls 63

Asian Meatball Soup
Recipe on page 54

Asian Meatball Soup

technique savvy

Lots of Meatballs!

The recipe for Easy Oven Meatballs makes plenty to enjoy now and still have some to freeze for another recipe. Prepare them as directed and cool the extras to room temperature. Place them on a tray in a single layer and freeze until firm, about 30 minutes. Transfer the meatballs to a freezer-weight reclosable plastic bag or an airtight container and freeze for up to 4 weeks. Defrost overnight in the refrigerator and they're ready for spaghetti, sandwiches, or to top with your favorite sauce.

Skip the Chinese take-out. Keep these versatile meatballs from Test Kitchen Manager Karen Hurych in the freezer to make it a cinch to prepare this incredibly flavorful soup on a busy weeknight.

- 1 tablespoon olive oil
- 1/2 cup finely chopped onion
- 1 tablespoon minced fresh ginger root
- 1 clove garlic, minced
- 1/2 recipe frozen Easy Oven Meatballs
- 1 box (32 ounces) reduced-sodium chicken broth
- 2 cups water
- 1 tablespoon soy sauce
- 1 teaspoon chili purée with garlic (optional)
- 2 cups fine egg noodles
- 1 cup thinly sliced bok choy
- 1 cup sliced mushrooms
- 1/2 cup diced red bell pepper

ready in 20 minutes

In Dutch oven or large saucepan, heat oil over medium-high heat. Add onion, ginger, and garlic; cook until tender, about 3 to 4 minutes. Add meatballs, broth, water, soy sauce, and chili purée, if desired; bring to a boil. Stir in noodles and vegetables. Cook until noodles are tender, about 3 to 4 minutes.

Makes 6-8 servings

TIP Chili purée with garlic adds a lot of heat. Use smaller amount for milder heat, or increase the amount for more zip.

Per serving

Calories 165
Fat 6 g
Cholesterol 55 mg
Sodium 548 mg
Carbohydrate 12 g
Fiber 1 g

Easy Oven Meatballs

- 1/2 cup milk
- 1/3 cup Italian seasoned bread crumbs
- 1 egg
- 2 to 3 teaspoons chili purée with garlic (optional)
- 1 pound lean ground beef
- 1 pound lean ground pork
- 1/3 cup finely chopped onion
- 1/2 teaspoon salt

prep time 15 minutes

In large bowl, stir together milk and bread crumbs; let stand for 5 minutes. Add egg and chili purée; stir until just combined. Crumble ground beef and pork into bowl; add onion and salt. Stir until combined (do not over mix).

Place meat mixture on large cutting board; pat into 8-inch square. Cut meat mixture into 8 rows by 8 rows, or about 1 tablespoon each. Shape each piece into ball; place on foil-lined 10 x 15-inch jellyroll pan. Bake in 475°F. oven until internal temperature is 165°F., about 20 to 25 minutes.

Makes 64 meatballs

Per meatball Calories 24; Fat 1 g; Cholesterol 12 mg; Sodium 38 mg; Carbohydrate 1 g; Fiber 0 g

Photograph on page 52

Tortellini Minestrone Soup

Minestrone means "big soup" in Italian. Packed with cheese-filled tortellini and plenty of hearty vegetables, this colorful soup is a complete meal.

- 1 tablespoon olive oil
- 3/4 cup finely chopped onion
- 2 cloves garlic, minced
- 1 teaspoon Italian herb seasoning
- 1 box (32 ounces) beef broth
- 1 can (14.5 ounces) diced Italian seasoned tomatoes
- 2 cups (1/2 of 20-ounce package) frozen cheese tortellini
- 1 can (15 ounces) cannellini beans, rinsed and drained
- 2 cups cubed zucchini
- 2 cups coarsely chopped baby spinach
- Grated parmesan cheese

prep time 15 minutes

In Dutch oven or large saucepan, heat olive oil over medium-high heat. Add onion, garlic, and Italian seasoning; cook stirring frequently until onion softens, about 2 to 3 minutes. Add broth and tomatoes; bring to a boil. Stir in tortellini, beans, and zucchini. Reduce heat and simmer until tortellini are tender, about 5 minutes.

Remove from heat; stir in spinach. Ladle into serving bowls; top with grated parmesan.

Makes 6-8 servings

LAURA'S Weeknight Tip *Everything you need for this soup can be stashed in your pantry and freezer for a last-minute meal. Frozen chopped onions and any combination of mixed vegetables can stand in for fresh when you're in a time crunch.*

technique savvy

Soup – Your Way

Whether you're an experienced cook or a novice in the kitchen, making a pot of soup is a cozy, comforting, and creative way to stir up something special for dinner. Many recipes – especially baked goods – depend on precise measurements, but soups and stews give you room to be flexible with ingredients. Add more of a favorite seasoning, a splash of wine, or whatever sounds good. Chopped a little too much onion or carrot? No problem. Don't know when you'll use that piece of zucchini or handful of spinach? Toss them into the pot. You'll add extra color, flavor, and nutrition to every delicious spoonful.

Per serving

Calories 161
Fat 4 g
Cholesterol 9 mg
Sodium 658 mg
Carbohydrate 24 g
Fiber 4 g

French Onion Soup

Caramelized onions, rich beefy broth, and gooey, melted cheese make this soup a memorable meal. C'est magnifique!

- 4 tablespoons olive oil
- 4 pounds onions, thinly sliced
- 2 packages (1 ounce each) au jus gravy mix
- 1/2 teaspoon ground black pepper
- 8 cups water
- 1 cup dry red wine
- Dierbergs Bakery Toasted French Bread Slices (crostini)
- 16 ounces gruyére cheese, grated (about 4 cups)

prep time 30 minutes

In Dutch oven or large saucepan, heat olive oil over medium-high heat. Add onions; cover and cook until onions wilt, about 10 minutes. Uncover and cook stirring frequently until onions are golden brown, about 20 to 25 minutes.

Stir in au jus gravy mix and pepper. Add water and wine; bring to a boil. Reduce heat, cover, and simmer for 20 minutes.

Ladle soup into oven-proof serving bowls; place on jellyroll pan. Top with crostini and grated cheese. Bake in 425°F. oven until bubbly and lightly browned, about 10 to 12 minutes.

Makes 6-8 servings

LAURA'S Weeknight Tip *Get creative while the soup simmers and put together a salad with whatever greens and fruit you have on hand. Our Greens and Fruit Salad (recipe on page 66) has some great tasting combinations.*

technique savvy

Soup On Hand

Most any soup tastes better when it's reheated because the flavors have time to blend. Make a big batch of your favorite to stash in the freezer for those nights when there's no time to cook.

Clear or broth-based soups and stews freeze best. Potatoes, pasta, and rice get mushy in the home freezer. Omit them from the batch you freeze and add them freshly-cooked as you reheat the soup. Avoid freezing soups with milk, cheese, or other dairy products as they will separate.

Prepare soups as directed, then cool uncovered to room temperature. Pour into individual or meal-sized containers, cover, label, and freeze for up to 4 weeks.

Per serving

Calories 438
Fat 26 g
Cholesterol 63 mg
Sodium 1024 mg
Carbohydrate 28 g
Fiber 3 g

Chicken Orzo Soup

Chicken soup is pure comfort in any language. Orzo pasta and Italian seasoning make this version a little more fun.

- 2 teaspoons olive oil
- 1 cup diced onion
- 1 cup diced celery
- 1 cup diced carrot
- 1 teaspoon Italian herb seasoning
- 1 pound boneless, skinless chicken breast halves, cut into bite-size pieces
- 1 box (32 ounces) reduced-sodium chicken broth
- 3/4 cup orzo or rosamarina pasta
- 1/4 teaspoon ground white pepper

ready in 30 minutes

In Dutch oven or large saucepan, heat olive oil over medium-high heat. Add onion, celery, carrot, and Italian seasoning; cook until softened, about 3 to 4 minutes. Add chicken; cook stirring frequently until no longer pink, about 3 minutes. Add broth, orzo, and pepper; bring to a boil. Reduce heat and simmer until pasta is tender, about 10 to 12 minutes.

Makes 6 servings

LAURA'S Weeknight Tip *Orzo is pasta that looks like rice, but any tiny pasta works in this delicious soup. Make it fun for the kids by using alphabet pasta instead of orzo.*

ingredient savvy

Lower-Sodium Broth

Canned beef, chicken, and vegetable broths make quick work of homemade soups and sauces. But they tend to be very high in sodium. Choosing broth labeled *lower* or *reduced* sodium is a great way to reduce the amount of salt in a recipe. Prepare the recipe as directed, substituting lower-sodium broth for the regular broth. Then just before serving, taste to see if the seasoning needs to be adjusted. You'll probably find that the flavors develop while simmering, and you won't even miss the extra salt!

Per serving

Calories 178
Fat 3 g
Cholesterol 29 mg
Sodium 417 mg
Carbohydrate 22 g
Fiber 2 g

Chicken and Broccoli Cheese Soup

Certified Culinary Professionals and St. Louis Post-Dispatch Food Columnists, Mary and the late Jack Billings, created this wonderful soup for one of their many classes at Dierbergs School of Cooking. It's perfect for a little midweek luxury!

- 4 1/2 tablespoons butter (divided)
- 1/2 cup hot water
- 1 teaspoon chicken base
- 1/4 cup flour
- 1/2 pound boneless, skinless chicken breast halves
- 1 large onion, diced
- 1/2 pound broccoli florets, chopped (about 2 cups)
- 2 cans (14 ounces each) chicken broth
- 1 cup heavy whipping cream
- 1/8 teaspoon ground black pepper
- 1 package (8 ounces) shredded sharp cheddar cheese
- Diced roma tomatoes (optional)

ready in 45 minutes

Place 2 1/2 tablespoons of the butter and water in 1-cup glass measure; microwave (high) until butter is melted, about 30 seconds. Stir in chicken base until dissolved. Whisk in flour; set aside.

In Dutch oven or large saucepan, melt remaining 2 tablespoons butter over medium-high heat. Add chicken; cook until seared on both sides. Add onion; cook until chicken and onion are browned, about 3 to 4 minutes. Reduce heat to medium-low and cook until internal temperature of chicken is 165°F., about 5 to 7 minutes. Remove chicken from skillet; cool slightly. Dice and set aside.

In same pan, cook broccoli stirring frequently over medium-high heat until bright green, about 3 minutes. Add chicken base mixture, broth, cream, and pepper; cook stirring constantly until thickened, about 10 minutes. Remove from heat. Stir in chicken along with any accumulated juices and cheese. If desired, garnish each serving with diced tomatoes.

Makes 6-8 servings

Laura's Weeknight Tip *This rich, hearty soup really is dinner in a bowl! A few crackers and a very simple fruit plate with apple wedges and small bunches of grapes are just enough to finish the meal.*

ingredient savvy

Soup Base

When your soup needs a little flavor boost, add a pinch or two of soup base to the pot. An updated version of the bouillon cube, these soup bases are a paste form of dehydrated chicken or beef stock that adds depth and richness to homemade soups and sauces. Check the label for suggested amounts and whether the product needs to be refrigerated after opening. Since most contain a significant amount of salt, omit salt from your recipe and adjust seasonings at the end of cooking. Look for jars of chicken and beef base in the soup aisle.

Per serving

Calories 302
Fat 25 g
Cholesterol 91 mg
Sodium 659 mg
Carbohydrate 8 g
Fiber 1 g

Loaded Potato Soup

Who can resist a baked potato with all the trimmings? Dierbergs School of Cooking instructor Jan Ford blends all of your favorite flavors into a quick, easy, and satisfying soup.

- 3 cups quartered baby red potatoes
- 4 slices bacon, diced
- 1/2 cup finely chopped onion
- 1/3 cup finely chopped celery
- 3 tablespoons butter
- 3 tablespoons flour
- 2 1/4 cups milk
- 1 ounce (1/4 cup) shredded sharp cheddar cheese
- 1 ounce (1/4 cup) shredded swiss cheese
- 1/4 cup chicken broth, milk, or water
- 1 tablespoon fresh marjoram, OR 1 teaspoon dried
- Salt and ground black pepper to taste
- 1 tablespoon minced fresh parsley
- 1/3 cup dairy sour cream
- 4 green onions, thinly sliced

ready in 30 minutes

In large saucepan, cook potatoes in boiling water until just tender; drain and set aside.

In medium skillet, cook bacon, onion, and celery over medium heat stirring frequently until bacon is crisp, about 7 minutes. Remove bacon mixture with slotted spoon; drain on paper towels.

In Dutch oven or large saucepan, melt butter over medium heat. Stir in flour. Gradually whisk in milk; cook whisking constantly until thickened, about 2 to 3 minutes. Remove from heat; stir in cheeses until melted. Add chicken broth, potatoes, bacon mixture, marjoram, salt, and pepper; cook over medium heat until warmed through.

Just before serving, stir in parsley. Ladle into serving bowls; garnish with sour cream and green onions.

Makes 4 servings

TIP If you like a thinner soup, increase broth to as much as one 14-ounce can.

technique savvy

Freezing Chopped Onions

If you use chopped onions in lots of recipes, don't let dinner time bring you to tears. As long as you have the cutting board out, chop more onions than you need at one time and freeze the rest. Divide into convenient-size portions and place in freezer-weight reclosable plastic bags. Label and freeze for up to 3 months.

Frozen chopped onions may be added directly to soups and stews – no need to thaw them. When a recipe calls for sautéing the onions, thaw them first. Then blot the onions dry with paper towels before cooking so they'll brown.

Per serving

Calories 465
Fat 27 g
Cholesterol 72 mg
Sodium 478 mg
Carbohydrate 34 g
Fiber 3 g

Hearty Veggie Chili Bowls

Made from ingredients that are easy to keep on hand, this zesty meatless chili is a winner. Kids and grown-ups alike will love the biscuit bowls, too.

- 1 can (11.5 ounces) 100% vegetable juice (V-8)
- 1 can (15.5 ounces) red kidney beans
- 1 can (15 ounces) black beans
- 1 can (14.5 ounces) diced tomatoes and green chiles
- 1 cup chopped zucchini
- 2/3 cup chopped onion
- 1 tablespoon chili powder
- 1 teaspoon ground cumin
- 1 can (17.3 ounces) refrigerated biscuits (any flavor)
- Shredded cheddar cheese (optional)
- Dairy sour cream (optional)

In Dutch oven or large saucepan, combine all ingredients except biscuits, cheese, and sour cream over medium-high heat; bring to a boil. Reduce heat, cover, and simmer stirring occasionally for 20 minutes.

Meanwhile, coat outside of eight 6-ounce custard cups with no-stick cooking spray; place upside-down on ungreased jellyroll pans. Separate dough into 8 biscuits; pat each biscuit into 4 1/2-inch round. **1** Press to fit over bottom and sides of cups. Bake in 375°F. oven until deep golden brown, about 14 to 16 minutes.

2 Carefully remove hot biscuit bowls from custard cups. Place bowls right-side up. Ladle chili into each biscuit bowl. If desired, top with cheese and sour cream.

Makes 8 servings

HEART-HEALTHY TIP Serve chili without the biscuit bowls.

Per serving Calories 123; Fat 1 g; Cholesterol 0 mg; Sodium 549 mg; Carbohydrate 22 g; Fiber 8 g

LAURA'S Weeknight Tip *If you like mild chili, use plain diced tomatoes and only 1/2 teaspoon ground cumin in this recipe. Serve on cooked elbow macaroni for quick chili mac.*

technique savvy

Step-by-Step Instructions

Per serving with biscuit bowl

Calories 303
Fat 9 g
Cholesterol 0 mg
Sodium 1199 mg
Carbohydrate 47 g
Fiber 8 g

FROM THE

garden

Greens and Fruit Salad 66

Mango Chutney Spinach Salad 67

Mediterranean Couscous Salad 68

Tomato and Artichoke Salad 69

Broccoli 71

Green Beans 72

Corn 74

Zucchini 75

Carrots 76

Cauliflower 77

Asparagus 78

Sugar and Spice Sweet Potatoes 80

Garlic Roasted Potatoes 80

Cheddar Cheese Sauce 81

Greens and Fruit Salad
Recipe on page 66

Greens and Fruit Salad

Oh, the possibilities! Try one of our combinations of crisp greens, juicy fruits, and crunchy sugared nuts. Or create your own – depending on the season.

8 cups mixed salad greens
1/4 cup thinly sliced sweet onion (Maui, Vidalia, red)
1/2 cup prepared raspberry vinaigrette
3 medium peaches or nectarines, sliced
1 cup blueberries
1 cup raspberries
4 ounces (1 cup) crumbled goat cheese
1 cup sugared walnuts

In large bowl, combine salad greens and onion. Drizzle vinaigrette over greens; toss until well mixed. Arrange salad on individual serving plates. Top with fruit, cheese, and nuts.

Makes 4-6 servings

VARIATIONS

Strawberry Mandarin Salad Use poppy seed dressing, 2 cups sliced strawberries, 1 can (11 ounces) drained mandarin oranges, feta cheese, and sugared almonds.

Makes 4-6 servings

Per serving Calories 237; Fat 17 g; Cholesterol 11 mg; Sodium 219 mg; Carbohydrate 18 g; Fiber 4 g

Apple, Pear, and Cranberry Salad Use pomegranate blueberry vinaigrette, 2 sliced medium apples, 2 sliced medium pears, 1 cup sweetened dried cranberries, gorgonzola cheese, and sugared pecans.

Makes 4-6 servings

Per serving Calories 359; Fat 18 g; Cholesterol 17 mg; Sodium 340 mg; Carbohydrate 45 g; Fiber 6 g

Photograph on page 64

technique savvy

Sugared Nuts

Any variety of nut can be glazed and sugared. They are so easy to make that you will want to keep a batch on hand as the perfect finishing touch for a lettuce and fruit salad.

To make sugared nuts, combine 1 cup sliced or slivered almonds, or coarsely chopped pecans or walnuts, and 2 tablespoons sugar in a small skillet. Cook stirring constantly over medium-low heat until sugar is caramelized and nuts are toasted, about 4 to 5 minutes. Place nuts on plate and cool completely. Break into pieces. Store in airtight container.

Per serving

Calories 334
Fat 25 g
Cholesterol 20 mg
Sodium 247 mg
Carbohydrate 25 g
Fiber 5 g

Mango Chutney Spinach Salad

Major Grey's (mango) chutney gives this warm bacon dressing just the right sweetness. Look for chutney in the condiment aisle.

- 3 slices bacon, chopped
- 1/4 cup Major Grey's chutney
- 2 tablespoons apple cider vinegar
- 1 bag (5 to 6 ounces) baby spinach, rinsed and drained
- 1 can (8 ounces) sliced water chestnuts, drained
- 1/3 cup slivered red onion
- 1/4 cup diced red bell pepper
- Coarsely ground black pepper

1 Place bacon in 2-cup glass measure; loosely cover with paper towel. Microwave (high) for 3 to 4 minutes, stirring halfway through cooking time, until crisp. **2** Remove bacon with slotted spoon; drain on paper towels. Add chutney and vinegar to drippings in glass measure. Microwave (high) for 1 minute; whisk to blend.

In large salad bowl, combine spinach, water chestnuts, red onion, and bell pepper. Drizzle warm dressing over salad; toss until well mixed. Sprinkle bacon over top. Season with pepper and serve immediately.

Makes 4 servings

LAURA'S Weeknight Tip *Grilled pork tenderloin will turn this salad into a delicious entrée. You can double the dressing and use half of it to baste the pork as it cooks. Then slice the pork into medallions and serve it on top of the salad. Even easier…use grilled chicken from Dierbergs Deli!*

technique savvy

Step-by-Step Instructions

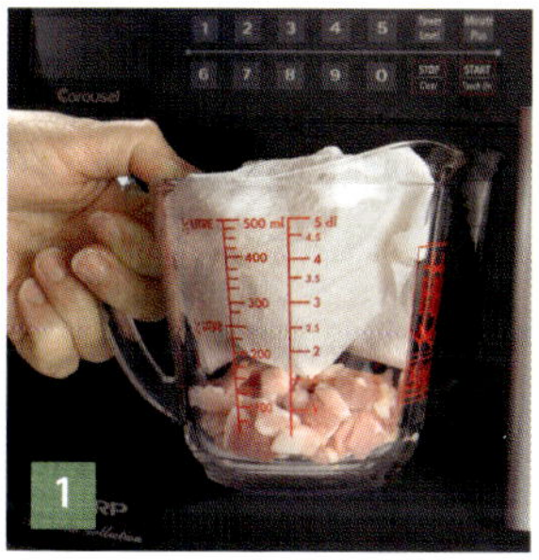

Per serving

Calories 218
Fat 13 g
Cholesterol 19 mg
Sodium 437 mg
Carbohydrate 22 g
Fiber 2 g

Mediterranean Couscous Salad

Staff Home Economist Therese Lewis created this colorful salad to showcase summer's best and brightest vegetables. On a hot summer evening, it can be a meal all by itself.

ingredient savvy

Couscous

These tiny pearls of pasta are at the heart of North African cuisine, but are right at home in all sorts of dishes. Look for boxes of couscous (KOOS-koos) in the rice and pasta section.

Couscous cooks very quickly so it's perfect for weeknight meals. Add extra flavor by cooking couscous in chicken broth instead of water, or stirring in your favorite seasonings. Serve it as you would pasta or rice, as a complement to grilled meats or hearty stews.

1 can (14 ounces) chicken broth
1 package (10 ounces) couscous (1 2/3 cups)
1 clove garlic, minced
Salt and ground black pepper to taste
Greek Dressing
1 can (15 ounces) garbanzo or black beans, rinsed and drained
1 pint grape or cherry tomatoes, halved
1 cucumber, peeled, seeded, and cubed (about 1 1/2 cups)
1 cup pitted kalamata olives, halved
1 package (4 ounces) crumbled herb-seasoned feta cheese
3 green onions, thinly sliced

In medium saucepan, bring chicken broth to boil over medium heat. Remove from heat; stir in couscous and garlic. Season with salt and pepper. Cover and let stand until liquid is absorbed, about 10 to 15 minutes.

Fluff couscous with fork. Place in large serving bowl; stir in 1/2 cup of the Dressing. Add beans, tomatoes, cucumber, olives, and feta cheese; stir to combine. Sprinkle green onion over top. Serve with remaining Dressing.

Makes 8-10 servings

TIP If desired, baby cucumbers can be used in place of regular cucumbers. No need to peel or seed them, just cut into cubes.

Greek Dressing

Grated peel and juice of 2 small lemons
1 teaspoon dried oregano
1/2 teaspoon garlic salt
1/2 teaspoon ground black pepper
1/2 cup olive oil

In small bowl, whisk together all ingredients except olive oil. Whisking vigorously, add olive oil in slow, steady stream until well blended.

Makes about 3/4 cup

Per serving

Calories 373
Fat 22 g
Cholesterol 9 mg
Sodium 540 mg
Carbohydrate 36 g
Fiber 4 g

Tomato and Artichoke Salad

Juicy tomatoes taste their best served at room temperature. They're even better when you team them with artichoke hearts, olives, and a tangy vinaigrette.

4 medium tomatoes (about 2 pounds)
Salt and ground black pepper to taste
1 jar (6 to 6.5 ounces) marinated artichoke hearts
1 can (2.25 ounces) sliced ripe olives, drained
2 tablespoons white wine vinegar
2 cloves garlic, minced
2 tablespoons chopped fresh parsley

Cut tomatoes into wedges. Arrange in single layer on large platter. Season with salt and pepper. In medium bowl, stir together artichoke hearts with marinade, olives, vinegar, garlic, and parsley. Spoon over tomatoes.

Makes 6-8 servings

TIP If desired, prepare salad; cover and chill for several hours or up to 24 hours. For best flavor, let salad stand at room temperature for about 20 minutes before serving.

LAURA'S Weeknight Tip *This salad makes a terrific veggie sandwich. Cut a baguette into 4-inch sections, and split each one in half. Spoon salad over the bottom halves and drizzle with some of the dressing. Add a lettuce leaf, a slice of mild provel cheese, and top it off with the remaining bread.*

ingredient savvy

Tomatoes

Few things are as delectable as a juicy, perfectly-ripened tomato. Choose tomatoes that are firm, heavy for their size, and give a little when gently squeezed.

For the very best flavor, don't refrigerate tomatoes. Cold temperatures dull the flavor. Store tomatoes uncovered at room temperature, away from direct sunlight.

For under-ripe tomatoes, try this trick: Pierce several holes in a paper bag. Add the tomatoes along with an apple and let stand at room temperature for a few days, checking occasionally.

Per serving

Calories 67
Fat 5 g
Cholesterol 0 mg
Sodium 142 mg
Carbohydrate 6 g
Fiber 1 g

Orzo and Broccoli Salad

Orzo and Broccoli Salad

Co-host of Dierbergs Presents Everybody Cooks *TV show, Cathy Chipley shares this colorful side dish infused with lively Mediterranean flavors. It's terrific served either warm or at room temperature.*

- 1 1/2 cups orzo or rosamarina pasta
- 2 cups fresh broccoli florets
- 1/4 cup olive oil
- 1/2 teaspoon crushed red pepper flakes
- 4 ounces (1 cup) feta cheese, crumbled
- 1 can (2.25 ounces) sliced ripe or kalamata olives, drained
- 3 tablespoons freshly grated asiago cheese
- 1/2 teaspoon dried basil
- 2 tablespoons pine nuts, toasted, OR 1/4 cup chopped walnuts, toasted

In large pot of lightly salted boiling water, cook orzo according to package directions, adding broccoli during last 2 minutes of suggested cooking time; drain well.

Meanwhile, combine olive oil and red pepper flakes in 1-cup glass measure. Microwave (high) for 1 minute.

In large bowl, toss cooked pasta and broccoli with warm olive oil mixture, feta, olives, asiago, and basil. Just before serving, top with pine nuts. Serve warm or at room temperature.

Makes 6-8 servings

Per serving Calories 266; Fat 15 g; Cholesterol 10 mg; Sodium 257 mg; Carbohydrate 26 g; Fiber 2 g

Lemon Almond Broccoli

Almonds add a tasty and healthful crunch to the usual side of plain broccoli. A twist of lemon peel brightens the flavor, too.

- 2 green onions, thinly sliced
- 2 tablespoons sliced almonds, toasted
- 1 tablespoon butter, melted
- 1 teaspoon grated lemon peel
- 2 cups broccoli florets, cooked

In small bowl, combine green onions, almonds, butter, and lemon peel. Sprinkle over cooked broccoli; toss until well mixed.

Makes 3-4 servings

Per serving Calories 60; Fat 5 g; Cholesterol 8 mg; Sodium 9 mg; Carbohydrate 3 g; Fiber 2 g

technique savvy

How To Cook Broccoli

TO MICROWAVE
Place 2 cups broccoli florets in shallow microwave-safe dish; cover and microwave (high) for 5 to 6 minutes or until crisp-tender. Let stand for 2 to 3 minutes.

TO STEAM
Pour 1 inch water into large saucepan; place steamer basket over water. Place 2 cups broccoli florets in basket. Bring water to a boil; cover and steam until crisp-tender, about 8 to 10 minutes.

TO SAUTÉ
In large nonstick skillet, heat 1 tablespoon olive oil over medium-high heat. Add 2 cups broccoli florets; cook stirring frequently until crisp-tender, about 4 to 5 minutes.

Garden Fresh Green Bean Salad

The vegetable that goes with everything gets a modern make-over that couldn't be easier or more delicious. Keep the ingredients on hand to round out any meal.

1 pound green beans, trimmed, halved, and cooked
1 pint grape or cherry tomatoes, halved
1/2 cup thinly slivered red onion
2 tablespoons red wine vinegar
1 tablespoon olive oil
1 tablespoon honey
3/4 teaspoon dried thyme
1/2 teaspoon salt
1 package (3 ounces) real bacon bits

In large bowl, combine cooked green beans, tomatoes, and onion. In small bowl, combine vinegar, oil, honey, thyme, and salt. Pour over vegetables; toss until well mixed. Just before serving, toss in bacon bits.

Makes 6 servings

Per serving Calories 125; Fat 5 g; Cholesterol 10 mg; Sodium 644 mg; Carbohydrate 13 g; Fiber 3 g

technique savvy

How To Cook Green Beans

TO MICROWAVE
Place 1 pound trimmed green beans in shallow microwave-safe dish; cover and microwave (high) for 6 to 8 minutes or until crisp-tender. Let stand for 2 to 3 minutes.

TO BOIL
In medium saucepan, bring 4 cups water to a boil. Add 1 pound trimmed green beans and cook for 7 minutes; drain.

TO ROAST
Place 1 pound trimmed green beans on foil-lined 10 x 15-inch jellyroll pan that has been lightly coated with no-stick cooking spray. Drizzle with 1 tablespoon olive oil; toss until well mixed. Spread green beans into single layer. Roast in 425°F. oven, stirring halfway through cooking time, until green beans are tender and lightly browned, about 20 to 25 minutes.

Basil Walnut Green Beans

Mellow walnuts, fresh basil, and a splash of vinegar take green beans from ordinary to extraordinary in about 1 minute. Easy enough for a weeknight, and special enough for company!

2 tablespoons butter
1/3 cup walnuts, coarsely chopped
1 clove garlic, minced
1/4 cup balsamic or red wine vinegar
1 tablespoon Dijon-style mustard
2 teaspoons minced fresh basil
Salt and ground black pepper to taste
1 pound green beans, trimmed, halved, and cooked

In 2-cup glass measure, combine butter, walnuts, and garlic. Microwave (high) for 1 minute or until butter melts. Add vinegar, mustard, basil, salt, and pepper; stir to combine. Pour over cooked green beans; toss until well mixed.

Makes 4-6 servings

Per serving Calories 120; Fat 9 g; Cholesterol 11 mg; Sodium 65 mg; Carbohydrate 9 g; Fiber 2 g

Garden Fresh Green Bean Salad

Fiesta Corn Salad

You're minutes away from a fiesta with this colorful salad. Try this zesty medley on grilled fish, burgers, or brats, too.

2 cans (11 ounces each) white shoepeg corn, drained
1 can (15 ounces) black beans, rinsed and drained
1 large avocado, pitted, peeled, and cubed
1 cup quartered grape or cherry tomatoes
4 green onions, thinly sliced
2 cloves garlic, minced
1/3 cup light dairy sour cream
1/4 cup fresh lime juice
1 tablespoon olive oil
2 teaspoons chili powder
Salt and ground black pepper to taste

In large bowl, combine all ingredients; gently toss to combine. Refrigerate for 30 to 45 minutes to blend flavors. Serve as side salad, sandwich relish, or with corn chips.

Makes 6-8 servings

TIP If desired, cook 6 ears corn-on-the-cob (see sidebar for directions). Cool corn; cut kernels from cob with serrated knife. Substitute 3 cups cooked corn for the 2 cans shoepeg corn. (6 ears corn yields about 3 cups kernels.)

Per serving Calories 207; Fat 7 g; Cholesterol 3 mg; Sodium 355 mg; Carbohydrate 30 g; Fiber 7 g

LAURA'S Weeknight Tip *This is a great double duty recipe. Leave out the avocado until the last minute. Serve some of it as a salad one night, and the rest as a topping for fajitas or quesadillas the next.*

technique savvy

How To Cook Corn-on-the-Cob

TO MICROWAVE
Remove tassels and dark outer husks from corn, leaving remaining husks intact. Place up to 6 ears in microwave, arranging in spoke fashion. Microwave (high) for 2 minutes per ear. Let corn stand for several minutes. Remove husks and silk from corn.

TO GRILL
Remove tassels and dark outer husks from corn, leaving remaining husks intact. Soak corn in husks in cold water for 20 minutes. Place corn on grid over medium-high heat. Grill turning frequently until kernels are bright yellow and tender, about 12 to 15 minutes. Remove husks and silk from corn.

TO BOIL
Remove husks and silk from corn. Bring large pot of water to boil over high heat. Add corn; bring water back to boil. Reduce heat and simmer for 4 minutes.

Summer Squash Medley

Turn this ubiquitous summer staple into something fabulous when you stir-fry it with tomatoes, mushrooms, and Italian herbs. It's great alongside grilled chicken or fish.

- 1 tablespoon olive oil
- 1 medium zucchini (about 1/2 pound), sliced 1/4-inch thick
- 1 medium yellow squash (about 1/2 pound), sliced 1/4-inch thick
- 1 cup sliced mushrooms
- 2 tablespoons grated parmesan cheese
- 1/2 teaspoon Italian herb seasoning
- 1/4 teaspoon seasoned salt
- 6 grape or cherry tomatoes, halved

In wok or large nonstick skillet, heat olive oil over medium-high heat until hot but not smoking. Add zucchini, yellow squash, and mushrooms; stir-fry until crisp-tender, about 3 to 5 minutes. Sprinkle parmesan cheese, Italian seasoning, and seasoned salt over top; toss until well mixed. Stir in tomatoes; cook until heated through, about 2 to 3 minutes.

Makes 4 servings

Per serving Calories 68; Fat 4 g; Cholesterol 2 mg; Sodium 142 mg; Carbohydrate 6 g; Fiber 2 g

Zucchini Roma

Four ingredients and four minutes are all you need to create this simply sensational side. You'll make this one often!

- 2 tablespoons butter
- 2 medium zucchini (about 1 pound), halved lengthwise, and sliced 1/2-inch thick
- 2 ounces (1/2 cup) shredded mozzarella cheese
- 1/3 cup Italian seasoned bread crumbs

In large nonstick skillet, melt butter over medium-high heat. Add zucchini; cook stirring frequently until crisp-tender, about 4 minutes. Remove from heat; place in serving dish. Sprinkle cheese and bread crumbs over top.

Makes 4 servings

Per serving Calories 149; Fat 10 g; Cholesterol 24 mg; Sodium 281 mg; Carbohydrate 11 g; Fiber 2 g

technique savvy

How To Cook Zucchini

TO MICROWAVE
Place 1 pound sliced zucchini in shallow microwave-safe dish; cover and microwave (high) for 4 to 5 minutes or until crisp-tender. Let stand for 2 to 3 minutes; drain.

TO GRILL
Halve zucchini lengthwise; brush with olive oil. Place on grid over medium-high heat; grill, turning frequently and brushing with additional olive oil as needed, until tender and lightly charred, about 6 to 8 minutes.

TO SAUTÉ
In large nonstick skillet, melt 1 to 2 tablespoons butter over medium heat. Add 1 pound sliced or chopped zucchini; cook stirring frequently until crisp-tender, about 5 minutes.

technique savvy

How To Cook Carrots

TO MICROWAVE
Place 1 pound baby carrots in shallow microwave-safe dish; cover and microwave (high) for 6 to 8 minutes or until crisp-tender. Let stand for 2 to 3 minutes.

TO STEAM
Pour 1 inch water into large saucepan; place steamer basket over water. Place 1 pound baby carrots in basket. Bring water to a boil; cover and steam until crisp-tender, about 5 to 6 minutes.

TO ROAST
Place 1 pound baby carrots on foil-lined 10 x 15-inch jellyroll pan that has been lightly coated with no-stick cooking spray. Drizzle with 1 tablespoon olive oil; toss until well mixed. Spread carrots into single layer. Roast in 425°F. oven, stirring halfway through cooking time, until carrots are tender and lightly browned, about 15 to 20 minutes.

Honeysuckle Carrots

Keep a bag of baby carrots on hand for a quick and convenient side dish. An orange and ginger glaze makes them something special any night of the week.

- 1/2 cup orange juice
- 2 teaspoons cornstarch
- 2 tablespoons honey
- 1 tablespoon butter
- 1 teaspoon minced fresh ginger root
- 1 bag (16 ounces) baby carrots, cooked

In 2-cup glass measure, dissolve cornstarch in orange juice. Add honey and butter. Microwave (high) for 2 minutes stirring halfway through cooking time until thickened and bubbly. Stir in ginger. Pour over cooked carrots; toss until well mixed.

Makes 8 servings

Per serving Calories 59; Fat 2 g; Cholesterol 4 mg; Sodium 45 mg; Carbohydrate 11 g; Fiber 1 g

Butter Crunch Carrots

Two minutes in the microwave is all it takes to make this sweet and savory topping for cooked carrots. The name says it all!

- 1/4 cup slivered almonds
- 3 tablespoons butter
- 2 tablespoons brown sugar
- 1/4 teaspoon lemon pepper seasoning
- 1 bag (16 ounces) baby carrots, cooked

In 1-cup glass measure, combine almonds, butter, brown sugar, and seasoning. Microwave (high) for 2 minutes stirring halfway through cooking time until sugar dissolves. Pour over cooked carrots; toss until well mixed.

Makes 8 servings

Per serving Calories 98; Fat 7 g; Cholesterol 12 mg; Sodium 63 mg; Carbohydrate 9 g; Fiber 2 g

Mediterranean Cauliflower

Grape tomatoes and thyme give cauliflower a bright, fresh flavor. A dusting of nutty asiago cheese is a nice finish.

2 tablespoons butter
2 cups cauliflower florets
2 green onions, thinly sliced
2 tablespoons water
6 grape or cherry tomatoes, halved
1/4 teaspoon dried thyme
Salt and ground black pepper to taste
2 tablespoons shredded asiago cheese

In large skillet, melt butter over medium heat. Add cauliflower; cook stirring occasionally for 2 minutes. Add green onions; cook stirring occasionally until cauliflower is crisp-tender, about 3 to 5 minutes. Add water; cover and steam for 1 to 2 minutes. Stir in tomatoes and seasonings; cook until heated through, about 2 minutes. Sprinkle asiago cheese over top.

Makes 3-4 servings

Per serving Calories 81; Fat 7 g; Cholesterol 19 mg; Sodium 44 mg; Carbohydrate 4 g; Fiber 2 g

Crun-Cheesy Cauliflower

Crumble cheesy snack crackers over cauliflower and add a drizzle of butter for a fast and fabulous vegetable fix-up that even the kids will love.

2 cups cauliflower florets, cooked
2 tablespoons butter, melted
1/2 cup crushed cheese-flavored crackers

Drizzle melted butter over top of cooked cauliflower. Sprinkle crushed crackers over top.

Makes 4 servings

Per serving Calories 123; Fat 9 g; Cholesterol 16 mg; Sodium 103 mg; Carbohydrate 9 g; Fiber 1 g

technique savvy

How To Cook Cauliflower

TO MICROWAVE
Place 2 cups cauliflower florets in shallow microwave-safe dish; cover and microwave (high) for 6 to 7 minutes or until crisp-tender. Let stand for 2 to 3 minutes.

TO STEAM
Pour 1 inch water into large saucepan; place steamer basket over water. Place 2 cups cauliflower florets in basket. Bring water to a boil; cover and steam until crisp-tender, about 7 to 8 minutes.

TO ROAST
Place 2 cups cauliflower florets on foil-lined 10 x 15-inch jellyroll pan that has been coated with no-stick cooking spray. Drizzle with 1 tablespoon olive oil; toss well to coat. Spread cauliflower into single layer. Roast in 425°F. oven, stirring halfway through cooking time, until tender and lightly browned, about 25 minutes.

technique savvy

How To Cook Asparagus

TO MICROWAVE
Place 1 pound asparagus spears in shallow microwave-safe dish; cover and microwave (high) for 4 to 5 minutes or until crisp-tender. Let stand for 2 to 3 minutes.

TO STEAM
Pour 1 inch water into large saucepan; place steamer basket over water. Place 1 pound asparagus spears in basket. Bring water to a boil; cover and steam until crisp-tender, about 5 to 7 minutes.

TO GRILL
Place asparagus spears on platter. Drizzle with olive oil; toss to coat. Season with salt and pepper to taste. Place diagonally on grid over medium-high heat; grill turning occasionally until crisp-tender and slightly charred, about 5 to 7 minutes.

Asparagus Gremolata

Gremolata is a light and tangy garnish of freshly grated lemon peel, parsley, and garlic. It's a quick and easy fix-up for tender asparagus spears.

1 pound asparagus, trimmed and cooked
2 tablespoons butter, melted
1 tablespoon minced fresh parsley
1 1/2 teaspoons grated lemon peel
1 clove garlic, minced
Salt and ground black pepper to taste

Drizzle melted butter over cooked asparagus. In small bowl, stir together parsley, lemon peel, and garlic. Sprinkle over asparagus; toss until well mixed. Season with salt and pepper.

Makes 4 servings

Per serving Calories 68; Fat 6 g; Cholesterol 16 mg; Sodium 3 mg; Carbohydrate 3 g; Fiber 1 g

Toasted Sesame Asparagus

Get asparagus dressed for dinner in no time. A sprinkle of sesame seeds adds a nutty crunch.

1 pound asparagus, trimmed and cooked
1 tablespoon butter, melted
1 tablespoon minced fresh parsley
1 tablespoon sesame seed, toasted
Salt and ground black pepper to taste

Drizzle melted butter over cooked asparagus. Sprinkle parsley and sesame seed over top; toss until well mixed. Season with salt and pepper.

Makes 4 servings

TIP To toast sesame seed, place seeds in small nonstick skillet. Cook stirring often over medium-high heat until golden brown, about 1 to 2 minutes. Remove from heat immediately.

Per serving Calories 51; Fat 4 g; Cholesterol 8 mg; Sodium 3 mg; Carbohydrate 3 g; Fiber 2 g

Asparagus Gremolata

Sugar and Spice Sweet Potatoes

Per serving

Calories 180
Fat 7 g
Cholesterol 0 mg
Sodium 63 mg
Carbohydrate 29 g
Fiber 4 g

Here's a tasty new way to enjoy sweet potatoes. These are so easy you will want to make them all year round.

- 2 pounds sweet potatoes, peeled and cut into bite-size pieces (about 6 cups)
- 3 tablespoons olive oil
- 3 tablespoons brown sugar
- 1 teaspoon ground cinnamon

Place potatoes on foil-lined 10 x 15-inch jellyroll pan that has been lightly coated with no-stick cooking spray. Drizzle oil over potatoes. In small bowl, combine brown sugar and cinnamon. Sprinkle over top; toss until well mixed. Roast in 425°F. oven stirring occasionally until tender, about 20 to 25 minutes.

Makes 6 servings

Garlic Roasted Potatoes

Per serving

Calories 170
Fat 7 g
Cholesterol 0 mg
Sodium 203 mg
Carbohydrate 25 g
Fiber 3 g

Less is more, unless you want more – and you will – of these outstanding potatoes. Try them with salmon, steak, or lamb chops.

- 2 pounds Yukon gold or small red potatoes, scrubbed and cut into bite-size pieces (about 6 cups)
- 3 tablespoons olive oil
- 6 cloves garlic, slivered
- 1 tablespoon snipped fresh rosemary, OR 1 teaspoon dried
- 1/2 teaspoon salt
- 1/2 teaspoon coarsely ground black pepper

Place potatoes on foil-lined 10 x 15-inch jellyroll pan that has been lightly coated with no-stick cooking spray. Drizzle oil over potatoes. Top with remaining ingredients; toss until well mixed. Roast in 425°F. oven stirring occasionally until tender and browned, about 35 to 40 minutes.

Makes 6 servings

Cheddar Cheese Sauce

Even the pickiest of eaters will be rendered powerless by this easy, cheesy sauce. It's guaranteed to make broccoli, cauliflower – just about anything – simply irresistible.

- 2 tablespoons butter
- 2 tablespoons flour
- 1 cup milk
- 3 ounces (3/4 cup) shredded cheddar cheese
- Salt and ground black pepper to taste

Place butter in 2-cup glass measure. Microwave (high) for 30 seconds or until butter is melted. Whisk in flour; microwave (high) for 30 seconds. Slowly whisk in milk. Microwave (high) stirring every 30 seconds until bubbly and thickened, about 2 minutes. Stir in cheese, salt, and pepper. Microwave (high) stirring every 30 seconds until sauce is thickened and smooth, about 1 minute.

Makes 1 1/2 cups

Laura's Weeknight Tip *If your kids are less than enthusiastic about eating vegetables, try this trick. Kids love to dip, so serve this cheesy sauce in small dishes and let them dip their vegetables at dinner time.*

technique savvy

Smooth Sauces

For a smooth sauce every time, blend the thickening agent – flour or cornstarch – with melted butter, oil, or cold liquid before stirring it into the pot. Adding flour directly to a hot mixture will create lumps that are impossible to get rid of. Stir the sauce frequently until it thickens. Then gradually stir in the shredded cheese until it melts.

Per 2 tablespoons

Calories 61
Fat 5 g
Cholesterol 14 mg
Sodium 53 mg
Carbohydrate 2 g
Fiber 0 g

FROM THE
sweet shoppe

Country-Style Peach Tart 84

Cobblestone Berry Crisp 85

Plum Upside-Down Cake 86

Peanut Butter Cup Bars 88

S'more Brownie Bars 89

Turtle Ice Cream Sundaes 90

Not-Fried Ice Cream 90

Country-Style Peach Tart
Recipe on page 84

Country-Style Peach Tart

technique savvy

Step-by-Step Instructions

There's no need to peel the peaches for this rustic, free-form tart. Serve it warm with a dollop of whipped cream.

- 1 refrigerated pie crust (1/2 of 15-ounce package)
- 3/4 cup flour
- 3/4 cup sugar
- 1/2 teaspoon ground cinnamon
- 1/4 teaspoon salt
- 4 cups sliced peaches (about 4 medium)
- 5 tablespoons cold butter, cut into pieces
- 1/2 cup coarsely chopped pecans

Unroll pie crust onto lightly floured surface. Roll dough lightly into 12-inch circle; place on baking sheet. In medium bowl, combine flour, sugar, cinnamon, and salt. Sprinkle 1/4 cup of the flour mixture over crust. **1** Arrange peaches on crust, leaving 1 1/2-inch border around edge. Using pastry blender, cut butter into remaining flour mixture until crumbly. Stir in pecans. Sprinkle topping over peaches. **2** Fold edge of dough over peaches, crimping as needed. Bake in 400°F. oven until crust is golden, about 25 to 30 minutes. Best served warm.

Makes 6-8 servings

VARIATION

Gingered Apple Tart Add 3 tablespoons finely chopped crystallized ginger to flour mixture. Substitute apples and walnuts for peaches and pecans. Bake for 25 to 30 minutes.

Per serving Calories 390; Fat 20 g; Cholesterol 25 mg; Sodium 185 mg; Carbohydrate 51 g; Fiber 2 g

Per serving

Calories 416
Fat 20 g
Cholesterol 25 mg
Sodium 182 mg
Carbohydrate 57 g
Fiber 4 g

Photograph on page 82

Cobblestone Berry Crisp

Chop a refrigerated pie crust, toss it with cinnamon-sugar, and you have a shortcut topping for this quick fruit crisp. Just pop it in the oven before dinner and it will be ready in time for dessert.

1/2 cup sugar
2 tablespoons cornstarch
1 tablespoon grated lime peel
2 tablespoons fresh lime juice
1/4 teaspoon salt
2 packages (12 ounces each) frozen blueberries (4 cups)
2 tablespoons sugar
1 teaspoon ground cinnamon
1 refrigerated pie crust (1/2 of 15-ounce package), cut into 1/2-inch pieces
Vanilla ice cream

In large microwave-safe bowl, combine the 1/2 cup sugar, cornstarch, lime peel and juice, and salt. Add blueberries; gently stir to combine. Microwave (high) for 5 minutes; stir. Microwave (high) stirring occasionally for 5 to 6 minutes, until mixture is bubbly and starts to thicken. Place in 8-inch square or 9-inch round baking dish that has been lightly coated with no-stick cooking spray.

In medium bowl, combine the 2 tablespoons sugar and cinnamon. Add pie crust pieces; toss until well mixed. Sprinkle evenly over berries. Bake in 375°F. oven until top is brown and juices bubble in center, about 20 to 25 minutes. Serve warm with vanilla ice cream.

Makes 6 servings

VARIATION

Cherry Almond Crisp Substitute 2 bags (12 ounces each) frozen dark sweet cherries for the blueberries. Omit lime peel and juice. Add 1 teaspoon almond extract to the thickened cherry mixture before placing it in baking dish.

Per serving Calories 321; Fat 9 g; Cholesterol 7 mg; Sodium 246 mg; Carbohydrate 58 g; Fiber 3 g

Fresh Blueberry Crisp When blueberries are in season, prepare filling as directed, substituting 4 cups fresh blueberries for frozen berries. Microwave (high) stirring occasionally for 5 to 6 minutes, or until mixture is bubbly and starts to thicken.

Per serving Calories 303; Fat 10 g; Cholesterol 7 mg; Sodium 243 mg; Carbohydrate 54 g; Fiber 3 g

ingredient savvy

Fresh vs. Frozen

Craving your favorite fruit dessert – out of season? Don't despair. Head to the Frozen Food Department. Many varieties of fruit are available frozen and work great in your favorite pie, crisp, or cobbler recipes.

Select frozen fruit that is dry-packed, meaning loose pieces packed without sugar. Use the same amount of frozen fruit as you would fresh, brushing off any extra ice crystals before measuring. Do not let the fruit thaw.

Use the maximum amount of thickener as called for in your recipe and toss the filling ingredients together. Then assemble and bake your recipe as directed, increasing the time as needed for the filling to become thick and bubbly. Pies may need anywhere from an extra 15 to 30 minutes baking time.

Per serving without ice cream

Calories 301
Fat 10 g
Cholesterol 7 mg
Sodium 243 mg
Carbohydrate 53 g
Fiber 3 g

Plum Upside-Down Cake

A classic American cake gets two delicious updates. Choose cozy cinnamon cake topped with tart, juicy plums or tangy lemon cake covered with plump blueberries for an easy weeknight dessert.

- 2/3 cup firmly packed brown sugar
- 5 tablespoons butter
- 2 teaspoons honey
- 4 medium plums, halved, pitted, and cut into thick slices
- 1 box (9 ounces) yellow cake mix (Jiffy)
- 1/2 teaspoon ground cinnamon
- 1/4 teaspoon almond extract

Lightly coat bottom and sides of 9-inch round cake pan with no-stick cooking spray. Add brown sugar, butter, and honey. Bake in 350°F. oven until butter is melted and mixture is bubbly, about 7 to 8 minutes. Arrange plum slices, slightly overlapping, in circular pattern to cover entire surface of pan. Let cool while preparing cake mix.

Prepare cake mix according to package directions, adding cinnamon and extract to batter. Pour over plums. Bake until wooden pick inserted in center comes out clean, about 30 minutes. Cool on wire rack for 15 minutes. Loosen sides of cake with thin knife and invert onto serving plate.

Makes 8 servings

VARIATION

Lemon Blueberry Upside-Down Cake Lightly coat bottom and sides of 9-inch round cake pan with no-stick cooking spray. Omit butter, brown sugar, honey, and plums. In medium bowl, combine 2 cups fresh or frozen blueberries, 1/2 cup sugar, and 1 tablespoon cornstarch; toss until well mixed. Place in pan. Bake in 350°F. oven until sugar is melted and mixture is bubbly, about 7 to 8 minutes.

Prepare cake mix as directed above, substituting 1 tablespoon grated lemon peel and 1 teaspoon vanilla extract for the cinnamon and almond extract. Pour over berries. Bake as directed above.

Per serving Calories 210; Fat 3 g; Cholesterol 26 mg; Sodium 213 mg; Carbohydrate 43 g; Fiber 1 g

technique savvy

Preheating the Oven

Preheating your oven may sound mundane, but it is an essential part of preparing a recipe. If the oven is not fully heated, your food will need more baking time and will likely be dried out or overcooked.

Be sure to adjust the oven racks to the correct position according to your recipe before you preheat. When the recipe doesn't specify, bake food on the center rack. Allow 10 minutes for your oven to preheat.

Per serving

Calories 294
Fat 11 g
Cholesterol 46 mg
Sodium 221 mg
Carbohydrate 48 g
Fiber 1 g

Lemon Blueberry
Upside-Down Cake

Peanut Butter Cup Bars

What's better than a fluffy, rich, creamy dessert chock-full of one of your favorite candies? Um…nothing we can think of!

- 1 1/2 cups chocolate sandwich cookie crumbs (about 15 cookies)
- 2 tablespoons butter, melted
- 1 package (8 ounces) cream cheese, softened
- 1 cup powdered sugar
- 1/2 cup creamy peanut butter
- 1 cup heavy whipping cream, whipped, OR 1 container (8 ounces) frozen non-dairy whipped topping, thawed
- 8 peanut butter cups, chilled and coarsely chopped (divided)

In medium bowl, combine cookie crumbs and butter. Press into bottom of 9-inch square baking pan that has been lightly coated with no-stick cooking spray. Bake in 350°F. oven for 8 minutes. Cool completely.

In large mixer bowl, beat cream cheese, powdered sugar, and peanut butter at medium speed until light and creamy. Fold in whipped cream. Fold in half of the chopped candies. Spread over crust. Sprinkle remaining chopped candies over top. Chill at least 3 hours. Cut into bars.

Makes 12 bars

TIP If using miniature or double peanut butter cups, use 3/4 cup chopped for the filling and 3/4 cup chopped to sprinkle over top.

technique savvy

Cookie Crumbs

Packaged cookies make terrific dessert crusts. Here's how to make quick work of crumbs.

First, eat one cookie to make sure they're good. Place about 6 cookies in the food processor. Eat another cookie. Pulse on/off until the crumbs have reached the desired consistency. Transfer the crumbs to a measuring cup. Eat one more cookie. Repeat process with remaining cookies.

Or make crumbs the old-fashioned way. Eat two cookies, drink a glass of milk, then place the rest of the cookies in a freezer-weight reclosable plastic bag. Seal the bag, squeezing out the air. Use a rolling pin to crush the cookies to the desired consistency.

Per serving

Calories 390
Fat 28 g
Cholesterol 54 mg
Sodium 217 mg
Carbohydrate 30 g
Fiber 1 g

S'more Brownie Bars

You don't need a campfire to indulge your inner child. We've turned this classic treat into brownie form so you can enjoy it anytime.

- $1\frac{1}{2}$ cups graham cracker crumbs
- $\frac{1}{4}$ cup sugar
- 6 tablespoons butter, melted
- 1 box (19.5 to 21 ounces) brownie mix
- 1 bag (10.5 ounces) miniature marshmallows
- $\frac{1}{2}$ cup semisweet chocolate chips

1 Mold foil around bottom side of 9 x 13-inch baking pan, extending foil about 1 inch above sides of pan. Remove foil; turn pan right-side up. Line pan with foil; lightly coat with no-stick cooking spray.

In medium bowl, combine crumbs, sugar, and butter until well mixed. Press mixture onto bottom of prepared pan. Prepare brownie mix according to package directions. Spread batter over crust. Bake in 350°F. oven for 25 minutes. Sprinkle marshmallows over hot brownies. Bake until marshmallows are lightly browned, about 5 minutes.

Place chocolate chips in small freezer-weight reclosable plastic bag; seal bag. Immerse bag in bowl of very hot water until chips are melted; wipe bag dry. Knead chocolate in bag until completely smooth. Snip off one corner of bag to make small hole. Drizzle chocolate over toasted marshmallows. Cool completely. 2 Lift out of pan onto cutting board. Cut into bars.

Makes 20-24 bars

technique savvy

Step-by-Step Instructions

Per serving

Calories 285
Fat 13 g
Cholesterol 26 mg
Sodium 145 mg
Carbohydrate 39 g
Fiber <1 g

Turtle Ice Cream Sundaes

Chocolate, caramel, pecans – what's not to love? Keep these on hand in the freezer for a family-friendly dessert at a moment's notice.

Per serving with 1 tablespoon caramel topping

Calories 690
Fat 43 g
Cholesterol 63 mg
Sodium 279 mg
Carbohydrate 74 g
Fiber 4 g

1/2 gallon vanilla ice cream
2 cups chocolate sandwich cookie crumbs (about 20 cookies)
1 bottle (7.25 ounces) chocolate-flavored hard-shell topping
1/2 cup caramel ice cream topping
1 cup chopped pecans, toasted

Scoop 8 ice cream balls. Place cookie crumbs in shallow dish. Roll each ice cream ball in crumbs to coat. Place ice cream balls, one at a time, on small plate. Drizzle chocolate topping over each, partially coating top and sides. (If at any point ice cream balls become too soft, return to freezer for a few minutes before continuing.) Freeze in covered container at least 2 hours or up to several days.

To serve, place ice cream balls in individual dessert dishes and drizzle with caramel sauce. Sprinkle pecans over top.

Makes 8 servings

Not-Fried Ice Cream

Our easy version of this restaurant favorite is a delicious make-ahead finale for any night of the week.

Per serving with 1 tablespoon honey

Calories 497
Fat 27 g
Cholesterol 80 mg
Sodium 126 mg
Carbohydrate 63 g
Fiber 2 g

1/4 cup butter
1/2 cup flour
1/3 cup flaked sweetened coconut
1/3 cup coarsely chopped pecans
2 tablespoons brown sugar
1/2 teaspoon ground cinnamon
1/2 gallon vanilla ice cream
1/2 cup honey

In large skillet, melt butter over medium-high heat. Add flour, coconut, pecans, brown sugar, and cinnamon. Cook stirring constantly until golden brown and crumbly, about 3 to 4 minutes. Remove from heat; cool completely.

Scoop 8 ice cream balls. Roll each ice cream ball in crumb mixture to coat. (If at any point ice cream balls become too soft, return to freezer for a few minutes before continuing.) Freeze in covered container at least 2 hours or up to several days.

To serve, place ice cream balls in individual dessert dishes and drizzle with honey.

Makes 8 servings

Recipe Standards

How many cooks does it take to develop just one recipe? Well, more than you would guess! Why? Because each recipe is carefully developed, tested and scrutinized with a seven-step process by Dierbergs' (very picky) home economists and critiqued by a (very willing) taste panel. And our taste panel isn't shy in the area of feedback! We get many honest opinions with their diverse, discriminating palates. Foolproof recipes? You bet! We've done all the cooking and baking and testing and tasting. The results are wonderfully successful and delicious.

The recipes in this cookbook were tested using the following standards unless otherwise indicated:

Eggs are large.

Butter is unsalted. Stick margarine may be substituted; do not substitute whipped butter, butter spreads, or soft margarines.

Milk is 2% or higher fat; using fat-free or low-fat may alter results.

Dairy Products are regular or light/reduced-fat; using fat-free may alter results unless indicated in the recipe.

Vegetable Oil is your favorite brand.

Olive Oil is virgin for cooking, extra virgin for dressings.

Flour is all-purpose.

Sugar is granulated.

Brown Sugar is firmly packed when measured.

Coarse Salt is kosher or sea salt.

Preheat Oven for 10 minutes before beginning to bake.

Baking Sheets are flat without sides.

Jellyroll Pans are baking sheets with sides.

Parchment Paper makes for easy cleanup and does not need to be greased unless indicated in the recipe. It is available with aluminum foil and plastic wrap.

Dicing and Chopping

To Freeze or Not To Freeze

Make weeknight cooking easy by keeping a well-stocked freezer. Be sure your freezer maintains a temperature of 0°F. or below. Always wrap food in airtight packages and label them, including the date.

Some foods lose flavor, texture, or quality when frozen. These items should not be stored in the freezer:

- Battered and fried foods
- Cooked egg whites and yolks, or whole eggs in the shell
- Desserts with cream fillings
- Soups and stews made with potatoes
- Soups and stews thickened with cornstarch or flour
- Stuffed chops or chicken breasts
- Mayonnaise
- Sour cream

Equivalents

Pinch or dash	= less than 1/8 teaspoon
1 tablespoon	= 3 teaspoons
1 fluid ounce	= 2 tablespoons
1/4 cup	= 4 tablespoons
1/3 cup	= 5 tablespoons + 1 teaspoon
1 cup	= 16 tablespoons, 8 fluid ounces, or 1/2 pint
1 pint	= 2 cups or 16 fluid ounces
1 quart	= 4 cups, 32 fluid ounces, or 2 pints
1 gallon	= 4 quarts or 128 fluid ounces
1 pound	= 16 ounces
2 slices bread	= 1 cup soft bread crumbs
1 medium lemon	= 3 tablespoons juice, 2 to 3 teaspoons zest
1 medium lime	= 1 1/2 to 2 tablespoons juice, 1 teaspoon zest
1 medium orange	= 1/3 to 1/2 cup juice, 1 1/2 to 2 tablespoons zest
1 stick butter	= 8 tablespoons, 1/2 cup, or 1/4 pound
1 cup uncooked rice	= 3 cups cooked rice
3/4 pound boneless, skinless chicken breast	= about 2 cups diced cooked chicken
1 bottle (750 ml) wine	= about 3 1/4 cups (25.4 fluid ounces)
4 ounces cheese	= 1 cup crumbled, grated or shredded

Minimum Safe Internal Temperatures

Use an instant read thermometer to determine the internal temperature of foods. Follow individual recipes for optimal end temperatures. Use the following chart as a guide for minimum safe temperatures.

Beef, medium-rare .... 145°F.
Beef, ground .... 160°F.
Fish .... 145°F.
Pork, chops or tenderloin .... 160°F.
Pork, roast .... 150°F.
Pork, ground or sausage .... 155°F.
Poultry .... 165°F.
Casseroles .... 165°F.
Previously cooked foods .... 165°F.

Dierbergs School of Cooking

Explore the world of cooking at Dierbergs, and have a little fun in our kitchen – and yours!

- Choose from dozens of topics from appetizers, entrées, or desserts, to seafood, wines, restaurant specialties, regional cooking styles, ethnic foods, heart-healthy cooking and much more.
- Classes taught by noted chefs, restaurateurs, cookbook authors, caterers, and staff instructors.
- Custom classes for birthday parties, special events, and corporate team-building events.

For more information on Dierbergs School of Cooking or cooking class schedules:
www.dierbergs.com

For information on Dierbergs cookbooks or magazine subscriptions:
publications@dierbergs.com

Dierbergs School of Cooking Since 1978

Southroads Center
Tesson Ferry and I-270
St. Louis, MO 63128

West Oak Center
Olive Boulevard and
Craig Road
Creve Coeur, MO 63141

Clarkson/Clayton Center
Clarkson and Clayton Roads
Ellisville, MO 63011

Bogey Hills Plaza
Zumbehl Road and I-70
St. Charles, MO 63303

Edwardsville Crossing
Troy Road and
Governor's Parkway
Edwardsville, IL 62025

636-812-1336 (Missouri)
618-622-5353 (Illinois)

Index

BEEF

Asian Meatball Soup, 54 ◆♥
Barbecued Beef Sandwiches, 45 ♥
Beef and Broccoli Stir-Fry, 33 ♥
Bistro Beef Medallions, 34 ◆♥
Easy Oven Meatballs, 54 ◆♥
French Onion Beef Sandwiches, 12
Hearty Beef Burgundy, 44 ◆♥
Ingredient Savvy
  Beef Petite Shoulder Tender, 34
  Meat For Stewing, 45
  Meat Loaf Mix, 11
Meat Loaf Italiano, 11
Mexican Flatbread Pizza, 19
Steak and Potato Pot Pie, 10 ◆
Technique Savvy
  Lots of Meatballs!, 54
  Slicing Raw Meat, 10
Vegetable Beef Barley Soup, 51 ◆♥
Weeknight Beef Stroganoff, 36 ♥

BREADS

Honey Wheat Knots, 23 ◆♥
Maple Harvest Cornbread, 21 ♥
Quick Herb Muffins, 21

CHICKEN

Chicken and Broccoli Cheese Soup, 59
Chicken and Broccoli Stir-Fry, 33 ♥
Chicken Orzo Soup, 58 ♥
Chicken Paprikash, 48 ♥
Chicken Piccata Penne, 27 ♥
Light and Easy Chicken Enchiladas, 17 ♥
Mediterranean Chicken Orzo, 26 ◆
Technique Savvy
  Chicken Tonight or Any Night, 17
  Slicing Raw Meat, 10
Weeknight Chicken Stroganoff, 36 ♥

CONTRIBUTED BY

Jack and Mary Billings, 59
Cathy Chipley, 71
Suzanne Corbett, 21
Loretta Evans, 16
Jan Ford, 61
Ginger Gall, 49
Karen Hurych, 54
Jennifer Kassel, 11
Therese Lewis, 68
Nancy Lorenz, 36
Pam Pahl, 41

DESSERTS

Cherry Almond Crisp, 85
Cobblestone Berry Crisp, 85
Country-Style Peach Tart, 84 ◆
Fresh Blueberry Crisp, 85
Gingered Apple Tart, 84
Lemon Blueberry Upside-Down
  Cake, 86 ◆♥
Not-Fried Ice Cream, 90
Peanut Butter Cup Bars, 88
Plum Upside-Down Cake, 86
S'more Brownie Bars, 89
Technique Savvy
  Cookie Crumbs, 88
  Preheating the Oven, 86
Turtle Ice Cream Sundaes, 90

FISH *See also Seafood*

Almond-Encrusted Cod, 15 ◆♥
Baja Fish Tacos, 39 ◆
Ingredient Savvy
  Albacore Tuna, 13
Open-Faced Tuna Melt, 13
Savory Salmon Cakes, 40
Technique Savvy
  Thawing Tilapia, 39
Wasabi-Encrusted Tilapia, 15 ♥

FRUITS

Apple, Pear, and Cranberry Salad, 66
Cherry Almond Crisp, 85
Cobblestone Berry Crisp, 85
Country-Style Peach Tart, 84 ◆
Fresh Blueberry Crisp, 85
Gingered Apple Tart, 84
Greens and Fruit Salad, 66 ◆
Ingredient Savvy
  Fresh vs. Frozen, 85
Lemon Blueberry Upside-Down
  Cake, 86 ◆♥
Plum Upside-Down Cake, 86
Strawberry Mandarin Salad, 66

INGREDIENT SAVVY

Albacore Tuna, 13
Arborio Rice, 37
Asian Sauces, 30
Barley, 51
Beef Petite Shoulder Tender, 34
Convenient Crumbs, 40
Cooking With Wine, 44
Couscous, 68
Fresh vs. Frozen, 85
Ginger Root, 32
Lower-Sodium Broth, 58
Meat For Stewing, 45
Meat Loaf Mix, 11
Mushrooms, 36
No-Boil Noodles, 16
Pickapeppa Sauce, 41
Say "Cheese," 12
Sherry, 29
Soup Base, 59
Tomatoes, 69

MEATLESS

Easy Weeknight Lasagna, 16 ♥
French Onion Soup, 57 ◆
Fresh Tomato Pizza, 19 ◆
Hearty Veggie Chili Bowls, 63 ◆♥
Mediterranean Couscous Salad, 68
Monterey Wild Mushroom Risotto, 37 ♥
Orzo and Broccoli Salad, 71 ◆
Southwest Black Bean Soup, 49 ♥
Tortellini Minestrone Soup, 55 ♥

PASTA/RICE

Chicken Orzo Soup, 58 ♥
Chicken Piccata Penne, 27 ♥
Easy Weeknight Lasagna, 16 ♥
Ingredient Savvy
Arborio Rice, 37
Couscous, 68
No-Boil Noodles, 16
Mediterranean Chicken Orzo, 26 ◆
Mediterranean Couscous Salad, 68
Monterey Wild Mushroom Risotto, 37 ♥
Orzo and Broccoli Salad, 71 ◆
Sausage-Stuffed Spaghetti Pie, 20
Skillet Turkey Tetrazzini, 29 ◆♥
Technique Savvy
Precooking Pasta, 27
To Rinse or Not To Rinse, 20
Tortellini Minestrone Soup, 55 ♥

PIZZA

Fresh Tomato Pizza, 19 ◆
Mexican Flatbread Pizza, 19

PORK

Asian Lettuce Wraps, 32 ♥
Asian Meatball Soup, 54 ◆♥
Easy Oven Meatballs, 54 ◆♥
Hoisin Pork Medallions with Asparagus, 30 ♥
Ingredient Savvy
Meat Loaf Mix, 11
Meat Loaf Italiano, 11
Pork and Broccoli Stir-Fry, 33 ♥
Pork Tenderloin Diane, 31 ♥
Sausage-Stuffed Spaghetti Pie, 20
Technique Savvy
Lots of Meatballs!, 54
Removing Silver Skin, 31
Slicing Raw Meat, 10
Teriyaki Pulled Pork, 47 ◆♥

SALADS

Apple, Pear, and Cranberry Salad, 66
Fiesta Corn Salad, 74
Garden Fresh Green Bean Salad, 72 ◆♥
Greens and Fruit Salad, 66 ◆
Mango Chutney Spinach Salad, 67
Mediterranean Couscous Salad, 68
Orzo and Broccoli Salad, 71 ◆
Strawberry Mandarin Salad, 66
Tomato and Artichoke Salad, 69 ♥

SANDWICHES

Asian Lettuce Wraps, 32 ♥
Barbecued Beef Sandwiches, 45 ♥
French Onion Beef Sandwiches, 12
Open-Faced Tuna Melt, 13
Teriyaki Pulled Pork, 47 ◆♥

SAUCES

Cheddar Cheese Sauce, 81
Ingredient Savvy
Asian Sauces, 30
Pickapeppa Sauce, 41
Technique Savvy
Smooth Sauces, 81

SEAFOOD *See also Fish*

Piquant Garlic Shrimp, 41 ♥
Savory Crab Cakes, 40

SLOW COOKER

Barbecued Beef Sandwiches, 45 ♥
Chicken Paprikash, 48 ♥
Hearty Beef Burgundy, 44 ◆♥
Southwest Black Bean Soup, 49 ♥
Technique Savvy
Slow Cooker Saves The Day, 48
Teriyaki Pulled Pork, 47 ◆♥
Vegetable Beef Barley Soup, 51 ◆♥

SOUPS

Asian Meatball Soup, 54 ◆♥
Chicken and Broccoli Cheese Soup, 59
Chicken Orzo Soup, 58 ♥
French Onion Soup, 57 ◆
Hearty Veggie Chili Bowls, 63 ◆♥
Ingredient Savvy
Lower-Sodium Broth, 58
Soup Base, 59
Loaded Potato Soup, 61 ◆
Southwest Black Bean Soup, 49 ♥
Technique Savvy
Soup On Hand, 57
Soup – Your Way, 55
Tortellini Minestrone Soup, 55 ♥
Vegetable Beef Barley Soup, 51 ◆♥

TECHNIQUE SAVVY

Chicken Tonight or Any Night, 17
Cookie Crumbs, 88
Cooking Dry Beans, 49
Freezing Chopped Onions, 61
How To Cook Asparagus, 78
How To Cook Broccoli, 71
How To Cook Carrots, 76
How To Cook Cauliflower, 77
How To Cook Corn-on-the-Cob, 74
How To Cook Green Beans, 72
How To Cook Zucchini, 75
Lots of Meatballs!, 54
Precooking Pasta, 27
Preheating The Oven, 86
Removing Silver Skin, 31
Slicing Raw Meat, 10
Slow Cooker Saves The Day, 48
Smooth Sauces, 81
Soup On Hand, 57
Soup – Your Way, 55
Stir Fry, 33
Sugared Nuts, 66
Thawing Tilapia, 39
To Rinse or Not To Rinse, 20

TURKEY

Skillet Turkey Tetrazzini, 29 ◆♥

VEGETABLES

Asparagus
- Asparagus Gremolata, 78 ◆
- Hoisin Pork Medallions with Asparagus, 30 ♥
- *How To Cook Asparagus, 78*
- Toasted Sesame Asparagus, 78

Broccoli
- Beef and Broccoli Stir-Fry, 33 ♥
- Chicken and Broccoli Cheese Soup, 59
- Chicken and Broccoli Stir-Fry, 33 ♥
- *How To Cook Broccoli, 71*
- Lemon Almond Broccoli, 71
- Orzo and Broccoli Salad, 71 ◆
- Pork and Broccoli Stir-Fry, 33 ♥

Carrots
- Butter Crunch Carrots, 76
- Honeysuckle Carrots, 76 ♥
- *How To Cook Carrots, 76*

Cauliflower
- Crun-Cheesy Cauliflower, 77
- *How To Cook Cauliflower, 77*
- Mediterranean Cauliflower, 77

Corn
- Fiesta Corn Salad, 74
- *How To Cook Corn-on-the-Cob, 74*

Green Beans
- Basil Walnut Green Beans, 72
- Garden Fresh Green Bean Salad, 72 ◆♥
- *How To Cook Green Beans, 72*

Potatoes
- Garlic Roasted Potatoes, 80
- Loaded Potato Soup, 61 ◆
- Steak and Potato Pot Pie, 10 ◆
- Sugar and Spice Sweet Potatoes, 80

Spinach
- Mango Chutney Spinach Salad, 67

Tomatoes
- Fresh Tomato Pizza, 19 ◆
- Tomato and Artichoke Salad, 69 ♥
- *Tomatoes, 69*

Zucchini
- *How To Cook Zucchini, 75*
- Summer Squash Medley, 75
- Zucchini Roma, 75

◆ Photograph of Recipe
♥ Heart Healthy Recipe
Items in italic are sidebars